The Voice of the

Infinite in the Small

The Voice of the

Infinite in the Small

Re-Visioning
the Insect-Human
Connection

Revised Edition

Joanne Elizabeth Lauck

FOREWORD BY
Thomas Berry

Shambhala
Boston & London
2002

Shambhala Publications, Inc.
Horticultural Hall
300 Massachusetts Avenue
Boston, Massachusetts 02115
www.shambhala.com

9 8 7 6 5 4 3 2 1

First Shambhala Edition
Printed in the United States of America

♻ This edition is printed on acid-free paper that meets the
American National Standards Institute Z39.48 Standard.
Distributed in the United States by Random House, Inc.,
and in Canada by Random House of Canada Ltd.

Book design by Judy Arisman/Arisman Design

Library of Congress Cataloging-in-Publication Data

Lauck, Joanne Elizabeth, 1947–
The voice of the infinite in the small: re-visioning the insect-
human connection/Joanne Elizabeth Lauck; foreword by
Thomas Berry—Rev. ed.
p.   cm.
ISBN 1-57062-959-5
1. Insects 2. Insects—Psychological aspects. 3. Insects—
Religious aspects. 4. Human-animal relationships. I. Title.
QL463.L28 2002
595.7—dc21   2002005363

To M. Naomi Lauck,

who is still cheering me on with love

You should try to hear the name the Holy One has for things.
We name everything according to the number of legs it has;
The other one names things according to what they have
inside.

— *Jelaluddin Rumi*
(version by Robert Bly)

Contents

Foreword

In his great vision that he had in 1872 when he was nine years old, the Sioux Indian Black Elk experienced a moment when he saw the entire universe dancing together to the song of the stallion in the heavens. Throughout his work, Black Elk insists on this great unity of the entire world of the living, telling us that "one should pay attention to even the smallest of crawling creatures, for these too may have a valuable lesson to teach us, and even the smallest ant may wish to communicate to a man."

In an even more intensive manner, Joanne Lauck addresses the intimate bonding of humans with the insects. To appreciate the relation of humans to these other modes of beings does not come easily for us in the Western cultural tradition. That we are so lacking in both our intellectual and our emotional appreciation of the insects is part of the retarded cultural development of the peoples of Western civilization.

We even associate our own vices with the animals: gluttony with the pig, deceit with the snake, malevolence with the mosquito. We avoid these animals, especially the insects, as beings that somehow should be destroyed as far as we are able, unless we could make them serve some obvious human need. We have little awareness that by losing any of the animal species, we are losing splendid and intimate modes of divine presence. By destroying some insect species, we could even completely upset the pattern of survival upon which we ourselves depend. We need to be reminded constantly of such basic realities as we pass through these critical early years of transition into the twenty-first century. In our ancient years of tribal existence, when we were awakening to our human form of consciousness, we had a deeper understanding of our unity with other life forms. We could speak of the various forms of life as "all our relations." These other life forms were our guardians, our ancestors, our teachers, our healers. We set up totem poles to indicate this relationship, we carved masks and kachinas, painted our bodies and our dwellings, and enacted rituals and ceremonies to indicate this relationship. When we needed assistance, we went to these other members of our great family.

As Chang Tsai, an official in the Chinese administration in the twelfth century, stated in the inscription that hung on the west wall of his office: "Heaven is my father and earth is my mother, and even such a small creature as I finds an intimate place in their midst. Therefore that which extends throughout the universe I consider as my body and that which directs the universe I consider as my nature. All people are my brothers and sisters and all things are my companions." We find such thoughts attractive, until we think of insects. Immediately we become ambivalent. We fail to realize that insect—in terms of species, of individuals, and of sheer volume of living matter—outnumber and outweigh all other forms of animal life combined. Since we do not know why they exist in such abundance, we project onto them our own desire for dominance and then react to them with fear. What we fail to realize is that they exist in such large numbers because they are necessary for the functioning of the earth and the survival of all life.

The real question, however, that needs discussion and that Lauck weaves in and out of each chapter is the inner psychic-spiritual attitude that we adopt toward insects. The insects belong to the same organic social order to which we belong. They are integral members of our own life community. We cannot live without them. To speak of a comprehensive compassion toward all insects is indeed challenging. Yet we cannot refuse the right to existence to any aspect of the universe. Every being came from the same source as every other being. Every being has its own unique yet needed role in relation to all the others. As soon as we reject any part of the universe, we have upset the order of things.

We must indeed protect ourselves against the harmful dimension of other modes of being, yet we easily develop a psychic imbalance in our irrational and unfounded fears. We begin to eliminate insects from any positive role in the integral functioning of the planet. Once we begin this process of rejecting, once we place ourselves at war with the insects, then it is not easy to determine just how far we will go in applying this process of species suppression. The sting of the insects is a language we need to understand. If we turn from this generalized attitude of antagonism to one of discernment, we discover a world of beauty, of skill, of communication, a world of genius for adaptation beyond anything that we could ourselves ever be able to accomplish.

We are missing fully half of nature when we eliminate insects from our world of interest. Considering the beauty of color and form and song added to our world and the increase in intelligence offered to us, it is utterly objectionable to impose our antagonism on the insect components of the Great Community of the Earth. Each of these tiny insects is, by definition, an animated being, a being with an anima, a soul; not a human soul indeed, but an insect soul, a thing of marvelous beauty expressing some aspect of the Divine.

In establishing our basic attitude toward the world about us, we might simply reflect on the awakening of consciousness in our earliest years. As soon as we awaken to consciousness, the universe comes to us, while we go out to the universe. This intimate presence of the universe to itself in each being is the deep excitement of existence. The word "universe," *uni-versa* in the Latin, indicates the turning of the grand diversity of things back toward their unity. I mention this tendency here since this book on insects is simply to indicate the intimate presence that exists between ourselves and the insects. The immediate corollary is that we and the insects depend on each other in some profound manner.

This was the primordial insight of the Taoists of ancient China: the movement of the Tao is "to turn." After differentiating, all things turn back to that primordial unity where each is fulfilled in the others. To go far is to come near. Such is the basic law of existence. We are at the moment of turning. The time has come for humans and the insects to turn toward each other. It is our way to wisdom, the source of our healing, our guidance into the twenty-first century.

Thomas Berry

$\mathcal{P}$reface

In 1998, when *The Voice of the Infinite in the Small* was first published, I opened the preface with a dream that writer Daniel Quinn had when he was six years old. Quinn called the dream his call of destiny in *Providence: The Story of a Fifty-Year Quest*. I consider it a transpersonal dream that applies to a whole generation of people, including myself, predisposed to make deep connections with other species and work on their behalf.

The dream still speaks to me in that way, and so I share it again. It opens in the dead of night as a young Quinn is walking home, past darkened and silent houses. Up ahead he sees that a tree has fallen and is blocking the sidewalk. As he approaches, a "great black beetle" scurries along the trunk toward him. Quinn shrinks back in fear, afraid of insects and worried that the beetle might blame him for cutting down the tree and destroying its home. But the beetle, who has "an aura of great wisdom and authority," speaks to him "in his head" and reassures him that it only wants to talk.

The beetle asks him, "You don't really belong here at all, do you? You don't feel much at home . . . in this world?" Quinn's eyes filled with tears at the beetle's insight. The insect continues, telling the boy that it is because he is not needed in this world. Upon hearing this, young Quinn feels a grief rise up in him that threatens to engulf him.

But then the beetle tells Quinn that the community of life—that is, all the nonhuman species (who live in a forest next to the sidewalk and are now at its edge watching the interchange)—desperately need his help. They want him to leave the sidewalk and enter the forest. "We'll all be there, waiting for you," says the beetle, but "it will mean almost giving up your life . . . [and] becoming one of us, . . . and we need to tell you the secret of our lives."

Without hesitating, young Quinn steps off the sidewalk to join them and wakes up. He bursts into tears. When his mother tries to comfort him, reassuring him that it was just a bad dream, he tells her that she doesn't understand, that he is crying because the dream was so beautiful.

Quinn knew from that early age that someday he would enter the forest where the non human species lived and help them. Twenty-five years later he would use the framework of this dream in his novel *Ishmael*. Instead of a beetle, however, a gorilla confronts the narrator of the story, offering to reveal secrets unknown to humans and inviting him to embark on a journey of discovery.

Ten years after Quinn had his beetle dream, I was tending a wagonful of dirt and worms in my backyard in Michigan. At four years old, a longing for connection with other species was already a strong and steady impulse within me.

Like many of my contemporaries wired in a similar fashion, I found my beetle equivalent and was compelled by intense life-shaping communions with other forms of life and modes of consciousness to push beyond the accepted cultural and scientific assumptions about them. My own life experiences found affirmation in the perennial wisdom of indigenous cultures that believed we were never alone—that we were immersed in a sentient world.

That view of the world as alive and conscious is growing, a response perhaps to global crises caused by paradigms that justify our separation from nature and rationalize an unconscionable destruction of the biosphere that has pushed thousands of species into extinction. Regardless of its origin, more people are asking critical questions and learning how to listen to the wisdom encoded in the natural world. It is a wisdom that has informed and guided indigenous peoples the world over. What has been commonly overlooked in our society, however, for reasons this book and its previous edition details, is the wisdom manifested in and by creeping creatures.

I described the first edition of *The Voice of the Infinite in the Small* as a journey into the shadow of the human psyche. Instead of focusing on the insects, I turned the spotlight on human beings and explored how our beliefs and fears have created an enemy where none exists. On the surface, not much has changed. The abuses that I originally detailed are still occurring. The largely unconscious forces that fuel our habit of enmity are still influencing the culture, still supporting our self-destructive use of insecticides.

What has changed is that a rising impulse to reconnect with these kinds of creatures and celebrate them, barely perceptible a decade ago, is making itself visible. Thomas Berry says that a return to rapprochement with insects is inevitable. He explains in the foreword that the culture has traveled as far away from these kinds of creatures as it can go and after separating, all things must turn back to an underlying unity where each is fulfilled in the other.

Evidence of this shift is all around us. Insect zoos and museums have sprung up all over the world. And you can now find a wide range of products with insect motifs, including paper clips, magnets, soap, metal sculptures, kites, sleeping bags, jewelry, U.S. postage stamps, notepaper, lunch boxes, clothing, and even insect-inspired furniture. I also see this new impulse in the array of insect movies that have come out in the last several years, like the entertaining *ANTZ, A Bug's Life,* and the stunning documentary (and book) *Microcosmos.* Even the new "dark" movies featuring insects that simply mirror our habitual fears, such as *Starship Troopers, Men in Black,* and *Mimic,* may be traced to something new stirring in the unconscious landscape of the culture—albeit twisted by our unexamined enmity.

This new and revised edition of *The Voice of the Infinite in the Small* enters at this period of turning, riding on the rising impulse to reconnect with these creatures and to reclaim the projections that have made them our adversaries. The forces and images that fill our imagination, especially after the horrific terrorist attacks of September 11, 2001 are bound up with the shadow—from what is occurring in our personal lives to what is happening globally.

I believe that undertaking the necessary shadow work to heal our broken relationship with insects and in the process restore a profoundly alienated aspect of our core identity promises benefits that extend beyond the specifics of the insect-human connection. Berry goes so far as to call this inevitable reconciliation with the insects our wisdom, the source of our healing, and our guidance into the twenty-first century. I think of it as a way to access a vital source of renewal and reveal the radiance hidden in what appears small and humble. It is also a unique opportunity to embrace otherness and learn how to blur the boundaries that separate one from another so that we can view the world through different eyes and respond with compassion from that

understanding. It is this aspect of the work that carries the most promise of helping us heal our human relationships.

The new edition is significantly different from the original, while
preserving, I hope, the qualities that a small number of passionate readers have loved. I believe it is easier to read. And I have added more stories to help the reader better imagine the possibilities of relationship.
We are wired for stories. In this edition they strengthen and illuminate
the message that Spirit moves through all creatures and that insects are
messengers and guides of the beneficent powers of creation.

My intention was never to try and to solve every issue that has created uproar and animosity in the insect-human connection but to reveal a blind spot in the culture and set the relationship between insects
and people on a more positive track. The new course requires a context
that elevates kinship bonds and the fact of our interdependence with
all species above our convenience, comfort, and economic concerns
and encourages us to seek correspondences between our worlds.

I'm a layperson, not an entomologist or a scientist, and so I have
written this book for other nonspecialists. The scientific discoveries
that I share in the book are ones that I came across in my reading. If
they delighted my imagination, I included them. I enjoy reading popular science books and magazines, looking for the threads that connect
to my own experiences and what I understand about the world intuitively. I am particularly enamored with the metaphors of what has
been called "new science" and the exciting implications of quantum
mechanics. It is a paradigm based on connections and potentiality, and
it is filled with mystery.

This work of changing the culture's view of insects has grown out of
the contributions of many others—the majority of whom I have referred to in the text. It is the work of the late Laurens van der Post, however, to whom I want to pay special tribute. He illuminated in his books
and lectures the "first" transcendent, creative pattern within each of us
(which he saw in its purest and most mature form in the Stone Age
hunters called Bushmen, also known as the San, of southern Africa),
explaining why an insect—the praying mantis—was chosen as the
Bushmen's highest representation of value and meaning or "the voice
of the infinite in the small." Van der Post believed—and it is an idea that
has greatly influenced my thinking—that the restoration of the despised and profoundly rejected wilderness or instinctual self inside us

(a foundation in spirit that is rooted to nature) is critical to our surviving the challenges of this time.

I have chosen after some deliberation not to include the scientific names of insects in the text. In doing so, I hope to appeal to the average person, who is largely unfamiliar with insects and uninterested in delving into the classification system that entomologists find so useful. Instead, I refer to insects using their common names and the broad categories that laypeople use. I believe it is only when an insect calls a person into its sphere of influence that he or she wants to know exactly what kind of insect it is and how it lives its life, and for that purpose there are other books available.

Although I continue to share a common purpose with the many entomologists who have devoted considerable energy and resources to changing the public's view of insects, my approach is radically different. I enter the territory with a deep love for the insects, an understanding of the dynamics of the human psyche, a belief that the microcosm reflects the macrocosm, and an abiding interest in the healing potential inherent in our relationship to all other species.

Joanne Lauck
December 2001

Acknowledgments

Although many people have supported me directly and indirectly as I worked on this revision of the original book, *The Voice of the Infinite in the Small*, my deepest gratitude and love continues to go to my parents—Emery and Naomi Lauck, who are with me in spirit: to my father for passing on his deep love of the natural world and encouraging me to always have a vision, and to my mother for her unconditional love and support over the years. I also want to thank my stepchildren, Ashley, Andy, and Matthew, for bringing the fire of transformation and renewal into my life and my nieces, Andrea Hill, Ellen and Beth Lauck, and Sarah and Laura Thomas, who have been the inspiration for my work with children in the schools.

Deep love and appreciation go to my sisters, Linda Buecken and Cheryl Thomas for their encouragement and for sharing my love of the "other ones." And to my brother, Tom Lauck for giving me a home that I cherish and for his patience and willingness to tutor me, not only in the art of computing but in the art of moving out into the world with clarity, integrity, and purpose.

Special love and deep gratitude go as well to Marcia Lauck, who has been friend, sister-in-law, and mentor for over twenty years. Marcia, an author herself, is the "universal dreamer" whose dream of the golden cockroach I include at the end of chapter 14. As the catalyst for my self-explorations and my guide, Marcia has freely shared her vision, knowledge, and heart with me over the years. In fact, it was she who first understood and taught me that my deep feelings for other species were not the eccentricity of a personality out of sync with cultural expectations, but the expression of an inner blueprint that would eventually lead me to begin writing and teaching about these "other nations of consciousness." Her influence in my life and my gratitude extend far beyond what I can express here.

I also want to acknowledge and give thanks to my dear friend Trisha Lamb Feuerstein. Trisha and her husband, Georg Feuerstein have supported this project in large and small ways from the start. Trisha, deeply called herself to work on behalf of cetaceans, has been sending me insect articles and information for years, and many of the stories included in the book are her discoveries.

Deep appreciation goes as well to Kendra Crossen Burroughs for her vision and enthusiastic support of the original book and for the central role she played in getting this new version out into the world through the excellent publishing house Shambhala Publications and with the help of Dave O'Neal and the rest of the editorial team. Kendra has also provided invaluable editorial assistance on this second edition.

Thanks also to my neighbor Pam van Dyck, an insect enthusiast for years, and to Lisa van Dyck, her daughter and a kindred spirit who has cared for my animal companions over the last ten years whenever I have had to travel to make presentations on the insect-human connection. And gratitude to other friends, old and new, who have provided encouragement and enthusiasm along the way, including a sister of the heart, Gwynn Popovac, the insect artist you will meet in chapter 1; my Canadian cousin Jim Lauck, who brought his teacher's eye to the original manuscript; my Brazilian sister Silvia Jorge, my cat sister Sherral Morford, who tends a homeless colony of cats with me; Scott Hess, whose enthusiasm brought the original book to the attention of the No Spray communities in Northern California; Touch drawing artist Deborah Koff-Chapin, whose images provide guidance; insect aficionado Hariana Chilstrom; Brian Crissey and Pam Meyer, my original publishers, who caught the vision and ran with it; writer and wildlife rehabilitator extraordinaire Phylis Rollins; Reiki healer and animal communicator Darlene Dressler (and Clarence, her basset hound), oldest friend and confidante, Diana Funicello; sister on the path Patricia Earl; and the one who walks and talks with angels, Jean Collins.

I also want to acknowledge my circle of animal lovers and writers, who, like me, found their essential selves in working on behalf of other species: Dawn Brunke, Sharon Callahan, Susan Chernak, Victoria Covell, Brooke Medicine Eagle, Morgaine Jurdan, Maraleen Manos-Jones, Rita Reynolds, Jeri Ryan, and Penelope Smith. And this page of acknowledgments would not be complete without thanking Brian Goddard, the young man featured in the stories about my "Thinking Like a Bug" class and who became my assistant after his memorable encounter with Cedar, the cockroach.

A new development in my work of helping people retrieve their projections and forego enemy-making revolves around mentoring at-risk youth and young adults—a group of people routinely misunderstood and marginalized by mainstream culture (see catalystforyouth.org). In light of this recent turn on the path, I want to take this opportunity to acknowledge and thank as my teachers and friends a group of young artists who live poised on the "edge of chaos" and are open to its inspiration and potential for transportation: Tony Landeros, Curtis Manzano, Erin Minjares, Louis Navarro, Mike Sandovol, Ernesto Solorio, and Anton Strila.

Last, but not least, I want to thank the inspiration of Spirit and the many creatures who have shared their wisdom with me, including those who keep me company now: my cats Susi, Moses, Bobbie, Scottie, and Rosie, each with a remarkable story of their own; my beloved dog, Jessie who shepherds all the animals when she is not chasing squirrels; Annie, my wild-born rat and gift from the rat gods; Rumi and Sweet Pea, my parakeets, who model devotion; Chloe and Hope, my irascible and engaging cockatiels; the twelve turtle doves who sing me to sleep each evening from their aviary outside my bedroom window; the colony of homeless cats who know the sound of my steps, and my cockroaches, who teach me daily about otherness. I am also deeply endebted to Mantis, under whose watchful presence this work was created and moves out into the world, and to Leaf, child of my heart, teacher, and the being in fur who started it all.

The Voice of the

Infinite in the Small

1. COMING HOME

We are all culturally hypnotized.
— *Willis Harman*

In Lewis Carroll's *Through the Looking Glass*, a gnat inquires of Alice, "What sort of insects do you rejoice in where you come from?" Puzzled by the question, Alice replies, "I don't rejoice in insects at all." In these lines, an ancient world that acknowledged and celebrated all life forms meets our modern world, which has little regard for insects and related creatures.* In the West we don't rejoice in insects. Most of our interactions with them, in fact, are fraught with anxiety and mistrust. If not actively hostile, we are at best, like Alice, ambivalent, our feelings colored by habitual enmity and fear.

If we rejoiced in insects, we would take delight in their presence and act on their behalf when needed. Yet, only a few people extend a helping hand when they see an insect in trouble, and only specialists

---

*As a convenience I use the term *insect*, usually reserved for six-legged invertebrates, to refer to all six-, eight-, and multilegged land-dwelling, creeping, and flying creatures commonly considered bugs or creepy crawlers.

act to save endangered insect species. Most of us feel that a few less insects in the world would be a good thing.

When I first began to investigate the insect-human connection, I was looking for stories of cooperation and kinship. What I found was a level of animosity that surprised and disturbed me. It was everywhere I looked—in the news, pop culture, scientific works, children's books, and even on the World Wide Web. I hadn't realized the amount of fear and hatred that governs typical responses to insects and found it to be far greater than any negative feelings we might harbor toward other species.

Attempts to explain these feelings typically focus on the insects: their independence, their strange appearance, and their tendency to appear in great numbers. But I wondered how much our assumptions colored what we saw when we looked at these creatures. And how much did a lack of knowledge about insects and the absence of a context to support kinship influence how we viewed our encounters with them?

The Belief in Insect as Adversary

Large and small battles against insects occur every day in Western industrialized society. Our belief in insects as adversaries shapes our interactions with them. It has given rise to the regulatory agencies and big-business conglomerates whose goal is to eradicate or control insects. Propaganda generated by these institutions simplifies the complexities of our relationship with the creatures and feeds us hostile images that perpetuate a militaristic stance toward thousands of species. The taproot, however, is our fear.

"I didn't know what it was, so I killed it" is what biologist Ronald Rood heard over and over again when he questioned people who brought him the dead bodies of insects or other unfamiliar creatures to identify. The curiosity natural in a nonthreatening situation was absent. They had killed it—just to be safe—to crush the fear invoked by the creature's presence.

A large part of our fear revolves around being bitten. Bug zappers, those glowing fixtures in suburban yards, keep those fears at bay, killing billions of insects each year. One entomologist said that all these devices do is amuse us; they are otherwise ineffective. Fewer than one-fourth of the insects killed are the ones with an appetite for blood. Any mirth, however, would be short-lived if we realized that when insects hit the zapper and explode, they spray bacteria and viruses in a radius of at least two meters.

Self-protection may motivate us to stop using bug zappers because compassion for the estimated seventy-one billion nontarget insects that are killed each year has not. In fact, there isn't much that influences our conviction that insects are adversaries. When our experiences do not substantiate our fears, we tend to discount the contradictory evidence. Convinced we are justified and acting realistically, we are quick to defend our aggressive stance and don't even see the opportunities that arise for a different, more positive relationship.

Stories of Kinship and Affinity

The stories of kinship, communion, and cooperation that I originally sought I found in certain religions, philosophies, and cultures that felt differently about insects and included them in their circle of community. In tribal societies, for instance, the strategies for dealing with biting insects and the discomfort of insect bites did not negate their feelings of kinship with these species. Consider an Eskimo tale found in Lawrence Millman's *A Kayak Full of Ghosts*, called "The Old Woman Who Was Kind to Insects." The story was told around a fire in West Greenland during a plague of mosquitoes:

> One winter an old woman was left behind by her family and tribe as they followed their winter prey. She was so old that she could barely chew anymore, so they only left her a few insects to eat. The woman looked at the insects and said: "I'm not going to eat these poor creatures. I am old and perhaps they are young. Perhaps a few are even children. I'd rather die first."
>
> Soon after, a fox entered her hut. It leaped up and started to bite her. The old woman thought it was all over. But the fox bit her repeatedly from head to toe, as if it were taking off her clothing. Soon all her skin fell away revealing a new younger skin underneath, for the grateful insects had instructed their friend the fox to rid her of her old skin.[1]

This story of compassion toward insects and its surprising reward gains added importance because of when it was told—when the air was thick with mosquitoes. No hero's tale of battle against mosquito foes, the story seeds the listener's imagination with images of respect and kinship, teaching the transformative power of compassion. It also underscores this tribe's belief in the bond between their people and all other species, even when the behavior of another species is painful or inconvenient.

I also found a few memorable stories by contemporary people like Gwynn Popovac, an artist from Sonoma, California, who discovered an essential aspect of her life's work after an encounter with an insect. The meeting happened years ago while Popovac was sitting on a boulder in the middle of a creek. A drab, many-jointed bug crawled onto the back of her hand. She almost obeyed a startle reflex and flung it away, but for some reason she checked herself and allowed it to crawl to the tip of her finger. There its back split open, and it extracted itself from its shell. This new creature was transparent and pulsated. Soon what looked like wads of cellophane began to uncrinkle and—"vibration by vibration"—became flat, glistening wings. "A few quivers more," recalls Popovac, "and this drab creature of the creek bed had changed into an iridescent creature of the air." She watched the dragonfly as it rested briefly and felt its vibration run from her fingertip to her arm and down her spine. Then it was gone, soaring downstream with a rustling of wings. The pleasing vibration stayed with her as she returned home and got out her oil paints, painting the dragonfly hovering over a stream. It was the first time Popovac had ever given center stage to an insect in a painting, having decided it was the best way to repay it for the experience.

And since that day Popovac has continued to repay the insects for the magic of that encounter and others that followed. Each of her exquisitely detailed insect portraits reveals her love of their form, their iridescence, and their color. Enshrined in decorative borders, suspended in time, each subject is given the respect it deserves under her skilled hand, and the viewer is left with a feeling of having glimpsed the essence of the creature, its mode of divinity, and the unblemished treasure that it is. Rudolf Steiner once said, "The artist does not bring the divine onto the Earth by letting it flow into the world; he [or she] raises the world into the sphere of the divine." And that is a fitting description of what Popovac has done for the insects, leading those who can follow to connections above and beyond cultural norms and bias.

We are at a turning point where each of us can choose to follow the connections in the hopes of being led to something essential and worthy of our attention. Even though in the West we have moved away from these links, thinking ourselves separate from other species, denying our connections hasn't dissolved them. And as our understanding of our profound interdependence with all species grows, only the fear-driven habits of enmity—which largely determine our present responses to insects—hold us to a false path and prevent us from finding the insect species whose presence can turn us toward our authentic selves.

In the following pages, I will reveal the habit that binds us to a narrow path of mistrust, indifference, and fear, influencing our perception and imagination. Awareness will lead to freedom. Simply by taking a hard look at the current state of affairs, we strip this hostile attitude of its covert power, clearing a path to the multifaceted, transformative power of the insect realm.

Creating a Hostile World

There are real reasons why we mistrust and fear insects. Few have much to do with the actual insect. Most involve misperceptions about them and about ourselves, and are tied to a multitude of beliefs about our place in the Earth community.

The current stance toward insects has roots that extend back to when we desacralized Nature and adopted a mechanistic model of the world—a collective decision explored in recent years through a great number of lenses. During that time, we transferred our trust to science and technology and turned a cautionary stance—that what is strange or unknown may be dangerous—into an absolute belief. Then we added to it, attributing to the strange and unknown an evil intent. It is understandable, then, given our beliefs, that we view the often bizarre-looking creatures suspiciously and arm ourselves against them.

By drawing our boundaries of self and community too small, we have created a world outside those lines that frightens us. Imbuing the unfamiliar and strange with malevolence has transformed the once-sacred Earth community into an environment populated by monsters. It has also exaggerated and distorted whatever survival instincts—whatever healthy fear—we had evolved as a species to keep us cautious and appropriately alert.

Today our animosity is largely habit and unexamined fear, fueled by a flow of hostile images and words that remind us that insects are adversaries. The widespread acceptance of this view as a realistic response makes its considerable influence virtually invisible—until we become aware of it. Then we will discover, as I did, that the evidence is all around us.

Our Assumptions at Work in Movies   In movies, we see our beliefs paraded before us in uninhibited display. These imaginative expressions reflect the mainstream's core assumptions and fears about insects and, entertainment aside, help to maintain our combative attitude.

In the last hundred years, movies consistently portrayed insects as hungry for power and human flesh. In many films, common insects assume immense proportions, often after some accident in a laboratory or a catastrophic natural event. Their appetite increases in proportion to their size. When they inevitably seek human prey, a hero-scientist must outwit them to save the terrorized human community.

In the film *The Deadly Mantis* (1957), a typical science-fiction thriller, a giant praying mantis hunts humans for food. And in *The Beginning of the End* (also 1957), flesh-hungry giant locusts ravage the Midwest. Forty years later the same theme is played out in *Independence Day,* in which aliens, described as swarming locusts, ruthlessly attack the Earth, trying to exterminate the human species.

In 1997 *Men in Black* made its debut, a rather comic sci-fi movie in which the ruthless extraterrestrial alien is now a cockroach, hated and feared by humans and other extraterrestrials alike. No matter that the cockroach villain has teeth like a shark and a lizardlike body, the real cockroaches that drop out of its sleeve throughout the movie are enough to evoke the loathing people feel toward this particular insect.

Scientific Discoveries Add Credibility   To provide variations on a standard theme, filmmakers keep their antennae tuned to scientific discoveries about insects, incorporating them into their scripts to make them more plausible. New findings either create a new insect problem or provide the heroic scientists with a critical advantage over insect monstrosities ravaging the human community.

The use of wasp enzymes and bee serum in the cosmetic industry led to a 1960 film called *Wasp Woman,* in which a cosmetic queen takes wasp enzymes to stay young and turns into a killer wasp. And in *Bug,* a 1975 movie, a scientist crosses a new insect species that feeds on carbon with a common cockroach and gets a flesh-eating insect. *The Nest*, perhaps a sequel, also features cockroaches that feed on humans.

The 1997 sci-fi thriller *Mimic* incorporates gene-altering biotechnology with the remarkable ability of many insects to camouflage themselves. And the psychological thriller *The Silence of the Lambs* relies on techniques from the field of forensic entomology to pair insects with a psychopathic killer.

Short Stories Reflect Our Beliefs Like movies, fiction also follows the culture's beliefs faithfully. In T. S. Eliot's short story "The Cocktail Party," the missionary heroine is staked near an anthill and tortured by swarming ants. Ants are also the culprits in William Patrick's thriller *Spirals* and carry a virus from a sealed lab to the outside world. In "Itching for Action," a short story by Charles Garofalo, fleas take revenge on a man who poisons dogs and cats.

Thomas M. Disch's 1965 story "The Roaches" incorporates layers of negative beliefs. The heroine, Marcia, is a lonely young woman who can't see a cockroach without wanting to scream. She spends every evening killing them in her apartment. The story's effectiveness depends on readers who are repelled by the look and mobility of cockroaches and horrified by the thought of thousands living behind their walls.

The intensity of Marcia's hatred and her single-minded pursuit of these insects create a link between herself and them. One day she discovers that they understand and obey her commands. Once aware of her powers over them, she sends them to kill her neighbors. After the deed they return to her, broadcasting one thought: "We love you we love you we love you." To her amazement she answers, "I love you too." The story ends as roaches from all over the city crawl toward their mistress. The story's message—that hating something can be an expression of hidden sympathies for the thing we hate—is a good insight into the nature of affinity. The idea that cockroaches will kill on command, however, reflects the common belief in the robotic mentality of insects and is a kind of infantile fantasy of power over others.

Comic Books Reflect the Culture's View Comic books are another medium that expresses the culture's beliefs about insects in an exaggerated fashion. A good example is "Winged Death Came Out of the Night," which features a generic bug that combines size, odor, claws, and piercing mandibles to engage the widest range of fears in the reader. The insect smashes against a screen door, startling a man alone in a cabin.

Each night the bug grows bigger, hurling itself against the door in unexplained fury. In a dream, the human-size bug tells the man scornfully, "You can't kill me, man! You can't keep me from getting you! My intelligence is greater than yours! We, the lowly bugs, shall rule the earth." The dream becomes reality the next day when the bug bursts through the screen and eats the man.

These are our fears and projections, our belief in the insect as adversary. It is also our belief in the malevolence of the unknown and unfamiliar. We imagine that given the chance, insects, possessed of an evil intent, want to take over the world and dominate us.

This tendency to attribute to insects our desire for power over others is also seen in articles on alien abductions. One UFO author, recalling the "flying bee hives" reported in the 1950s and other sightings and accounts of abductions by insectoid aliens, painstakingly describes what these insect aliens could do to human abductees.

But is the will to dominate another species in the insect, or is it in the human personality? Our beliefs about insects and our readiness to think the worst of them color our experiences with real insects and transform the natural world into an alien landscape populated by robotic and malevolent specks of life. Anxiety levels elevated, we become increasingly isolated from the natural world, pitted against the imagined ill will of the Earth community.

The Language of War

Whereas we might expect the popular media to reflect our fears and fantasies, we don't expect it in news reports about insects. Yet it is there, in written form as well as reported live. A newspaper reporter under the spell of the cultural bias, for example, writes about a "vicious" fly biting innocent people unfortunate enough to live in the fly's territory. According to this news item, the fly is a "savage animal" that rampages across the county looking for people to attack. Another news item, about a company that manufactures biological insecticides, describes an "insidious new weapon against humanity's ancient enemy— the lowly cockroach."

Insect-related advertising on television and in newspapers and magazines, a tool of the industries that make their money killing insects, reminds us at every turn that insects lie waiting for a chance to hurt us or our property or to spread filth and disease. A woman on a television insecticide commercial tells the viewers in a confidential tone, "They deserve to die." Few of us question her statement. Fewer still identify it as an expression of hatred or realize that there are real and dire consequences—both psychological and physiological—to hating anything.

We simply don't take issue when insects are called aggressive, vicious, or malevolent. In fact, we are more likely to object and dismiss as sentimentality descriptions of insect behavior using favorable characteristics. Worse, cultural pressure shames those who might naturally respond compassionately to individual insects. Offenders are ridiculed by those who would uphold the culture's condemnation of insects and our right to kill what we find offensive.

Ironically, the tendency to anthropomorphize, or attribute human characteristics to, other species, a taboo of science, is often accepted without comment in scientific circles when the traits projected are negative. The literature is filled with reports of other species that act "spitefully," "greedily," or "cruelly." When, however, a species displays friendship, trust, or curiosity, scientists are quick to use negative or neutral language to prevent accusations of naiveté, romanticism, or ridicule by their colleagues. It seems that no one is automatically immune to the influence of the collective bias simply by the weight of his or her academic credentials.

Celebrating Our Hostility

Our hostility toward insects also appears in community activities. In fact, we often stage events to celebrate it. An archery club on the West Coast, for instance, holds an annual bug shoot where people pay a fee to shoot at replicas of worms, snails, and insects. Although the public might protest if models of dogs and cats were used, no one objects to the multilegged targets.

Mosquitoes are a favorite recipient of group hostility. Each year a small Texan town hosts a mosquito festival to lure tourists to their area. Townspeople pass out tiny swatters to participants to keep the mosquitoes away. One year, however, the eighty-four species of mosquitoes native to the state were noticeably absent, so there were not enough insects to kill. The mayor was unhappy about the dearth of the normally abundant mosquitoes—but he made the best of it. In the opening ceremony, he held up a jar with a live mosquito in it and then opened the jar and killed the insect ceremoniously with a "Texas-size" swatter as the crowd cheered.

Attempts to balance the prejudice toward insects and promote an appreciation for them are often contaminated by our unexamined beliefs. A case in point is the popular hands-on exhibition on insects touring the country's museums and featuring six huge, robotic insects. It could have been called Backyard Wonders but was named Backyard Monsters by its creators.

A few years ago, a local art gallery in the San Francisco Bay area that prides itself on its innovative exhibitions featured mixed-media artworks devoted to insects. One "artist" killed flies and mounted their dead bodies on paper so that they spelled the word "flypaper." Prejudice passed for creativity, and the audience was appreciative and amused.

When art reflects the limitations of the popular culture, it becomes little more than a propaganda device, reflecting not vision but our blind spots and narrow interpretation of life. A contemporary British artist uses live insects in his exhibits. In one of his displays, houseflies are hatched and killed by an electric fly zapper so that the observers of the exhibit will become uncomfortable and realize they are like the hapless flies. No one protests the needless deaths of the flies.

Teaching Prejudice

The message we give our children is understandably in line with our beliefs. We train their imaginations, instilling hostile images that uphold the cultural stereotypes of other creatures. This type of indoctrination also prevents undue curiosity from interfering with the official view—especially if the insect has been categorized as a pest.

Our control orientation toward the natural world, taught from grade school on, emphasizes that every plant and animal must fit our human-centered agenda to be of value on the Earth. Having divided all species into beneficial ones or pests, we are quick to ask, "What good is it?" The answer given determines how we feel about that insect, and those judged as pests are stripped of all rights and targeted for extermination on sight.

Our teaching materials naturally reflect the biases we have come to view as reality. A web site geared toward children joined a new science center and calls itself "The Yuckiest Site on the Internet" because it presents photos of "humankind's worst enemy: the cockroach." In its online learning center, Rodney the Cockroach offers facts about cockroaches that are contaminated by a pest-management orientation and the culture's condemnation of these creatures.

Teaching hatred under the guise of education is effective. The site's message board includes an entry from a young visitor who shares his "fun" roach-killing methods: "Turn a fan vertical and drop one in [*splat*]." Lest we think this unusual, a major technology institute teamed up with an insecticide company to sponsor a cockroach-killing exhibit for children. Billed as an educational event, it was well attended.

A "find out about science" book for young children on cockroaches follows the same line of thinking, with illustrations showing adults and children killing insects in a variety of ways. The text explains that some insects, like cockroaches, are simply pests. Another illustration shows a boy's foot about to come crashing down on a cockroach to illustrate the function of two appendages that help alert the insect to danger. This is scientific information presented with an appeal to the hostile imagination.

What this book teaches is that human beings don't like certain insects and that it is okay to kill what we don't like. By the age of ten, the information will be embedded in children's minds. As adults, they will probably not remember why they hate them. Their ingrained response will feel natural.

These same negatively conditioned individuals will be likely to accept the popular theory that people dislike and fear insects because they look so different from us. They may also accept the theory that insect fear as it exists in modern society is a protective mechanism, a genetic holdover from a time when humans were still learning which insects were dangerous. They may not even consider the possibility that their responses are exaggerated and distorted by simple conditioning and the lack of a context that would encourage kinship and appreciation.

Organic Controls Keep the Insect as Enemy

After Rachel Carson's exposé on insecticides, *Silent Spring*, hit the bookstores in the 1960s, the growing concern about using toxic chemicals to fight insects increased. Our new awareness, however, did not change our belief in insects as adversaries. We still wanted them dead; we just didn't want to kill ourselves in the process—or poison creatures we liked. New products flooded the market. Advertising kept its aggressive tone. Headlines from organic gardening magazines read like military news: "Be Ready for the Annual Beetle Invasion."

Today, the official view of insects continues to support a dangerously high use of toxic chemicals despite the overwhelming evidence of their danger. New studies substantiate old fears with an alarming frequency. For example, Stanford University researchers recently linked home pesticide use to Parkinson's disease. And the connections between pesticides and cancer, birth defects, hormonal disruptions, and genetic alterations are already well documented.

In the environment, pesticides destroy beneficial soil organisms, escalating soil erosion and nutrient loss. Pesticides seep into groundwater, streams, and lakes, contaminating our drinking water and damaging aquatic ecosystems. Pesticide use also leads to secondary insect infestations that necessitate further applications, putting us on a pesticide treadmill.

Biological Pest Control   One alternative solution that safeguards our belief in insect as adversary is called biological pest control—using insects to kill other insects. We have imported insects from other countries to prey on local species, setting aside the complexities and interrelationship between plants and insects in the target habitat. John McLaughlin of the U.S. Department of Agriculture admits that biological pest control "is a bit of a crapshoot, so you don't release just one species; you try to introduce several." Sometimes it appears to have worked; other times it definitely has not. Sometimes the imported species has become the enemy preying on and threatening species that were not even supposed to be part of the game.

Genetically engineered plants have also entered the battlefield. Engineered to resist specific insects, their effectiveness has been shown to decrease over time as insects mutate to survive. Our response is to add another gene to the formula to address that resistance. Applying one fix on top of another gone awry is standard operating procedure despite the fact that hundreds of cases of resistance by mutation have been recorded.

Upping the ante, scientists have made genetically engineered insects to carry on the war, ignoring protests from angry groups who call it "ecological dynamite." In an attempt to assuage concern, one scientist told reporters, "We can use genes the same way we use insecticides." This is not very reassuring. Scientists do not really know for certain what they are unleashing in the environment. They admit their understanding of insect behavior and ecology is far from complete. They are also under considerable pressure to act because their research is funded by organizations that require efficient short-term solutions. More important, most scientists lack the psychological maturity to unplug the war machine and harness genetic technological prowess in service of the nonhostile imagination. Only then might an appropriate response to a complex problem be found.

Mythologist Joseph Campbell pointed out that the popular culture never rises above issues of power and deals with this theme in all its variations. It is in this mode, then, that we are caught between opposites: either we kill the insects or we are defeated by them. We rarely see a third possibility. We scarcely put down our weapons long enough to consider the effect we might have if we entered the insect world with empathy and compassion—like the old Eskimo woman who was kind to insects. Perhaps we underestimate the powers of Providence that would suddenly appear if we could align ourselves with the Earth and its small multilegged creatures. It is time to try.

Re-visioning Our Connection to Insects

Leaving the battlefield would be a simple matter if all it involved were presenting the right facts about an insect in the right way. But knowing how to live in harmony with insects has less to do with insect biology and behavior than it has to do with untangling the threads of self-deception, misperception, and fear that prevent us from including insects in our circle of community.

Depth psychologist James Hillman maintains that the insect problem is in our heads. He says that unless we develop an inner ecology to stop us from acting out our fears, we will become increasingly isolated and continue to infect, pollute, and poison the world in an attempt to eradicate what we perceive as evil. Our self-destructive behavior starts when we imagine that they are intent on harming us and so we attack them first and continue attacking them with pesticides until we risk poisoning ourselves and the environment beyond repair.

Transforming Ourselves   To unplug from the perception of insect as adversary—and not only unplug but radically alter the way we perceive and relate to insects—we must be willing to change ourselves. The required transformation promises to rattle our most cherished ideas but will serve us in the end. Anytime we let go of assumptions we blindly adopted as children and prejudices we retain as adults, we move under the influence of a powerful catalyst for insight and growth in directions unforeseen.

Part of our task is clearing the lens through which we see another and becoming more psychologically sophisticated. We must learn, for instance, how enemies, personal and collective, are created in the human psyche. We must also bring a sharp and discriminating eye to the propaganda around us. When we take our instructions from organizations that tell us that "the only good bug is a dead bug," we expend great amounts of energy fighting insect phantoms. After all, waging war on insects is a $3.5 billion business.

A further challenge involves scrutinizing our notions of sickness and health and who causes what disease, and then rerouting research dollars into preventative measures. With insects and microbes mutating, and diseases like tuberculosis and malaria increasingly drug-resistant and on the rise, it is clear we need a different conceptual base underlying medicine, and one that adds more complexity to our formulations and treatment strategies.

Finding a New Context   After rooting out the beliefs that set up the war with insects, we will be ready for a new context to help us translate our interactions with them. The context sets the stage and determines whether we enter a battlefield, an amusement park, or a temple when we meet an insect. The right context will help us leave the current good-versus-evil drama and discover something heroic and of great merit in changing our customary stance. It will also provide us with guidelines for how to respond.

Stories are the vehicle through which any cultural worldview or commonly held beliefs are disseminated and upheld in the population. From the story we tell ourselves about who we are and how the world works, an environmental ethic, sound or unsound, emerges.

A new life-serving story that weaves new scientific discoveries and ancient truths about our interdependence with other species will be the ground from which an appropriate ethic about insects will emerge. Indigenous practices and stories like "The Old Woman Who Was Kind to Insects" are a response to an understanding of that bond. Studying the ways of tribal societies may help us find a contemporary expression aligned with the truth of our profound interconnectedness. Then we can teach the children.

Having briefly entered and marked the territory—the existing bias against insects, the beliefs that have created our habits of enmity, the forms that uphold it, and the nature of the change that will free us for rejoicing—we are ready to embark on the journey back to our native place. By transforming ourselves, we can forgo our fugitive status and come home, finally, to an Earth community that awaits our return.

2. Clearing *the* Lens

In the beginning we create the enemy.

—*Sam Keen*

Each generation has learned from the previous one to project a good measure of hostility onto insects and then react to them accordingly. Children watch their parents respond to the creatures around them and imitate their reactions. I recently witnessed this kind of modeling behavior in a local crafts store. I was standing in an aisle amid a display of assorted plastic crickets and ladybugs created to add interest to floral arrangements, when a woman with a toddler in hand walked by. The woman pointed to the plastic insects and said, "Oh, Jeffrey, look, bugs! Ick!" "Ick," echoed the child, the lesson learned without protest.

This kind of instruction, given without thinking, is commonplace. Teaching disgust or fear too often stops a child from exploring the connection further—at least until time and insight have tempered the experience. The celebrated wildlife researcher Jane Goodall tells in her memoir, *Reason for Hope,* about an incident that happened when she was less than a year old. As described to her by a family member, she was in a stroller parked outside a store while her nanny shopped inside. A dragonfly swooped around her, and she screamed. A well-intentioned man passing by swung at the insect with a rolled-up newspaper, knocking it to the ground, and then stepped on it. Little Jane screamed all the way home. She was so hysterical that the family doctor was called to calm her with a sedative.

Sixty years later, Goodall tried to remember why she had been so terrified. She closed her eyes and was transported back in time. She saw herself lying in her nursery crib mesmerized by a big blue dragonfly that had flown in through the open window. Just then her nanny came in and chased the insect out, telling the young girl that its long tail was a stinger. No wonder she was frightened, Goodall thought, when a few months later a second dragonfly flew near her. It didn't mean, though, that she wanted someone to kill it. Suddenly the memory returned vividly, and she could see the insect with the shimmering blue wings crushed on the sidewalk. She knew even at that young age that it had died because she had screamed in fright, and so she screamed again and again in outrage and from a terrible sense of guilt.

Fear is a powerful force that shapes how we see the world and respond to it. Our eyes are not machines that simply reflect the world back to us without distortion. What we see is always subject to interpretation. Like Goodall, if we are afraid of dragonflies and believe they might sting us, we will feel threatened when they fly around us. It will not occur to us that they might just be curious about our scent or the color of our clothing. But if we have learned that insects are friendly, we might decide, like one six-year-old boy, that they simply want to kiss us.

Mitchell Hall writes in *Orion Nature Quarterly* of the time when a dragonfly brushed the cheek of his young son, Ezra. "That dragonfly kissed me," the boy matter-of-factly told his mother. Later that afternoon, Ezra hurt himself and started to cry. Hall was holding him when a dragonfly flew out of the canopy of a nearby tree. The insect buzzed around in a circle just above Ezra's head. When Hall pointed it out, the boy stopped crying to look at the insect. Hall told him that the dragonfly had come to let Ezra know that he loved him. Ezra calmed right down, and the insect flew away to the tree.

Seeing Truly Seeing an insect or any creature as it is, without fear and judgment obscuring our perception, isn't easy. When we do, we open ourselves to the most vital and significant facts arising out of the moment. It's called "beginner's mind," a state of dynamic receptiveness that meditators seek. Zen masters teach that this state of mind is the space or attitude from which all wisdom arises, and it takes practice to experience it.

Thoreau believed that looking at and seeing something were two different acts, and that only the act of seeing involved understanding and genuine meeting. The naturalist Annie Dillard said that only when you love something or have spent time learning about it can you see its reality.

Dillard's insight is echoed by Nobel Prize laureate Barbara McClintock, who conducted her genetic research on corn by getting to know each plant intimately. McClintock's deep reverence for Nature and ability to unite with whatever she studied enhanced her vision and led to her discovery of gene transposition in corn.

So, to look at insects rightly, we must have, as McClintock would assert, "a feeling for the organism" composed of empathy, appreciation, and enough knowledge to respond appropriately when we meet them—enough knowledge to know that the long abdomen of the dragonfly is not a stinger, enough sensitivity to prevent us from passing on our fears to others.

Neither loving toward insects nor knowledgeable about them, we view them through a shadowed lens. Our opinions and judgments shield us from the anxiety of being in the presence of a consciousness so different from our own. But we lose a deep feeling connection to other creatures when we trade the mystery of another's existence for a neat bundle of classifications and a pooling of unexamined emotions. We also lose our ability to see accurately and respond appropriately when we attribute dark motives to other beings and cast them as enemies.

Enemy-Making

Enemy-making depends on a psychological defense mechanism called projection. Projections interfere with our ability to see and relate humanely to another, be it insect or person. When a projection is operating, we attribute qualities and motives to the other, creating an identity in line with our own needs and beliefs and often far removed from the other's true nature.

Identifying our projections is the first step toward seeing others—human or nonhuman—as they exist outside of our fears, needs, and opinions. Projections reside in what psychologists call the Shadow, a part of the personality that contains qualities made unconscious so that traits deemed good and acceptable can be emphasized and developed. But these Shadow qualities don't disappear. They come out as attacks on others in order to feel good about who we are. Self-righteousness and ridicule are signs that the Shadow is operating in a situation.

The creation of a Shadow is a universal phenomenon, a pattern formed as a child's personality develops. Each child learns its culture's acceptable ways of looking and acting, modified only by the parent's values. All other qualities contrary to the culture's and family's ideas of what is good and appropriate are relegated to the child's unconscious Shadow. But repressing qualities does not eliminate them. They continue to function, unsupervized and unchecked, projected out into the world onto others.

Group Shadow   Groups, like individuals, have a Shadow that contains repressed qualities incongruent with the way members of the group like to think of themselves. The Shadow of Western culture is expressed collectively as the Enemy, the personification of evil typically seen in minority nationalities, races, and religions. In turn, "Americans" carry the projections for extremists like Osama bin Laden and totalitarian leaders like Saddam Hussein and their followers.

In Sam Keen's insightful book *Faces of the Enemy*, he points out that both the personal and the collective Shadow help people avoid looking at their own hostilities, which are always projected out onto someone else. Propaganda is an essential component of preserving the Shadow projections toward a particular target, because it demonizes the individual or group while simplifying the issues and glossing over contrary evidence. The collective Shadow's influence compels us to find public enemies, replacing one nation with another, one leader with another, one species with another, as power shifts and economic and political alliances change. The wars that follow then, Keen observes, are little more than attempts to kill those parts of ourselves we despise and deny having.

The fact that we project our rejected qualities onto another doesn't automatically mean that the other is innocent of these projections. But the intensity of our fear, repulsion, or dislike reflects the strength of the repressed energies within us and is not a response to the traits as they actually exist in another. In fact, we can't really know how much is in the other until we suspend our beliefs and study the source of our projections. When we have done our personal work and understood our complicity, we will have defused the hot buttons that cause us to react with self-righteousness and militancy. We also will have freed ourselves to see another accurately and choose an appropriate response.

Faces of the Enemy   Although Keen is referring to the faces of human enemies, the psychological realities apply to any situation in which, denying our hostility, we project it out into the world. Insects are an easy hook for our projections because of their strange appearance and habits and their disregard for our economic agendas. To aid the enemy-making process, insects are often paired with humans. In 1994, for instance, when the Haldeman diaries implicated Richard Nixon in the Watergate cover-up, *San Jose Mercury News* cartoonist Scott Willis drew a cockroach with Nixon's head; the association between Nixon's behavior and our belief in the contemptibility of this insect was readily understood.

During Operation Desert Storm, political cartoonist D. B. Johnson drew a fly with Iraqi president Saddam Hussein's head and a hand with a fly swatter ready to annihilate the fly man. More recently, an editorial called the war against terrorism a "flyswatter war," linking flies with terrorists. No one, of course, protests, although (as we will see in a later chapter) the fly has many more redeeming qualities than the humans it is paired with.

Projections prevent us from seeing our actions and motivations clearly. James Hillman says that our fears about insects—that is, of their multiplicity, monstrosity, autonomy, and parasitic propensity— are actually fears of *our* attributes, and it is *our* prolific use of deadly chemicals that has infested every bit of the environment. It seems, observes Hillman, that we are mimicking the "enemy," having become the dangerous ones who infest places and spray insecticides as if by automatic reflex.

Reinventing Ourselves   As individuals, if we could comprehend the psychological truth of projection, we might take a second look at insects and others who disturb us. Simply by understanding how we create the insect as enemy, for instance, we begin the process of retrieving the projection.

The goal is nothing less than to radically change ourselves, to create, as Keen suggests, a friendly human being who is animated by kindness and compassion. It is this potential inside each of us that already knows how to respond to and even rejoice in insects.

As long as our projections rule our vision, dictating what we see and experience, we will defend our view of insect as enemy. By moving our focus from the creature to the eyes that see it and the mind that interprets it, we open the door to the complexities of those species against which we fight with such ferocity. We also dispel the free-floating anxiety and vague fears that pool beneath our awareness and urge us to war.

The Insect-Human Connection

The insect-human connection is not a fabricated bond but a firm and abiding link with many components. There is a strong physical aspect. Besides having the same basic DNA (we share key genes with insects that produce, among other features, eyes, legs, and even hearts), we need insects to survive as a species. We cannot live on the Earth for more than a few months without their recycling, harvesting, and pollinating services.

Our physical survival may also depend in part on the chemical prowess of the insect kingdom. Any one of the million new insect species that scientists say await discovery and identification could provide scientific information, new products, and pharmaceuticals of great value. And insects are even a potential source of food with substantial nutritive value.

These biological links, strong as they are, however, are not enough to free the insect from its role as adversary. Facts don't inspire us to care and conserve, much less celebrate insects. Feelings fuel action, and positive feelings are the gateway to responding appropriately and welcoming them into our community.

Psychological Links to Insects　Our psychological links to insects are as strong as our physical links, although not so well known. We are emotionally and psychologically closer to other species than we have acknowledged in modern times. Just being in the natural world has been shown to invoke within us a sense of completeness. Without its presence, when we reside in a purely human-oriented environment, we suffer from emotional loss and unrealized potential. We even lose a measurable degree of vitality and general health.

Many of us sense this dependence when we are outside in Nature. Encounters with other species heighten our awareness and return us to an energetic state of being. Insects frequently surprise and arouse us. Were we more open, they could awaken us out of our complacency, returning us to an alert, watchful state of being. As teachers, they continually invite us closer to inspect and reflect on their ways.

In *The Buddha Got Enlightened under a Tree,* Rick Fields observed that meditating outside in Nature lets you see its dangers and distractions as messengers. When Fields was on retreat in Colorado, he found himself wallowing in self-pity, unable to crawl out of it until a yellow jacket landed on his bare stomach one morning. It stung him and flew off. The pain brought awareness and his self-pity, and indulgence vanished. It was a small but critical turning point in his retreat, and he thought it worked as well, as if not better than, the "encouragement stick" wielded by watchful monitors in traditional Zen meditation halls.

An Epiphany Awareness of our affinity with other species enhances our sense of self. When we identify with another creature, even an insect, the blurring of boundaries facilitates a natural compassion and can even heighten our awareness of the mystery of life.

Such a meeting was a life-shaping event for cosmologist Brian Swimme one Halloween night. He was crouched down in the street to relieve pressure on his back after making the rounds of the neighborhood with his wife and sons. As his family went on, leaving him to rest, he stared at the pavement, which was wet from a recent rain. A little insect crawled by with wings plastered to the asphalt. It occurred to Swimme that insects had been around for four hundred million years, but only recently, in terms of evolution, had they been forced to deal with cars and roads and a radically altered landscape. And their environment has been changed without any regard for them or any other species.

Although he knew that insects were intelligent and had an astonishing capacity for adaptation, he also knew that at any moment a car could go by and extinguish the small life in front of him. He felt as though the creature was asking something from him; as if the universe itself was asking him to do something about the whole situation. For a brief moment, which he would later describe to an interviewer from *The Sun* magazine as an epiphany, he identified so completely with the insect that he felt himself to be just a suffering creature there with another suffering creature.

> I was seeing, through this insect, all the creatures that were suffering and all the species that were disappearing. And, for some reason, I was seeing the situation from their point of view. It was like stepping inside this amazing universe story. I realized that I could have been that insect. Or I could have . . . surfaced anywhere in the flow of creation. That realization became a source of connection and compassion for me. It redefined what it means to be human.[1]

Biophilia   Our psychological ties to insects also stem from "biophilia," a term coined by ant authority Edward Wilson for our inborn capacity to love all life forms. Biophilia implies that our relationship to other species plays a role in our mental health. How we translate the affiliation, then—allowing, blocking, or distorting its expression—merits our attention.

Assuming a biophilic affiliation to insects, its healthy expression might include rejoicing. If blocked or distorted by the prejudice of the culture, however, we might respond instead—and to our detriment—with malice, fear, and ridicule.

Environmental psychologist James Swan has posed the appealing idea of an "inner zoo." He says in his book *Nature as Teacher and Healer* that our core identity is filled with natural images that resonate with each aspect of the natural world. Perhaps the recent development of insect zoos and butterfly aviaries around the world was prompted by impulses arising from our inner insect kingdom. And if so, what happens to this inner zoo when the same aspects in the natural world no longer exist?

Consider that if a need for other species and a longing for connection are encoded in our psyche, and if our interior is populated with the creatures of the world, then the persistent exclusion of so many species from our circle of concern and community means we are expending great amounts of energy excluding parts of ourselves. It also means that what we do to insects we do to our inner menagerie. When we destroy an aspect of the natural world, or when a species becomes extinct, we lose a piece of ourselves. Ecological restoration is at its essence a restoration of ourselves, a retrieval and revival of the disowned parts of self.

The Primitive Self

At the center of the human psyche is a natural intuitive and instinctive self at home in the natural world. Laurens van der Post called this fundamental identity our "primitive" or "wilderness" self. He saw it standing "in rags and tatters, the lowest of the low in the hierarchy of the contemporary mind."[2] No mere alarmist, van der Post believed that the resurrection of this wilderness person was absolutely vital to our continuation as a species.

Judging from the number of insect species and their importance to the ecosystem, it seems that our wilderness self must have a great fondness for creeping creatures. Perhaps it builds our complex responses to events from basic qualities they embody. If so, the number and importance of insects in the world mean that our current beliefs and the animosity that these beliefs create are a false overlay on an extended identity that encircles all life forms.

That extended identity is the focus of an emerging paradigm called deep ecology. Deep ecologists like Joanna Macy and John Seed tell us that our identities extend over the world and that as we relate to a living, self-regulating Earth, we will experience ourselves as part of the collective intelligence of all life forms—part of every ecosystem, every creature on Earth. We might dare to ask, then, who is this fly aspect or this cockroach inside us? And more important, how can we hold and heal these misunderstood, mistreated, and hated aspects of ourselves?

Journey to Wholeness Simply by knowing that the wilderness self exists, we start the retrieval process. Within us is a longing for wholeness—for our true nature—and an impulse to move toward it. Psychologists tell us we can only inhabit that nature more fully when we act to reclaim the missing parts. It is an inward journey that Carl Jung called individuation, which involves persistent self-reflection and self-correction. Having strayed from our instinctual human wholeness—our wilderness self—we actualize it only by repeated acts of choice.

Consciously choosing to cultivate a feeling for insects, we take a giant step toward healing this aspect of our psyche that has been battered by our hostility toward these species.

It may comfort some and disturb others to realize that we may already have guides back to our native place and helpers to redeem these lost aspects of self. There are insect species zealous in their efforts to remain close to us. When we abandoned our primitive selves, moving away from the natural world and into artificial living environments, certain insects followed us, moving into the cracks and crevices we couldn't plug. Maybe it is these species, the ones that insist on sharing our living space and that carry the heaviest burden of our ill will, who are the messengers of our insect self. How many, then, are we in conflict with? How many parts of ourselves have we condemned to hell, and at what point do we see their appearance not as something unpleasant to deal with but as a remarkable opportunity to stop the war and make peace?

If we can stay open to this possibility and give our hearts and imaginations free rein, there is immense power for positive change in our current struggles with certain species. Jane Goodall believes that she has spent her whole life trying to assuage the guilt she felt for the dragonfly's death, which was for her a symbol of our inhumanity to people and animals alike. She wonders if the insect was part of a larger plan to bring a message to a little child and set her on her life's course. If so, all she can say to her God is: "Message received and understood."[3]

We too might pray that our job is as straightforward as relinquishing our current stance toward the insects and letting the lens through which we see them clear. Seeing for the first time, we become beginners, and all possibilities for understanding and compassion are once again present in the moment.

3. INSECTS *as* GUIDES *and* MESSENGERS

One should pay attention to even the smallest crawling
creature, for these too may have a valuable lesson to teach us.

—Black Elk

Across diverse indigenous cultures, the more simply constituted
multitude of creeping creatures were thought to respond more readily
to the creative impulse of the Divine. In fact, their simplicity was believed to have been carefully designed so that they might be ready
emissaries of these powers. Today, however, the understanding that insects are messengers has been largely lost except in certain wisdom traditions. When a bee flew into the beard of Dawn Boy, the spiritual
teacher of psychologist, poet, and author Brooke Medicine Eagle, she
laughed. But Dawn Boy lectured her sternly, telling her that the bee's
action was a message from his spiritual elder, who spoke regularly to
him through the insect world.

Later, when Brooke Medicine Eagle began to pay attention to insects,
she noticed that a specific kind would appear just before one of her spiritual elders dropped by for a visit. Repeated experiences convinced her
that these insects were indeed messengers from these individuals.

The Beetle Messenger   Often insects arrive at a critical juncture in our lives, their presence an event that weaves our inner and outer worlds together in what we call a meaningful coincidence. It was a beetle, in fact, that brought this phenomenon to the attention of Carl Jung. The event occurred while Jung was listening to a patient describe a dream she had about the sacred Egyptian scarab beetle. As he listened to the dream, his back to a closed window, he heard a slight tapping sound. Turning around, Jung saw a flying insect knocking against the window glass from the outside. He opened the window, and a beetle flew in. Jung caught it and held it gently in his hand, studying it. He recognized the beetle as a species as close to a golden scarab beetle that one could find in that region of Switzerland where they were.

In Egyptian mythology the beetle is a potent symbol of rebirth. Its appearance in the dream of Jung's patient and then in his office was a significant event in his patient's therapy. Until that day, she had made no progress but clung to a rigid view of the world that only an irrational, acausal event—like the beetle's uncanny appearance—could break. And so it did: after that session, she began to change. Jung named the coincidence "synchronicity," and his investigation of the phenomenon led him to conclude that these occurrences emerge from another order of reality outside our conscious control.

The interweavings of the outer world with our subjective one are usually experienced as a form of internal and psychological help. Inner and outer worlds come together in a manner that speaks specifically to us, and we sense the Divine at work. Some numinous power has reached out and touched us. These correspondences tell us that all is connected. Feelings, intentions, thoughts, dreams, and intuitions are tied to outer activity and the physical world of biology and physics. Insects are frequently the messengers that alert us to these connections.

Phil Cousineau calls these connections "soul moments." In his book by the same name, he tells of the time he wrote to photographer and yoga instructor Trish O'Reilly, inviting her to contribute to his collection of accounts of meaningful coincidences. He included the story about Jung and the scarab beetle in his letter. The letter prompted her to reflect on her own experiences of synergy and coincidence. After musing on the subject, she reentered her day with a heightened awareness of the mystery and grace of life. As she walked through the front yard on her way to the mailbox, she was surrounded by hundreds of blue-green scarab beetles. She felt as though she were dreaming, so strange and splendorous was this sight of the air thick with the iridescent creatures. But she wasn't dreaming. The beetles stayed for thirty-six hours and then disappeared as quickly as they had arrived.

Insects as Spiritual Directors Traditional tribal peoples revered life in all its forms, so they naturally accorded insects value and respect and looked to them for information and help in meeting their own life challenges. Sometimes they sought the specific attribute of the creature. For example, warriors preparing to fight might invoke the protection of the butterfly, which exemplified elusiveness. A weaver, by contrast, would evoke the patience and industry of a spider.

Native people also acknowledged the invisible forces at work behind physical form, recognizing that everything emanated from a hidden spiritual realm. Native ceremonies created pathways between the physical world and the spiritual world to enlist the cooperation of the forces operating from this realm and influencing the physical world.

It was the tradition in many indigenous cultures to take as a spiritual guide the first creature that caught one's eye at the start of the day. It was understood that whoever commanded your attention—insect or otherwise—had sought you out, knowing inexplicably that its particular guidance was needed on some level.

Likewise, an expectant mother in these societies would look for the creature or aspect of Nature—whether rainbow, beaver, or ant—that presented itself to her during her pregnancy. She would know intuitively that its spirit wanted to communicate its connection to the unborn child. And when a creature appeared in a dream or vision, it was acknowledged as a reflection of the Creator as well as an intermediary link to what was sacred in the world. The dream was investigated and interpreted within this context and its message puzzled out—and, if called for, acted upon.

Underlying all such behavior was the intuitive knowledge that an encounter with any species was not haphazard or accidental, but an intentional, purposive meeting carrying immense healing potential and gifts for the recipient. If you approached the creature with genuine humility and intuition, you could be healed on the level you needed to be healed and gifted in unforeseen ways.

Different Eyes

The practices of tribal peoples offer us important lessons in interdependence. They also provide us with evidence that we are not by nature a hostile species; we can unlearn our habits of hatred. Many examples exist of nonhostile human cultures, including the Stone Age tribe of Bushmen in southern Africa, the more culturally sophisticated tribes like the Hodi of Venezuela, and the Chewong from the tropical rainforests of Malaysia.

The Chewong teach that every species inherently deserves human respect and that each possesses a unique worldview. Their stories explained that the intent and behavior of any individual creature, even when it is threatening or disconcerting to humans, arises out of its unique view. This insight encouraged them to bring compassion and understanding to every encounter with other life forms.

Implicit rules that governed ethical behavior toward others arose from this core belief in the value of every species. Acceptable behavior for human beings—what was deemed good—included the need to accord respect to other species, regardless of size or appearance. Hurting or ridiculing another creature was strictly forbidden.

If we overlay the Chewong worldview on our culture, we find it does not fit. Picking and choosing whom we value based on what they do for us, we behave and react as dictated by our human-created hierarchical system. The belief that we are at the top of the heap and entitled to exploit other species and do with them anything we deem fit means that those below us live only by our permission. And the ones at the bottom rungs are stripped unceremoniously of any rights, including the right to pursue their life without undue human intervention. Acted out in films and plays, presented in short story or novel form, or delivered as truth in scientific journals, news reports, and commercials, the stories we tell ourselves reflect our limited understanding of life and our broken relationship to Nature.

Native Stories versus Modern Tales

It is through our stories that we set up and transmit an understanding of insects as guides and messengers or as the enemy. Predictably, there is a great difference between native insect stories and tales generated by citizens of our industrial society. In "Caterpillars," a short story by British writer E. F. Benson, the narrator encounters a pyramid of immense luminous caterpillars a foot or more in length, with crablike pincers and gaping mouths in featureless faces. Mysteriously, they notice him and drop to the floor and move toward him. Their numbers, impersonality, and sheer vitality lend weight to the man's conviction that they are possessed of a malevolent supernatural mind that lets them choose a target at will.

In contrast, when fear, destructive acts, or even death occurs in native stories, the context is different. The reason why an animal pursues a person is spelled out. Often the main character is punished for harming another species or acting in a disrespectful manner. For instance, a story from the Sandy Lake Cree of Ontario, whose homeland is thick with mosquitoes, tells of an ill-tempered warrior who is angry about being stung by the insects. He scoops up a handful of mosquitoes one summer day, keeping them captive until winter. On a bitterly cold morning, he dumps them in the snow and watches them die. The following summer the mosquitoes pursue and bite him relentlessly until he dies from loss of blood. The message of the story is clear: Malicious behavior toward another species will not be tolerated.

The Biting or Stinging Message   In tribal cultures, a biting or stinging insect was not necessarily something to avoid. People believed that knowledge or attributes could be transmitted between human beings and other species through the act of biting or stinging. Biting creates the connection, perhaps by a mingling of fluids, and allows the insect to impart knowledge or its particular medicine to the human.

Traditionally, shamans attained their vocation as healers, seers, and visionaries through an experience of wounding, death, and rebirth. Animals—including biting and stinging insects—were typically the vehicles for acquainting novices with this transformative suffering. Experiences that we might consider merely misfortune—sickness, decrepitude, and pain—would strengthen the shaman-initiate in preparation for his or her vocation.

If we return to Benson's caterpillar story, we find no initiation, no final transformation, and no transmission of attributes, information, or power. The caterpillars wield no spiritual power. They are personifications of appetite and amoral intent, bringing only death, and a horrible

31

one at that. We are led to believe that the hero does not provoke the attack but is instead an innocent victim of the mindless hunger of the caterpillars. We finish the story feeling, understandably, that we too are vulnerable to unswerving, demonic forces that prey on the innocent.

Opportunities Disguised as Misfortune

That adversity—like being stung by an insect—is a gift is an ancient idea. When wielded by the soul, misfortune can be useful, and those that bring it to us may be seen as benefactors. Eastern religions teach that adversity provides an opportunity for willing individuals to deepen their faith and cultivate certain qualities. In both Buddhism and shamanism, when pain and distress are confronted directly, they are transformed into manifestations of wisdom. Weaknesses become strengths and the source of compassion for others.

Gyelsay Togmay Sangpo, the thirteenth-century Tibetan author of *The Thirty-seven Practices of Bodhisattvas*, tells the story that while he was at a monastery studying Mahayana texts on training the mind, he cared for a destitute man covered with lice. One day he found the man huddled in a hollow by the side of the road, driven out of town by those repulsed by his filthiness. Togmay Sangpo took the man back to the monastery and gave him a clean coat and other necessities before sending him on his way.

Then he wondered what to do with the lice in the man's old coat. He knew they would die if he just threw the coat away, so he put it on, determined to nourish these small creatures with his own blood. They fed well, but soon Togmay Sangpo was depleted and no longer able to attend to his studies. Still he would not be swayed from his decision to feed them. He told his concerned friends that in past lives he had lost one body after another in meaningless ways and that this time he would make a gift of his body. After seventeen days, the lice began to die naturally and no new ones were born. He picked out the dead lice, saying mantras over them, grinding up their bodies, and mixing them with clay to make votive candles out of them for the lice's benefit (a practice usually done with the bones of people revered and cherished for their kindness). Togmay Sangpo's fellow monks learned from his example that any adverse circumstance could be turned into a condition conducive to spiritual development.[1]

Battling Lice   Today we believe we must combat all adversity with heroic measures. We have lost the context that once instructed us in transforming misfortunes into blessings, so we try to end the unpleasantness as quickly as possible. The author of a juvenile book on lice teaches the cultural view to our children by introducing the louse as a creature "almost universally despised by both human and beast" and at its best "a nasty little pest that seems to serve no good purpose." As parents, teachers, and librarians, we don't object, because we think that the author is right. In the West, we are appalled by head and body lice, and battle them with strong chemical treatments. In fact, the presence of head lice is often seen as a cause for shame, although a lice specialist says that lice actually prefer clean hair.

Few of us wonder if there is another way to think about lice, not knowing that native people accepted their presence with aplomb. In a charming Navajo creation myth, Louse pleads for his life, telling Monsterslayer that if he is killed, people will have to live without lice and suffer loneliness.

Native peoples on every continent also had a strategy for keeping lice populations down—they simply ate them. Most believed that eating lice was healthy (and it probably is), and people picked off and ate lice from family members and friends as an act of courtesy, favor, and friendship. Others ate their own lice and deloused members of the opposite sex as a gesture of intimacy or to absorb some of the character of a departed soul that had temporarily assumed the form of a louse.

Although we are repulsed at this environmental and human-friendly strategy for dealing with lice, our preferred method of chemical warfare—especially against head lice—has only created "superlice" resistant to pesticides and able to live and breed on us with ease.

Pure Compassion   Native cultures were not the only ones to work with adversity in a positive way. From Buddhist teachings comes the story of Maitreya,[2] the Buddha of Loving-kindness, who takes the form of a maggot to provide Master Asanga with an opportunity to express compassion. Asanga has gone into retreat with the intention of developing pure compassion. He meditates on Maitreya for twelve years, without results. Discouraged, he leaves the retreat and on his return home meets a dog whose lower body is covered by maggots. Asanga wants to remove them to relieve the dog, but he knows that the worms need flesh to live, so he cuts a slice from his own leg to feed them. Then he considers how to remove them without injuring them and decides he must lick them off gently with his tongue. So he leans over to do so, and the dog and maggots disappear. In their place is Maitreya Buddha, who tells the awestruck Asanga that he has been with him from the very beginning of his retreat but could not be seen until that moment of pure compassion.

The Gift of the Parasite   Experiences that begin in adversity and end in blessing are still occurring today. In his book *To Be Healed by the Earth,* Cleveland psychologist Warren Grossman tells how a parasite changed his life, placing him on the path of a healer. Prior to the encounter, Grossman was comfortable in his chosen profession, complacent even. He knew psychotherapy's limitations—it wasn't a cure—but he was satisfied that it helped a little.

One year, a cold winter prompted him to take a vacation in Brazil. While there, he acquired a parasite that laid its eggs in his liver and left him desperately ill. He flew home and was told he had a week to live. He didn't die, although he remained dangerously sick for a year.

Each day, as he lingered between life and death, he went outside and lay on the ground. It was there that his perception began to change. He began to feel how the Earth was alive, flowing with energy. Soon he could actually see the energy in the trees and shrubs around him. Gradually his own energy returned and with it his strength, but his way of seeing had changed forever. "My values, beliefs and goals were different. I started having this experience of seeing light coming from all living organisms." Gradually he found that he could do more good as a healer than as a psychotherapist.

Although in his book Grossman did not acknowledge the gift of the parasite, perhaps someday he will see it as the divine instrument of his deepening.

Affinities

Without instruction and openness to all species—yes, even lice, maggots, parasites, and mosquitoes—we miss the opportunities they bring us, the lessons on how to work effectively with adversity and allow it to change us. We also short-circuit the links that could lend us strength and assurance. Few of us today ever discover the insect species that mirrors some vital aspect of our identity and has the ability to help us move toward a more authentic version of ourselves. Most of us don't recognize the other species—especially if they have many legs—from whom we might particularly learn and benefit by observing their unique way of being in the world.

Each of us has innate affinities for particular species that are activated by the sight of them. They move us to wonder—or fear and loathing if the creature is misunderstood or condemned by the culture. Fear hints at a connection. The creature you fear has power and commands your attention when you are near it, and beneath the fear is fascination.

Affinities triggered by fear and expressed as hatred are also tied to fears of the unknown. If power or energy comes in a form unexpected, a form outside normal classifications, we often mistake it for evil. We have forgotten the shamanic context that would help us understand the raw intensity and sometimes strange packaging of transformational forces. If an insect is connected to an aspect of our essential self, we may fear it and the unknown territory within us (the unconscious) that is its domain. Maybe we sense the creature's alchemical power and its intention to change us, so we run in terror from the dying that must precede transformation and new understanding.

As laypeople we find little evidence of an innate emotional connection with creeping creatures, especially to the over ten thousand species classified as pests. We have closed the door on affinity with these species and so leave people with a special inner link with mosquitoes or lice cut off from an aspect of their essential selves. Some people find it anyway, with enough time and opportunity to investigate the creature that draws their attention. It is well known in certain circles, for instance, that scientists who have devoted years to the study of lice regard them with a kind of affection. Lice researcher W. Moore fed over seven hundred lice on his own body twice a day. Between meals he is reported to have tucked them away carefully in a nice warm box.

Hans Zinsser wrote a book on lice because he wanted to "present the case of the louse in the humane spirit which a long intimacy" had taught him. During his experiments he had come to regard "these little creatures [with] what we may call, without exaggeration, an affectionate sympathy."

There are even those who are moved to awe by parasites. Daniel Brooks, a zoologist at the University of Toronto, thinks parasites are "splendid creatures." Much of his career has been spent dispelling myths about them—like the misconception that they are primitive and degenerate beings. He teaches that "parasites are successful, innovative creatures . . . [and that] if you compare them with related species that are free-living, parasites are often more complex. They give you a healthy respect for the power of little things."[3]

When we have an affinity for a creature that is loved, we accept it more readily, noticing that it activates some unknown ability within us, so that one part of us is always looking for it even when our mind is elsewhere. Thomas Eisner, who credits his many discoveries to his observation of insects in the wild, was primed to see insects and related creatures. He says, "I used to be able to drive along at night, stop, go backwards and pick up a millipede I had noticed out of the corner of my eye. . . ."

Art historian James Elkins, who wrote a book on the nature of seeing, says he was entranced by moths as a boy and hunted for them at night. He learned to see the particular shape of their bodies, the slight shadow they cast as they pressed against a tree, and the faint difference between their patterned wings and the texture of tree bark. Twenty years later, he still has the ability to spot them even though he stopped consciously looking for them long ago. He thinks that something in his unconscious must still be scanning the environment for a moth shape. When it finds one, it breaks into his conscious thoughts to alert him.

Comic Heroes   In popular culture, we see evidence of special connections with certain species in comic heroes like the Astonishing Ant Man, Spiderman, and Spiderwoman, and in villains like the Beetle and the Fly. Each of these characters takes on the power of the species for which he or she is named. But the original event that gave them insect attributes does not stem from conscious affinity with the creature, nor is the insect given any credit or respect for its innate abilities.

An example of affinity skewed by the culture's condemnation of the insect is seen in an artist who became obsessed with fleas and left the art world to create (or reinvent) the flea circus. Featured in an interview article in a prominent alternative magazine, this artist recently brought her fleas to "perform" at the illustrious San Francisco Exploratorium, a museum of science, art, and human perception.

The artist claims that her act has allowed her to investigate the connection between humans and animals. But I wonder, given the nature of her show, whether the only information she seeks is facts that will allow her to control the fleas. Like the flea circus masters of three hundred years ago (considered the epitome of cleverness), this artist also glues costumes to the body of every flea in her sideshow. Once they are attired, she gets the insects to perform feats of strength, such as pulling a toy train thousands of times their own weight by subjecting them to light—a stimulus, she learned, that they greatly dislike. Because the ropes that tie them to the train are adhered to their bodies, the captive fleas pull the vehicle as part of their desperate effort to get out of the light.

In the flea orchestra, the fleas are not only glued into chairs, they have tiny instruments glued to their legs. As they struggle in vain to escape, the movement of their legs gives the impression that they are playing the instruments. In another act, two fleas with formal attire glued to their bodies are then glued together—back to back. Their panic and frantic attempts to escape make them whirl in a circle like two dancers. Our dislike for these creatures and our vague anxiety about their disease-carrying potential (although the flea that likes to feed on people rarely carries the plague bacteria) suppress what might under other circumstances invoke a response of outrage to such acts of cruelty to living things.

The artist explains her own lack of feeling for the fleas (she doesn't bother to feed them and says she doesn't care if they die in the show or afterward) as the attitude of a scientist who just creates experiments and observes the results. Equally disturbing is the lack of awareness of the interviewer, who presents the show as artistic and tells the reader that the artist has "brilliantly melded science, ecology, aesthetics, and humor into her current body of work" and that "there's something refreshingly honest in her act—something primal, raw, and unedited."[4] But if there is humor in such a show, it is the dark ridicule associated with Shadow material. And what is primal is not abuse of other life forms, but our genuine connection to all other species, an affinity characterized in native societies by wonder and respect.

A more healthy expression of an affinity for fleas has found its way across culturally sanctioned prejudices. What marks it as healthy is its link to heartfulness, however rationalized. For instance, a friend of the naturalist John Ray is reported to have given bed and board to a favorite flea, admitting it at certain times to suck the palm of his hand for nourishment. After sharing three months of friendship and easy com-patibility, the flea died from the cold, and the man grieved.

We are hard-wired for empathy, according to a 2001 study con-ducted at the French Institute of Health and Medical Research in Lyons. This empathy instinct for understanding another's behavior in-volves seeing the other in action and then mentally projecting our-selves into that situation. Identifying with an insect like a flea isn't much different from identifying with any other species—including our fellow human beings. When we are open to them, the identification is just there, and we readily see ourselves in them and their situation. In his essay "Self-Realization," philosopher Arne Naess tells of the time he was looking under a microscope at two chemicals interacting when a flea jumped off a nearby animal and landed in the acid pool. Unable to save it, Naess watched it die. "Its movements were dreadfully expres-sive. What I felt was, naturally, a painful compassion and empathy."[5] Later he realized that if he had been alienated from the flea, failing to recognize anything in it that was like himself, the flea's plight would have left him indifferent. Compassion and empathy always arise from identifying with the other.

Investigating so-called pest species in a heartfelt way can facilitate our transformation. As Sam Keen reminds us, within the image of the enemy, we will see our own faces reflected most clearly.

Reinventing Ourselves

Real change begins with imagining ourselves in a new way. Con-temporary storyteller and author Brenda Peterson leads groups of in-ner-city teenagers in role-playing other species. She has discovered that these streetwise, disaffected youth identify with other species in a profound way. Their ease and eagerness in assuming the viewpoint of another species suggest to Peterson that Nature is not "out there," but inside.

Peterson believes it is our own spiritual relationship to other species that must evolve, and that imagination acts as a mutually nurturing umbilical cord between our bodies and the planet. When children claim another species as their ally—not just as their imaginary friend, but as the creature that has sought contact with them—it changes their outer world.

The Council of All Beings   A form of group work called the Council of All Beings—based on the writings and work of Pat Fleming, Joanna Macy, Arne Naess, and John Seed—weaves people and the natural world together. It awakens in participants the commitment and courage to act in behalf of the Earth community. People in the council come together and learn to act not on behalf of themselves or their human ideas, but for the sake of the Earth and its inhabitants.

Several years ago, when I created an elective course at a local elementary school to teach children how to stand in good relationship to other species, I used the model of the Council of All Beings to teach them how to act on behalf of insects. The children already understood that many species were endangered. They also knew about habitat loss and the general plight of the Earth community. But I wanted them to use their imaginations and feel what it must be like to be a disliked, mistreated, or endangered species. I also wanted them to understand that each creature has its own view of reality.

I encouraged the children to find elements of behavior and ways of communicating that were similar to the ways humans respond and then to discover how the creature differed from us and how it adapted to its life circumstances, an orientation that educator Peter Kelly calls "biological empathy."

The children assumed the viewpoint of invertebrates with the enthusiasm normally reserved for furred and feathered creatures. In fact, the shift to seeing the world through another creature's eyes happened easily for most of them. The uprooting process that encourages our children to detach themselves from the living world and rely only on concepts and language had not yet progressed very far.

In the second week I introduced six different insects, intending to assign each child to one group. Once assigned, they would make a mask of their insect and learn enough about it to speak on its behalf in the council.

To introduce the fly, I showed a slide of a gold fly necklace worn proudly by Egyptian officers in ancient Egypt, explaining that officers would present gold flies to their men as a reward for heroic deeds in battle. I also told them about the North American Blackfoot tribe's Fly Society for warriors and ended by sharing anecdotes about a friendship between a man and a housefly (a true story included in the chapter "The Wise Counsel of Big Fly").

As the first class period ended, I asked the children to be aware of their interactions with insects during the week and to note unusual behavior. They were particularly intrigued with the possibility that an insect with whom they had a special connection might make its presence known to them in the course of the day or in a dream.

One animated young boy named Brian was filled with images of the latest horror films featuring insects. A natural comic, he disrupted the lesson, entertaining his classmates with imitations of insects as demons running amok. I wondered if he would even stay in the group, as my parent helpers were ready to send him to the office. But the next week Brian came back and pulled me aside to tell me a dream he'd had the night before. In the dream, he had been threatened by Jason, the psychopathic killer in a series of popular horror films. Suddenly, a human-size fly appeared with a sword and went after Jason, defending the terrified boy.

I congratulated Brian on remembering the dream and having the fly as his defender. He beamed with satisfaction and asked to be assigned to the fly group so he could make a fly mask. He had claimed the fly as his ally—or perhaps the fly had claimed him.

Affinity for a particular creature is always a gift, linked inexplicably to our essential nature. Perhaps the species that mirrors some aspect of our wilderness identity waits, with insect diligence, at the entrance to our conscious awareness. Maybe we have only to become aware of our projections and seed our imaginations with new ideas and stories to create a pathway that permits their entry and helps us stay attentive to their messages.

Let's begin now, disarmed by the new realization of our deep and abiding connection with insects—and a good measure of goodwill and faith—to investigate some common species. We can start, like Brian, with flies.

4. My Lord Who Hums

Everything in Oneness has a purpose. There are no freaks, misfits, or accidents. There are only things that humans do not understand.

—*Regal Black Swan, in*
Mutant Message Down Under *by Marlo Morgan*

Caught among our fears of decay, disease, and death, flies are easy to condemn and execute as pests. They personify all the annoyances that prevent us, or so we think, from being really content. Their numbers and a few species' proximity to humans make them easy scapegoats for the uncertainties of life that plague us.

I suspect our lives would change if we understood and could mediate our responses to flies. By redrawing our circle of community to include these winged wonders with kaleidoscope eyes, we automatically expand our comfort zone. One less enemy, fewer battles. Including flies in our circle of concern might even mean that we have made peace with some of the fears that keep us pushing life away.

Deep ecologist, educator, and author Joanna Macy learned how to expand her circle of concern to flies after one fell into her tea during her first summer in Tibet. She was in a meeting with local Buddhists, intent on pushing through plans for a craft cooperative. A fly fell into her tea. It was a minor occurrence for Macy, who thought herself to be undisturbed by insects. She must have shown some reaction, though, because Choegyal Rinpoche, an eighteen-year-old lama, leaned forward in sympathy and asked her what was wrong. She assured him that it was nothing—just a fly in her tea. When he still seemed concerned, Macy assumed he was just being empathetic, so she reassured him again that it was not a problem and set her cup aside. But he continued to show great concern and finally put his finger into her teacup and with great care lifted the fly out and left the room with it.

The conversation resumed, and Macy's attention returned to the meeting. When Choegyal Rinpoche reentered the room, he was smiling. He walked over to her and quietly reported that the fly would be all right. He had placed the tea-soaked creature on a leafy bush near the door and had stayed until it began to fan its wings. They could confidently, he assured Macy, expect the fly to take flight soon.

That is what Macy remembered of that afternoon: not the elaborate plans and final agreements, but Choegyal's telling that the fly would live. She felt laughter in her heart and delight at the notion of concerning herself with the well-being of a fly. Choegyal's great compassion, revealed in the obvious pleasure in his face, conveyed clearly that she was missing a great deal by not extending her concern to all beings.

If something sputters inside us in indignation at the thought of helping a fly, it may only be self-importance arising out of a narrow band of awareness. Our sense of self expands when we extend our compassion to insects. It is an appropriate response to our interdependence. The question is not how to connect with a fly—we are already connected. The question is how to translate that connection into appropriate behavior. Helping one in need is always a good place to start.

Since most of us don't love flies, and few of us know anything about them, our opinions emerge from the cultural consensus on flies. That by itself will block a natural compassionate response to a fly in trouble.

A few fly species are already extinct, and many are threatened. It isn't something that concerns people. In fact, some people think that the world would be better off without flies—not a thoughtful or educated opinion, but a common one. It is supported by the official policy that divides all creatures into two categories: beneficial species and pest species. Flies are pests. The designation keeps our belief in flies as the enemy intact. What best serves the stereotype of flies as annoying, biting, disease-carrying pests is to eliminate the distinctions that complicate the issue and sweep the varied behaviors of flies into a homogeneous and manageable heap.

The Importance of Flies

I knew the picture was skewed against flies when I first started to read about them, so I was surprised to learn that the majority of entomologists agree that flies are the second most important insect on the planet—with bees and wasps taking first place. Then I wondered how we could hate a species so vital to our life on Earth.

One of the jobs that flies perform is pollination. They also dispose of decaying animal and vegetable matter, serve as food for many other animals, and destroy and feed on populations of insects that would otherwise multiply rapidly and upset the balance of countless plant and insect relationships.

Immature flies, or maggots, are also important. Indigenous people valued them as food, as do other species. They knew intuitively what science has now verified: maggots are nutritious.

What a maggot eats depends on what kind of a fly it will become. For some it is aphids and for others bulbs. The majority feed on something dead and high in protein like garbage, dung, dead animals, or even untreated wounds and the dead surface skin of live animals, including humans. Although we tend to abhor such an appetite, maggots are valuable *because* they break down and recycle carrion so effectively. In fact, without their services, we humans could not smell the roses for the stench of decaying matter.

In the West, we object to the way maggots look and move. We don't like land creatures without legs—especially ones that ingest foul substances. In a recent book on taking a "new look" at hated creatures, the author shares his not-so-new reaction to maggots in his compost pile calling them one of the most "disgusting sights" imaginable. His chapter on flies is laced with expressions of his repulsion, and even when he learns that the maggots in his compost pile are creating soil-enriching material, he is unwilling to let them be.

One of the sources he studied to learn about flies was a natural history of flies written by a distinguished entomologist. That authority called flies a "subject of disgust" because of their penchant for dead matter. In fact, all the information this esteemed expert conveys is couched in emotional terms. Disgust is, after all, a learned response. Every culture teaches its members what is disgusting and what is not. Children develop their disgust reaction by observing the facial expressions and reactions of their parents and teachers. And what is disgusting to members of one culture may not be disgusting to members of another. What allows us to eat shrimp and escargot, for example, and refuse maggots and caterpillars is the bias of our particular culture.

The tendency to describe another species and its behavior in terms of the emotions invoked in the observer is common and an easy way to transmit prejudice. The adjectives this entomologist chooses to describe different fly species ("aggressively advanced," "little nuisances," "pesky," "maddening," and "infuriating") slant the information he presents and do little to advance our understanding of flies. If his readers share the prejudice, they won't even notice the dark cast. Small wonder that one of them—the writer trying to take a new look at flies—ends up killing all the maggots in his compost pile with satisfaction. Not a very new look at flies.

A New Look at Maggots

A new look might include the role of blowfly maggots in forensic science. In a homicide, these creatures are used to pinpoint the time of death, because blowflies, important as pollinators of several crop plants, turn to dead meat for a place to lay their eggs.

A new look would also include the old knowledge that maggots are instruments of healing. During the Civil War, wounded men often had to wait several days before receiving help. Female flies, attracted to a soldier's decaying flesh, laid eggs in his open wounds. The eggs hatched in several hours, and the maggots began feeding on the decaying and dead tissue—painlessly to the soldier and without damaging healthy tissue. Not only did these tiny creatures eat the bacteria that caused gangrene, they excreted substances later found to accelerate healing and prevent the need for amputation in most cases. The same healing ability was brought to the forefront again during World War I, when similar circumstances brought maggots and men together.

The ability of these creatures to promote healing is due to urea and other antibacterial substances that they exude. In the 1940s, when scientists learned to synthesize and manufacture these substances, most forgot the gift of the maggots.

Today, as many bacteria prove resistant to antibiotics, maggots are returning to service to clear away dead tissue on patients who can't tolerate surgery but suffer severe bedsores, burns, bone infections, and tumors. It is a role largely unknown and unappreciated by a public who continues their proclamations of disgust over maggots.

The Fly as Skilled Navigator

As adults, flies also have many laudable abilities. In times past their impressive flight speeds and navigational abilities won them the admiration of people in diverse cultures.

Flies are indeed fast. Most can travel at more than fifty miles per hour, and the male deer botfly has been clocked at a speed of several hundred miles an hour when pursued. These inherent flying skills earned flies the attention and respect of warriors in ancient cultures. As I told the children in my "Thinking Like a Bug" class, Egyptian officers presented flies fashioned from ivory, bronze, and gold to their men as a reward for valor and tenacity in battle. Being associated with the fly in this culture was an honor.

Among the North American Blackfoot tribe, members of the Fly Society recognized and admired the insect's ability to harass the enemy without being captured or killed. Certain warriors were summoned by a dream or vision to join the Fly Society, where they sought to emulate the insect and gain its powers. Identification with another species, invoked and enacted during ceremonial rituals, was an acceptable way to acknowledge, celebrate, and embody its unique strengths and talents.

Baalzebub

The hum associated with the flight of all flies varies with the speed of their wing beat. The housefly, for instance, beats its wings 345 times per second, humming in the key of F in the middle octave.

The sound of a fly humming was not always a source of irritation. Scholars report that in ancient times the word *zebub* referred to a fly's humming or buzzing. And since *Baal* meant Lord, the name for the once revered Philistine god Baalzebub—healer, "Conductor of Souls," and oracular deity—can be translated as "My Lord Who Hums" or "My Lord Who Murmurs."

The modern meaning of Baalzebub, or "Lord of the Flies," comes from the Judeo-Christian tradition, in which this deity was identified with putrefaction and destruction. Baalzebub was derisively called the "God of the Dunghill" in an attempt to ridicule and undermine the influence of earlier religions and deities. The resulting religious doctrine left most insects, masters of destructuring life during its down cycle, not only excluded but despised.

Flies were considered demons or devils, living embodiments of evil, sin, and pestilence. Actual flies suffered from this twisted association of their natural connection with death and decay as stories from the dominant religious traditions transformed them into despicable creatures who deserve to be killed on sight. And savagery was added to the condemnation in William Golding's classic novel *Lord of the Flies*.

Projecting the shadow aspects of Christian ideology onto certain creatures provided those who embraced the religion with easy targets for their hostility. Those who bought the mechanistic view of the natural world and the militaristic orientation of medicine also had a target. When flies were implicated in the spread of disease, their damnation was secured. And once accomplished, the contributions of the fly and the complexities inherent in our relationship with them were buried.

Fly as Monster

No longer a sacred presence to humans, the fly has become a target, perfectly acceptable to kill on sight. Our stores stock fly swatters in decorator colors, and our stories and films help us maintain an adversarial stance and teach it to each new generation.

Monster-making is a popular religious and secular activity. By focusing on a few species of flies and the bacteria that live on and about them, and by calling on our hostile imagination to pull our emotional strings with images of flies feeding on feces and then coming to call, we are all too ready to believe that flies are monsters.

The demonizing of any species depends on the perception and belief in our inherent separateness from them and the tangent belief in their evil or amoral intent. George Langelaan's short story "The Fly," written in 1957 and made into a movie the following year, joins human body with fly body in an attempt to horrify us. And it does. We no longer understand that the complete or partial transformation of human to animal is an expression of our fundamental unity with Nature—the reemergence of life energy in another form. We see it instead as an object of repugnance and fear.

Mesmerized and delighted with these kinds of horror films, the public welcomed *The Return of the Fly* in 1959 and *Curse of the Fly* in 1965. In 1986 filmmakers remade the original movie, taking full advantage of studio technology to create even more spectacular special effects. Perhaps our consistent response to and fascination with this subject is a distortion of a deeper, more authentic understanding of our interdependence with other species.

In the original short story, the scientist-victim meddles with the powers of Nature in his attempt to manipulate atoms. After disintegrating the family cat, he tries again with himself as the subject, unaware that a fly has joined him in the chamber. The transmission of atoms results in his human features being replaced by fly features. The fly is changed too and now has the scientist's head.

Predictably, no attempt is made in the story or film to describe the fly's reaction (or the cat's). We rarely enter the world of an insect imaginatively and respond with empathy out of that identification. We might be surprised if we did. Imagine the fly's horror when it discovers it has a human head—inadequate to its fly tasks.

If we look at the story symbolically, we move past being entertained by our horror and catch a glimpse of the flies in our psyches that move unbidden and unwelcome into our inner chamber. Their presence is an unexpected part of the equation and fouls our attempts to manipulate the forces of transformation in service of the ego's desires.

The Official View of Flies

The link between flies and filth prevents contemporary people from accepting and understanding the presence of flies in the world. We loathe the decay and garbage we help create, and the fly who recycles it.

Our children also learn to hate flies early in life. A popular Marvel comic book character, the Fly is an unsavory man who is transformed into a fly and becomes little more than the voice of our projections as he condemns his appetite for garbage, calling it a depraved act.

Educational attempts to balance the prejudice toward flies and promote an appreciation for them are also vulnerable to contamination from our biases. A documentary on flies is titled *Backyard Monsters*. And a juvenile book on flies begins with the statement, "The best thing that can be said about flies is that they are a nuisance."

With their imagination thus seeded and the cultural view clearly spelled out, children have their opinion formed for them. Most children's books also list the kinds of flies that bite and annoy people and the diseases they cause or carry. After reading it, it is unlikely that anyone will have a good feeling toward flies. And the statements are presented as facts, so we are not likely to question this straightforward indictment of flies. But the issues surrounding our beliefs about sickness and health, and who causes what illness, and under what conditions, are neither simple nor clearly defined.

Sickness and Health The complexities of human sickness and health extend far beyond the scope of this book. A reasonable objective might be to throw some doubt on the official version of flies and pinpoint the fears that allow us to accept the story at face value.

One of the things that stops people from extending concern and protection to flies is the prevalent fear of disease. We all learned from our parents and teachers that flies spread diseases. We carry the image of flies crawling on revolting substances and then landing on our food, transferring bacteria in the process. When specialists announced that houseflies carry over two million microorganisms, what were we suppose to think? We didn't have a context to process that information. The number could only feed the hostile imagination. And it did. The bacteria count upheld the view of flies as death-wielding, disease-carrying creatures that deserve to die.

If we liked bacteria, their high counts wouldn't disturb us. We generally think of them as shrewd and malevolent specks of life that ride winged carriers to make trouble for their human hosts. But a microscopic view tells us that all surfaces, including our bodies and our food, are already teeming with life invisible to the naked human eye. It is a fact that does not engender comfort but it is something we need to accept. And accepting it puts the popular bacteria counts in an appropriate context.

In his book *Furtive Fauna*, biology professor Roger M. Knutson reassures his readers that none of the bacteria on a fly are likely to cause disease in people. In fact, he says, we all—flies and humans—have pretty much the same sort of organisms living on us anyway, and the flies just follow our example and move them around from one person to the next with little physical consequence. Good mental and physical hygiene and community sanitation measures are usually enough to provide reasonable protection.

The Bacteria in Our Midst

Learning more about bacteria could also ease our fears, impressing us with their abilities and making us more comfortable with their invisible presence in our lives. They are the dominant life forms on the planet, our ancestors and contemporary associates. To detail their influence would require several volumes, but in short, all life depends on them.

One of their strongest assets is their genetic fluidity. They have a single gene pool. It means every strain of bacteria has free access to the chemical power of the entire bacterial kingdom. They can exchange genes quickly and reversibly—and do all the time. It is how they adapt to changing environmental conditions. It is also how they defend themselves against our antibacterial products and learn to resist our antibiotics.

The concept of bacteria species is convenient but essentially meaningless in the face of such fluid boundaries. Outdated too is the traditional medical paradigm regarding cause and effect and the agents of disease. It is far more complex then that. No organism, bacterium included, exists by itself. Instead, each one coevolves with all the elements in its natural surroundings seeking a state of equilibrium or homeostasis. It is generally accepted that the bacteria and viruses identified in new infectious diseases are not new at all; they simply have never been identified with human diseases before.

When new diseases do occur, we can be sure that some equilibrium has been disturbed. So a thorough treatise on diseases in which flies are involved as carriers will invariably implicate the burgeoning human population and its disruption of existing balances between species.

Marc Lappé, who views disease as an evolutionary process, links every new disease or illness with upsets in the natural balance of existing ecosystems. Every time we clear a forest, build a road, or change a waterway, we abruptly open a habitat. Some species indigenous to the original balance die out, while others enter or leave the disturbed area and find new opportunities to multiply before natural checks are in place again.

Ferreting Out the Truth

Most books on flies state without elaboration that houseflies spread disease because of their appetites for dead things and their habit of softening food by spitting up a substance that liquefies it. It is the rare individual who questions what he or she reads about other species. If we did question, we would enter a tangled web of human complicity. It is much easier to just make flies the enemy.

Flies and Cholera   In a recent juvenile book on insects, for example, the entomologist author states without elaboration that houseflies are implicated in cholera, a sometimes lethal diarrheal disease. It sounds like a closed case. It prompted me to take a look at cholera. My investigation revealed that the bacteria associated with cholera's symptoms thrive in contaminated water. Outbreaks occur during periods of transition, particularly during the growth of new cities when good sanitation is lacking.

Deadly bacteria strains that stay destructive to their hosts can only afford to be deadly because something lets them be easily transmitted from host to host—so they don't have to worry about keeping one host alive. Cholera needs water, not flies, for transmission. Overcrowded living conditions without adequate sanitation permit an easy transmission of cholera from one person to another.

If they can't be transmitted easily, bacteria generally evolve toward a relatively mild state of coexistence with their hosts to avoid dying when their host dies. In fact a direct correlation exists between how deadly a diarrheal bacterium (including cholera) is allowed to stay and its ability to be transmitted by water. What this means is that water purification could transform deadly pathogens into milder ones—and records indicate that this has happened.

Killing flies, however, is often easier and less expensive than addressing overpopulation and sanitation problems or even finding an effective cholera vaccine. Governments rally people to join together against a common enemy. The Philippine government recently offered a bounty on flies, blaming them for spreading cholera in Manila. The outbreak was traced to an abandoned reservoir used as a public toilet by slum dwellers.

Adding further mystery to the subject of cholera is the fact that people can interact with most strains of cholera bacteria, which are also found in contaminated water, and not get sick. The situation is complex, and there is much that is not understood. To implicate the fly in books written for children—without elaboration—supports enemy-making and does a disservice to both children and flies.

The same author links flies to two other waterborne diarrheal diseases, typhoid and dysentery, all without elaboration.[1] My brief investigation of these diseases indicated that, as in the case of cholera, the presence of flies is not central to these afflictions, nor is the absence of flies linked to effective prevention of their spread.

Even if we accept the fact that heavily populated areas without adequate sanitation are conducive to an increase of flies that breed and feed on sewage, we also need to mention the nature of these waterborne diseases as well as implicating humans as likely carriers. A warning about the health risks to humans and other species (and the likelihood of creating secondary insect infestations) of using insecticides to wipe out fly populations is also appropriate. Given the dangers of pesticide use, improving sanitation (or developing vaccines) may be the only reasonable course of action.

I suspect that an investigation of any disease related to the fly would result in a similar web of interrelated events and conditions that we found in our brief look at cholera. It means that making simplistic cause-and-effect conclusions is inappropriate. In the case of flies, the bottom line is that with normal attention to mental and physical hygiene and the benefits of modern sanitation practices, Knutson is right. We have little to worry about from houseflies and other species with an appetite for dead and dying matter. In fact, we need them desperately. Fly populations increase in proportion to our own, so when we overcrowd areas and cannot dispose of our waste products efficiently, they arrive to help. It's their job.

Invitation to Sickness

Looking at it from another angle, even if flies were to carry a new strain of bacteria to us, it doesn't necessarily mean that we would get sick. Susceptibility also plays a big role. Biologist Lynn Margulis discounts the idea that microbes by themselves cause disease as too simplistic. Whether a person becomes sick is dependent on many personal, cultural, and environmental conditions, not just the characteristics of a given microbe. "We are infected by potentially dangerous microbes all the time without getting sick," says Margulis, "and some infections are actually beneficial in maintaining good health and proper body metabolism."[2]

It is generally accepted that any weakness or deterioration of the immune system creates a susceptibility, an invitation to sickness. War, famine, and revolution weaken us. So do prolonged anger and depression. It is also well substantiated that nearly all of the ectoparasite-borne diseases like the plague and several louse-borne fevers are not present in insects or in us until there are destructive situations produced by human activity.

Agents of disease surround us. A relatively well person can often interact with them and not get sick. A growing number of physicians agree that internal factors determine the nature of our relationship with such agents. This means diseases are not single entities but complex relationships between many internal and external factors and are greatly influenced by fluctuations in our immune system.

It also means that we can relax about our relationship with flies, work on inner and outer harmony in our lives, rein in our imaginations, and permit flies to recycle waste matter without unnecessary intervention.

Making Peace   Knutson concludes that getting rid of all flies, viewed as desirable by some, would produce more serious problems than any trouble they might cause. The world needs flies. People need flies. A feeling for them, more natural than the average person might suspect, will quicken and grow once we confront the fears that keep us from extending our concern to them.

Making peace with the bacteria around and on us is as life-serving as it is realistic. It not only relieves the fly of its role as "heavy," it promotes a healthy acceptance of life that correctly orients us in relationship to the Earth community. If we let our fears about bacteria run wild, the knowledge of a strange and foreign kingdom in our midst could paralyze us with fear. More information, if turned over to the storytellers, might better direct our imagination. Stories, if they did not ease our concerns, could at least promote acceptance of a world in which our planetary elders, omnipotent and life-creating, live like tiny gods in our midst.

The Dark Side of Existence

We have typically upheld our behavior toward flies and other species we have dismissed or judged as hostile, invasive, or life-threatening with great energy and conviction. The intensity of our judgments indicates that our attitude has roots that extend still further than the issues we have touched on so far. In the final analysis, our responses to flies may be but one thread in a larger pattern that is at odds with the essence of existence itself.

Perhaps one reason we keep trying to eliminate parts of our world is that we lack a life-sustaining, supportive context in which to move through our own human passages of life—toward the inevitable death of our bodies. We live with impermanence on every level, on a foundation of mystery, and deny it resoundingly, preferring not to be reminded of death and decay. To our youth-oriented culture, aging and death negate life. To scientists and others under the spell of a model of life that excludes consciousness, death is also the end and dying a process that requires heroic intervention.

Re-visioning Our Lives Cultivating a feeling for flies may be a simple step that ultimately entails a radical re-visioning of our lives. It may require coming to different terms with the impermanent yet enduring natural world and its cycles of death and decay, as well as our own changing bodies. When we read about flies softening their food with digestive juices tainted with their previous meal, which might indeed be feces or decomposing flesh, we become nauseated. It confirms our belief in their despicable nature and satisfies the projection. We also don't want to know that honey is partially dried bee vomit, and that butterflies seek and sip urine and sweat—facts likely to spoil any positive projections we have accorded these insects.

Life secretes substances beyond our naming. Out of touch with our own secretions—the saliva that accompanies our food, the perspiration that regulates our body temperature, the slime that allows us to procreate, or the protective layers of mucus that keep our stomach from digesting itself and trap the dirt and germs that rush into our lungs with each breath—we focus on the fly and detest in this creature the processes and qualities we deny or hate in ourselves.

Healing begins when we dare to become conscious of our violent and irrational ways and the mythologizing that makes flies or any other species our enemy. If we adhered to the idea that all life forms are a valuable and necessary part of the Earth, the change in our culture would be deep. Its rumbling would be felt in all corners of our lives, toppling the inner and outer structures built on false security and misplaced superiority. People would be open to new experiences, have fresh questions, and encourage science to investigate the nature of susceptibility and its role in the treatment and prevention of diseases for which other species act as carriers. Giving up inflated ideas about controlling and dominating the Earth, we might learn to participate in its community and accept that we may not always get our way. And finding our natural place, we could celebrate our interdependence, the miraculous fact of our lives, and the equally miraculous existence of flies.

5. The COUNSEL of BIG FLY

[Pray] that we may apprehend and rejoice in that everlasting truth in which the highest angel and the fly and the soul are equal.

—*Meister Eckhart*

One of the most well-known figures in American Indian mythology of the Southwest tribes is Big Fly. A revered mentor, Big Fly mediates between the Navajo people and their gods as the voice of the Holy Spirit and appears frequently in sand paintings. Navajo legends tell of Big Fly counseling members of the tribe by sitting on or behind the ear of a person who needed instruction and whispering answers to questions or forecasting future events.

Big Fly is thought to have a physical counterpart, a local fly in the region. I imagine that when these people saw such a fly near them, they would quiet themselves in the hopes of attracting its attention and receiving the benefit of its counsel, perhaps received as the voice of intuition.

The Ahanti tribe of West Africa paid homage to a fly god, and it is likely that this being also had a physical counterpart, a local fly whose presence this tribe welcomed. And the well-known flute-playing

Kokopelli personified the spirit of the local Assassin or Robber fly in a Hopi tribe kachina, although rarely portrayed as an insect. Perhaps artists removed his extra legs (as they did his prominent phallus) to make him more acceptable to nonnatives when kachinas became popular as art.

In the West we don't pay attention to flies except to wave them away from us in mild annoyance or, if we are particularly exasperated, to attempt killing them. We typically imbue these small creatures, not with wise counsel, but with a malicious intent and then respond to that projection. If they are flying around us, we interpret their proximity as aggressive, although we might just as easily interpret it as playful. We don't know how to respond when they violate our boundaries with their quick, darting movements, or when their numbers prevent us from tracking their movements effectively.

We prefer our companion species to have obvious points of kinship. The fly offers us little in terms of physical similarities, and their size prevents us from looking them in the eye. Yet, even with these inherent restrictions, if we replaced the perception of malevolent purpose by an imaginative, nonaggressive one, we would respond differently to them.

Flies as Relatives Finding correspondences between people and other species is a time-honored tradition in all cultures prior to the industrialized age. Since flies were relatives in tribal cultures, it was natural to tell stories about them as we might about a special cousin or uncle. In many indigenous stories, flies were heroes who applied their flying or biting skills in service of the tribe. Other tales explained the appearance and behavior of local species, like the story of Blue Fly from the South American Luiseño Indians. In this tale, Blue Fly twirled a stick so long to create fire for an ancestor's mourning ceremony that he couldn't stop and still makes the movement today.

Attempts to understand and explain another species' unique viewpoint were always made from close observations and within a context of interdependence. It is easy to imagine adults entertaining their children with stories of Fly, seeding their imaginations with images of kinship.

A haiku poem by Issa, the Japanese farmer-poet, compares the fly to people praying.

THE COUNSEL OF BIG FLY

> The flies in the temple
> imitate the hands
> of the people with prayer beads.[1]

Images like this one also stir the imagination and create good feelings.

Insects in Fairy Tales   If we understood the symbolic role of flies in our dreaming and in myths and fairy tales, we might also be on friendlier terms with their physical counterparts. In fairy tales, for example, people and animals represent energies operating within the total human psyche. The dramas portray the universal growth process, which can be viewed as an inner journey toward wholeness. In these tales, insects often arrive to sort things out and perform tasks that the hero or heroine is unable to perform. As allies, they befriend the hero or heroine and play an essential role in helping him or her overcome challenges. In a Vietnamese story called "The Gentleman of the Flies," the hero allows the flies that invade his house to stay and, being a kind person, even takes care to feed them. Later, when he wants to win the hand of a princess, the flies help him accomplish the impossible tasks set by her father the king.

In dream and myth, the house typically symbolizes the known and conscious part of the self. So what is to be done when flies "invade" our house/psyche? Although the full interpretation of a story like "The Gentleman of the Flies" lies outside the objective of this telling, it might be enough to say that the story promises that many unforeseen benefits come to one who can welcome the intrusion and befriend the small invaders. The friends of flies are the ones who benefit from the insect's gratitude—usually when they need uncommon help.

Fly Souls

That flies were souls searching for rebirth was a common belief in ancient cultures. Myths tell of souls taking the form of a fly and seeking to enter a woman's body to be reborn as a human. Underlying this belief was another one: that *all* creatures possess a soul that animates the body and survives its death.

Ancient Egyptians held this view of flies and wore as jewelry fly amulets symbolizing the human spirit and modeled after iridescent flies living in the region. Even today in some rural villages of Egypt, local traditions forbid the killing of certain flies believed to be inhabited by the souls of friends and neighbors.

The South American Auraucanian Indians believe that departed tribesmen, chiefs in particular, take one form of horseflies. Flies that appear at their ceremonies and celebrations are welcomed as a sign that their dead kinsmen are sharing in the feast.

Religions like Hinduism and Buddhism and native societies that teach the doctrine of reincarnation viewed death as a change of form—not an extinction of life. Since physical form was impermanent and the soul was permanent and indestructible, it seemed reasonable that the soul would inhabit one form after another, for each was involved in this cyclic process of death and rebirth. In his 1927 collection of Japanese stories Lafcadio Hearn includes the story of Tama, a devout maidservant who becomes a fly after her unexpected death so she can prompt her former employers to have the Buddhist services performed on her behalf. In Buddhist teachings, flies are sentient beings that may even have been our mothers, fathers, or grandparents in previous lives.

In the West our association of flies with death is one of the reasons we don't like them. Death is not a popular subject despite elaborate descriptions of life after death from our dominant religious traditions. Our dislike for flies has unmistakable ties to their association with decaying, dying, and dead things, essential preoccupations in the great round of living and dying. Perhaps flies are just unwelcome reminders that physical life is terminal and there are bigger forces than our will and our intellect that act on and in us.

Surrendering to Flies

The Australian aborigines, like other indigenous cultures, understood that everything in life has a purpose. By living intimately with the Earth and its creatures, these people develop a profound understanding of each creature's role—including the swarms of bush flies that visit them regularly. They respond to the presence of these flies with an acceptance and appreciation that we would do well to emulate.

In *Mutant Message Down Under*, a fictionalized account of an actual event, author Marlo Morgan tells of joining an Australian aboriginal tribe on a walkabout, inadvertently bringing with her the baggage of her Western beliefs. At dawn she saw hordes of bush flies traveling in black masses. She gagged and choked as the flies descended, covering her body and crawling into her ears, nose, eyes, and throat. The tribal people around her had a sense of where and when the flies would appear, so they stopped and waited passively, and soon thousands of flies covered their bodies.

Finally, after several encounters with the bush flies, the aboriginal leader, Regal Black Swan, took Morgan aside and explained to her that everything in life had a purpose. "There are no freaks, misfits or accidents," he said. "There are only things that humans do not understand."

He told her that she only believed bush flies were hellish because she wasn't wise and didn't understand how necessary and beneficial they really were.

> They crawl down our ears and clean out the wax and sand that we get from sleeping each night. Do you see we have perfect hearing? Yes, they climb up our nose and clean it out too. . . . It is going to get much hotter in the days to come, and you will suffer if you do not have a clean nose. . . . The flies crawl and cling to our body and take off everything that is eliminated. . . . See how soft and smooth our skin is and look at yours. . . . You need the flies to clean your skin, and someday we will come to the place where the flies have laid the larvae, and again we will be provided with a meal."[2]

Regal Black Swan looked intently at Morgan, ending his talk by reminding her that humans cannot exist if every unpleasant thing is eliminated instead of understood. "When the flies come, we surrender. Perhaps you are ready to do the same."

Taking his words to heart, when she next heard the bush flies approaching, she followed the tribe's example. In her imagination, she went to an expensive health spa and pictured trained technicians cleaning her entire body. When the flies left, she returned from her mental trip, understanding that surrender was the appropriate response.

The Descent Surrender means defeat in our culture. Encouraged not to give in to anything, we are taught instead to persevere and overcome obstacles whenever they present themselves. We all understand Morgan's initial response to the bush flies—that holding oneself in stiff resistance to something unpleasant. We think it will help us endure, but it only leaves us stressed and fatigued by the fight and in exactly the same place for the next encounter.

What fights with us during these times is larger than our desires, opinions, and measurement tools. These are the initiatory forces of creation that push us to grow beyond our ideas of who we are and what life is about. They push us toward the soul, toward what is most genuine and unique in each of us. Rainer Maria Rilke reminds us in his poem "A Man Watching" that "what is extraordinary and eternal does not want to be bent by us. . . ."

> What we choose to fight is so tiny!
> What fights with us is so big!
> If only we would let ourselves be dominated
> as things do by some immense storm,
> we would become strong too, and not need names.[3]

We are sons and daughters of a lopsided society, too often stuck in the heroic stance when surrender is the required response. Few of us have learned how to surrender—even the idea is foreign in our culture. We don't have instructions for the life-enhancing psychological descent into the abyss and the journey out again. It was replaced some three hundred years ago with a blueprint for controlling life and the faith that scientists would eliminate anything unpleasant. Yet it is this journey down into the depths, understood by ancient cultures and our wilderness selves, that is a necessary part of all life's passages. Being open to the inevitable descent transforms experience into wisdom. Without it, the same experience leaves us with only the taste of defeat.

The Descent of Inanna There are many myths of descent reentering the culture today through the efforts of pioneers like poet Robert Bly and storytellers Clarissa Pinkola Estés and Michael Meade. And in all descents there is the death of a false self that has possessed us and a turning toward the true self. The oldest myth of this motif is known as the descent of Inanna, the Sumerian queen of Heaven and Earth. Inanna's journey to the Netherworld is a story about surrender. As she passes through the seven gates of the underworld, ruled by Ereshkigal, Queen of the Great Below, Inanna is stripped and finally killed. Interestingly, her restoration occurs because Enki, the god of water and wisdom, sends two flylike creatures into the Netherworld. Once there, they commiserate with Ereshkigal as she moans over the dead. Ereshkigal is so grateful for the empathy, for the compassionate response to her grief, that she hands over Inanna's corpse, and it is taken above and restored to life.

Therapist and author Sylvia Brinton Perera considers the descent, ensuing death, and rebirth a mirror of the rhythmic nature of the seasons and a model for our own psychological-spiritual journeys. Inanna's surrender is not based upon passivity but upon an openness to being acted upon. This stance lets us go down into the depths and allow the death of our known identity. Something familiar is lost, but a life more in keeping with our deeper values is offered to us.

When we encounter the extraordinary and eternal, an event or experience outside our control and understanding, it can feel negative if we are accustomed to resisting change. If we can't stop railing against life and adopting the heroic or the victim stance, we may experience only the stripping aspect of the descent, without its cleansing and promise of renewal.

The forces that fight with us during life's initiations require respect and surrender. They demand that we recognize their validity and accord them a power equal to the powers of growth and expansion glorified in today's world. For without openness to this side of life, to the decay-sensing, death-wielding forces of transformation—the flies' domain—we will be worked on invasively, pitilessly, against our personal will, because our will, what we want, is too small.

Leaving Heaven and Hell   Stephen Levine, a pioneer in the investigation of conscious living and dying, says that most people live their lives in an incessant alternation between heaven and hell. Getting what they want, they are in heaven. Losing it, or never getting it at all, they drop to what their mind tells them is hell. But hell is just the resistance to what is. It is the fight against the bush flies' presence, and heaven is their absence. Trapped in this dichotomy, the mind fluctuates between thinking itself fortunate or unfortunate, and our responses arise from its pronouncement about the situation. And that judgment, congruent with our projections, bars us from experiencing the world as it exists apart from our mental baggage. It also blocks the informative and transformative energies that seek to deepen us.

The world made in the image of what we think we want will too often be a constricted and brittle place, shaped by fear and shadow projections. By trying to eliminate what we have perceived as unpleasant and achieve what we believe to be heavenly, we have cut ourselves off from the wellspring of life and declared war against beneficial forces in the natural world and in our psyches.

Perhaps one way around this deadening dichotomy of heaven or hell lies in changing what we desire. If our desire is big enough, it could work for us. If we want to understand Oneness, the fundamental unity of Creation, if we want to understand the worldview of every living thing, if we want to preserve biodiversity, we may only need to suspend our opinions and stay open to Nature and its creatures as they present themselves. We may only need to surrender. By giving up our false autonomous stance, we could cultivate a loving openness to all life, a loving openness to flies.

Losing Irreplaceable Wonders

The statistics of declining populations of species have reached alarming proportions. Something is drastically wrong or we wouldn't have allowed, or even participated in, the vast destruction of our planet, well documented in a slew of recent books. Although entomologists have identified thousands of fly species, we are starting to realize that having a dead insect pinned in a collection does not mean we know anything about that creature and the part it plays in its ecosystem.

Entomologists in California recently tried to get endangered or threatened status for seven eight-legged creatures and six insects. They were all rejected, all deemed "insufficiently endangered" to make the list. "Wise-use" groups like the National Wilderness Institute don't want to protect what it calls "ugly little life forms." In fact, they want the nation to abandon the Endangered Species Act, whose purpose is to protect all species, and let the public's preference for certain creatures guide the official decision-making process, a regressive move that would harm us all.

Experts tell us that when a species declines, it is a warning and the first indication that something is drastically wrong. Not to act at that point is a crime of omission that will return to haunt us.

Threatened Flies Several years ago the inch-long, Delhi Sands flower-loving fly became the first fly to be put on the endangered list— in spite of great resistance on the part of some. The Delhi Sands fly has eyes that change colors with reflected light and plays a key ecological role even though it only lives a few weeks in its San Bernadino, California, habitat. That habitat has now been reduced to five hundred acres, or 3 percent of its original size. Its cousin the El Segundo flower-loving fly vanished in the early 1960s.

Even if it can survive in such a small area, its struggle is not over. Protecting a fly outrages a lot of people, and some have moved to have it taken off the endangered species list. Any insect like the fly has a hard time getting protection and keeping it, regardless of its role in its habitat. Arguments against protecting it will draw power from our unexamined consensus on flies. Propaganda will reduce the issue to people versus flies or jobs versus flies.

The Endangered Species Act excludes insects we have judged as pests that "present an overwhelming and overriding risk to man." But the risks are economic, not life-threatening. We don't want to risk losing money or risk being inconvenienced or made uncomfortable. With sad irony, the real risk to people is not flies or other insects labeled pests, but the years of waging war against them with toxic chemicals that damage entire ecosystems. Rachel Carson gave us a wake-up call. It wasn't enough. Pesticide use remains at a dangerously high level.

Our persistence in dividing up the "oneness" of the world into good species and bad species and then trying to eliminate the bad ones ruptures the web of relationship on which our lives depend. To wage war against any species is to wage war against ourselves. Likewise, to refuse aid to a species threatened by extinction is to abandon an aspect of ourselves and diminish all life on Earth.

To respond appropriately to the crisis of endangered species, we must reexamine and discard current practices and models of the world that have not served life and not allow a handful of policymakers to determine who lives and who dies. For starters, we would make far fewer mistakes if we assumed every insect was a valuable part of its habitat. That assumption alone would alter the status quo while we cultivate a genuine regard for them.

Communicating with Flies

The evidence of our multifaceted interdependence with other species, outside what traditional scientific investigation has revealed, has led to another phenomenon generating interest and gaining acceptance in the popular culture: interspecies communication.

Interspecies communication, a rich area of research, has been dismissed by institutionalized science because it does not fit within conventional paradigms. Although modern physics and many other branches of science have moved beyond the mechanistic theory of life, traditional biology is still dominated by it, reducing other species to complex machines incapable of communication.

The phenomenon of interspecies communication, however, has not gone away. In fact, accounts of such communication and the uncanny behavior of animals are growing. World-renowned biologist and animal-lover Rupert Sheldrake believes it is an area where scientific research can be carried out by amateurs—people who do something simply because they love it. Following his own advice, he conducted five years of extensive research involving thousands of people who own and work with animals. He proved that there are invisible bonds connecting animals to each other, to us, and to their homes in powerful ways.

A "conversation" with a coyote sent Derrick Jensen, the author of *A Language Older Than Words*, on a search for others who had had similar experiences. He soon discovered that he wasn't alone. Most people he asked said that they had them too but kept quiet about it because they didn't want others to think they were crazy.

I've had "conversations" as well with my animal companions. My first spontaneous interspecies communication, however, was with insects, years before I took up the work of speaking in their behalf, but right after I read J. Allen Boone's story of Freddie the fly, which I share in the next section. Those inexplicable and unplanned occurrences have kept the door open in my mind about others who practice interspecies communication on a regular basis.

Many who love animals have been drawn to this field already, and interspecies communication workshops are offered around the world. Pioneer interspecies communicator and author Penelope Smith has instructed hundreds of people in this art, believing that it is our legacy. Smith communicates with insects like flies and mosquitoes in the same manner that she does with furred and feathered species—telepathically. Tested by skeptics and ignored by scientists, Smith has demonstrated repeatedly, under many circumstances, that when she engages other species in this way, something occurs between them to affect their behavior.

According to Smith, communicating sincerely with insects yields harmonious results. When insects are approached as intelligent beings with whom cooperation is possible, people achieve the results they want. Smith believes that the most important element is an attitude of nonresistance and being willing to validate another's viewpoint. When Smith attempts the communication to resolve a problem, she initially listens to their reasons for doing what they do and agrees to help them meet their needs. Even the listening process, however, is a foreign one for those not familiar with quieting the mind and stopping its whirl of thoughts. The art of listening can be cultivated, though, Smith insists, and devotes most of her time to this kind of training.

Universal Mind

Smith's ability may be evidence of a kind of nonlocality that is an integral part of quantum theory. It implies that there are connections at a distance that institutionalized science has not at present recognized. Physician and author Larry Dossey believes that some kind of universal nonlocal mind connects all living things, arguing that this makes good biological sense because it is an asset to survival.

In indigenous cultures, it was the shaman who had a special rapport with other species and advised the tribe on how to be in right relationship to them. The shaman's hard-won knowledge arose in part from initiatory experiences with other species and disciplined awareness.

Without contemporary shamans available to guide us today, we are left with the challenge of developing our own shamanistic abilities. We don't have to wait until our scientists discover the physical basis for Smith's communication or explain the levels of consciousness that native shamans have detected and mastered. A personal experience can do more to uproot old habits of perceptions than anything we might hear or read.

Befriending Flies Some precedents for befriending a fly exist. Colman of Galway, friend and correspondent of Saint Columba, reports that this hermit-saint lived in a clay hut with room for only himself, a cock, a fly, and a mouse. He fed and spoke to them kindly, and they became his friends. They each had a job. The fly, it was said, kept the saint's place in his books. And when his friends died, the saint wrote of his grief.

Following native wisdom, Sara Willow, a writer and the founder of a web site called "AnimalSpirit," encourages others to learn from any creature they encounter in the course of daily life. From the fly, Willow learned how to hold herself still, because the fly would only stay on her extended finger when she was practicing stillness.

For most of us, learning from insects or communicating with them is a possibility that only direct experience can verify. At some point we must be willing to set aside our self-consciousness and fear of looking and acting foolish, and try it. Psychiatrist Gale Cooper did just that one summer day while sitting in her dining room. A fly buzzed past her, making a futile attempt to penetrate the window. Without thinking and without changing her position, she offered to take the fly outside and extended her index finger. The fly circled, then landed on her finger and stayed while she walked outside. Cooper knew inexplicably that the fly had understood her, and that knowledge brought tears to her eyes—she had touched the great mystery of connection to other species.

Few published stories counteract the common view of flies as pests, much less suggest the possibility of communication or even friendship. Yet, when any individual stops acting in accordance with a wrong perception, the possibility for something new, something positive, emerges. Novelist J. R. Ackerly writes that when his mother "was losing her faculties" she formed a friendship with a fly. He never saw the fly, but his mother spoke about it a lot and talked to it. It lived in the bathroom, and although she made a bit of a joke about it, she was serious enough to give it bread crumbs each day, spreading them along the rim of the bathtub as she bathed.

Without a context that would allow for our having a relationship with a fly, we are likely to condemn or dismiss those who claim to have entered this terrain. One reviewer of a previous edition of this book was outraged by the inclusion of such stories, calling them "cheap assertions." Ackerly assumed his mother was simply becoming demented. Perhaps she was only losing her judgments and opinions and returning to a natural state of mind, cleared of projections and open to the possibilities of the moment. And maybe we don't have to fear being thought crazy to begin cultivating a friendship with a fly.

Freddie the Fly   The late J. Allen Boone provides us with a model for befriending a fly in *Kinship with All Life*. In this classic on interspecies communication, he relates how he was called into relationship with a housefly he named Freddie.

Boone learned that if he approached other species with a genuine willingness to learn, he found an intelligent being on the other side of the relationship. One day, after many successful interactions with an assortment of species, Boone noticed that a fly appeared to be following him from room to room. He wondered if communication was possible with this life form and decided to try. He wrote down the fly's admirable characteristics, the first step that seemed to set the stage for a dialogue to occur. With list in hand, he sent the fly appreciative thoughts, mentally asking it to land on his finger. The fly responded, flying to Boone's finger and walking up and down its length with a vigorous step.

Over the next couple of weeks, Boone and Freddie played games and generally explored their relationship. Sometimes Boone would mark his finger with different colored inks, sectioning it. He would then ask Freddie to fly to a particular color, and Freddie, demonstrating his ability to understand what Boone asked, would do it without hesitation.

When word spread about Freddie, visitors came to meet him. One visitor was an actor who at Boone's suggestion asked Freddie to light on his finger. But each time the man directed his request to Freddie, the fly flew instead from Boone's finger to the ceiling. Freddie's actions puzzled Boone. Freddie was usually as curious about visitors as they were about him. Finally, Boone questioned the man closely, and the actor admitted sheepishly that he had always hated and killed flies. Boone decided that Freddie was aware of the man's real feelings about flies and demonstrated that awareness by refusing to interact with him.

Before Freddie, Boone didn't like anything about flies, and with echolike precision his thoughts dictated his experience. He expected flies to be unfriendly, and they were. He expected them to annoy him, and they did. He expected to be bitten, and he was. When he changed his attitude about flies, he reports that he was never bothered again, even in fly-infested jungles.

There is a reality and a wisdom to any creature outside of our fears, judgments, and opinions. Indigenous people knew that every creature, including the fly, had the power to impart a revelation and reveal an aspect of the whole. Freddie the fly taught Boone that when people address other species as a "thou" instead of as an "it," and extend courtesy and appreciation, kinship and communion become possible.

The Flies' Lesson   Karen Hild and others at a Sathya Sai Baba retreat held in a New Mexican Buddhist monastery learned a great lesson from the flies around them. In the dining hall, dozens of flies landed on their hands and food, annoying everyone there. Of course, as practitioners of nonviolence, the Buddhists didn't do anything about the flies.

The retreat was a silent retreat, until one person fell out of a tree and broke his leg. Silence gave way to animated discussions over the event. Hild and her friend were talking about the fall when they noticed flies buzzing around their heads and trying to land on their mouths. It reminded Hild of how Freddie the fly had buzzed around Boone when he had a message for him. She wondered if these flies were trying to tell them something. Perhaps their indulging in ordinary conversation was inappropriate. To test the theory, they stopped talking and the flies left, only to return when they began speaking again. Hild's friend shared the incident with Sathya Sai Baba who wanted her to relate the experience to the group. Hild was reluctant, as she was uncomfortable speaking in groups, and it took another fly visit to convince her it was important to do so.

The second visit occurred just before the meeting. A fly landed beside her and stayed. Hild saw it as an opportunity to verify whether or not she should share the previous fly experience with the group. "I silently recognized the Divine Source in the fly and put my finger down beside it [asking] . . . Lord, if you want me to relate the story to the group, please jump up on my finger." And the fly did just that, half flying, half jumping up on her finger so quickly that it startled her.

Hild told the story to the group, including this last experience. Several people looked at her with disbelief written all over their faces, but others were keenly interested and asked her where they could read the story of Freddie.

The final kick to Hild's story is that from that point on, until the retreat was over, the flies in the dining hall never bothered any of the humans again. They were still present in droves but landed and stayed by the window as though the heightened awareness of the participants had been their goal all along.[4]

By following Boone's example and adopting a genuinely friendly view, we may discover for ourselves that we too can communicate with flies, including them in our circle of community and coming to their aid when they need help. And then, when the gnat asks us what insect we rejoice in where we come from, we might even say with enthusiasm: "The fly!"

According flies appreciation and respect is a radical approach to co-existence that requires some initial effort and perseverance on our part. But when flies are acknowledged individually with a simple gesture of courtesy, or as a species for their navigational skills or their superior recycling and pollinating abilities, we have the foundation for an environmental ethic based on a feeling for flies. We also open the door to the possibility of rejoicing in flies. And knowing them by their proper names, we might call on their advice and ask them to witness our inevitable descents and help secure our release and return. We might also seek Big Fly's counsel as we navigate the complexities of these times and, once again, hear My Lord Who Hums in the aerial visitor who enters our awareness.

6. DIVINE GENIUS

The roach, its shining back and hair thin feet / creaks the tiles
night's music / which means we are safe / we are never alone.

—*Linda Hogan*

Elisavietta Ritchie writes of a lonely year in Malaysia after her marriage of twenty-three years failed. Through a succession of long evenings as she sat up late at night writing, a cockroach appeared and stayed near her. The insect appeared to be observing her, or perhaps it was merely keeping her company. She felt a sort of gratitude for its presence.

Gratitude is not something usually accorded cockroaches, although they are admired begrudgingly by the scientific world because they are survivors.

Learning how to survive in a mental ward until securing his freedom is what Eddy Rubin sought when his parents had him committed at age fifteen. In a letter to *The Sun* magazine, Rubin says he spent the first few nights in a padded cell. Stripped of all his possessions—including his glasses, although he was legally blind without them—he could hear taunts from other patients outside his cell. After a while, he noticed a movement out of the corner of his eye, a brown blur. He got closer and closer until he could see that it was a cockroach. Although he'd never liked these insects before, he was glad for the company. He followed the roach around the floor, watching it run up and down the mattress, clean itself, and search for food. Suddenly it disappeared into a small crack in the wall. It had escaped. At that moment Rubin knew he had witnessed a lesson that would lead to his own freedom. If the cockroach could discover a way out of apparent imprisonment, so could he. And he did.

Stories of positive interactions between humans and cockroaches are unusual. Several stories, published as curiosities, feature prisoners. In 1938 a man jailed in Texas claimed to have trained a cockroach to come to his solitary confinement cell when he whistled. And in 1995 the *Weekly World News* featured an inmate with a pet cockroach that he fed bits of cheese and walked around his cell using a tiny thread as a leash. But this only became news when a guard killed the roach and the prisoner sued the prison.

Contact with cockroaches by those outside prisons and hospitals are unwanted contacts that elicit loathing, not interest or admiration. It is the rare individual who is curious about these elders on our planet or who wonders how these insects will survive their greatest test of adaptability—sharing the world with a hostile and burgeoning human population.

When species were ranked according to their popularity in a 1980 study at Yale, no one was surprised that the cockroach came in last, even beating the mosquito. A love of warmth, darkness, and our leftover food has placed a few species in a proximity to us that some find unbearable. The thought of their unseen activities, carried on in darkness, disgusts or scares us. We imagine them living sordid lives behind our walls, and companies who make millions selling products to kill them tell us that thousands wait hidden in our midst for an opportunity to spread filth, transmit disease, and take over our living spaces.

The cockroach's association with filth—our filth—overrides the fact that these benign creatures do not bite or sting or have any capacity to directly hurt humans. Biologist Ronald Rood maintains that cockroaches are harmless to human beings and seldom carry any bacteria that would adversely affect us.

Many research efforts have tried to link cockroaches to specific diseases as though eager to find a justification for the culture's hatred. Yet all evidence is circumstantial. Never have cockroaches been linked directly in the transmission of human infectious diseases. Most scientists agree that their disease-carrying reputation is quite undeserved. Cockroaches tend to stay healthy throughout their life. And even when cockroaches gain access to food before people eat it, they leave no contamination that could not just as easily enter in another way. But most of us don't know this, or we don't believe it. Our response to their presence is so strong that of the four thousand known cockroach species, the four or five species that live almost exclusively with humans account for approximately 25 percent of the total insecticide use in the United States.

Cockroaches and Dirt

People with cockroaches in their homes often call them by other names, such as water bugs, Croton bugs, Bombay canaries, or palmetto bugs to avoid being accused of keeping a dirty home. The belief that the presence of cockroaches in our homes points to a less than stellar character and slovenly habits runs through our literature and movies and may explain the results of a survey in which people named cockroaches as the most embarrassing insect. Their presence is a cause for shame and an accusation. For the person living an unexamined life, ridding their homes of these insects is a way to escape judgment.

Ironically, no matter how clean we keep our homes, in warm regions cockroaches are likely to be our roommates. They rarely miss an opportunity to eat and can exist easily on a wide variety of substances including the glue from book bindings. They can chew almost anything, hard or soft, and because they can sense just a few molecules of food, they rarely miss even a crumb. In dire circumstances they can even survive without food for three months and without water for one.

Since some cockroach species live amid our garbage and in our drains, most people assume they are dirty, but they are surprisingly clean in their habits. By performing contortions similar to a cat grooming itself, cockroaches pass every accessible part of their feet and antennae through their mouth parts. And they also wash themselves vigorously after being touched by human beings. It is a fact that must have amused Mary James, for in her novel *Shoebag*, a twist on Kafka's *Metamorphosis*, she features a young cockroach that wakes up one morning to discover that he has turned into a little boy. As a bacteria-laden human being, he is then shunned by his insect family and friends.

Instead of imaging that cockroaches are up to no good behind the walls, it would be more accurate to imagine them grooming themselves for hours. Since these activities occur in the darkness of hiding places, we are unaware of the time they spend on these ablutions each day. We are also unaware because pesticide companies don't want us to make comparisons between cockroaches and creatures we like—such as cats. It's not good for business.

Cockroaches and Allergies

Recently, cockroaches have been linked with human allergies. A major newspaper reports with a familiar venomous tone that now "there is another reason to hate cockroaches:" these "universally hated" creatures are a major cause of winter allergies and asthma. The news item was based on recent research demonstrating that inhaling the chemicals in the crumbling outer shell of a dead cockroach produces the same effect on allergic people as ragweed pollen or cat dander.

The correlation is not as cut and dried, however, as you might think. Allergies are complex afflictions, and their source is not easily identified. In fact, the root cause of the symptoms we label allergy remains a mystery. What is known is that allergies are two to ten times more common now than they were forty years ago. A recent book on environmental medicine attributes the increase to the load of toxic chemicals in the air, food, and water, which, in turn, build up in the body. It also cites the vastly increased indoor air pollution levels—a result of materials used in the construction of modern buildings and our modern farming methods, which produce food laced with chemicals and deficient in essential nutrients.

Because even the most ethical reporter and the most prestigious newspaper can unwittingly transmit the influence of the culture shadow, it is up to us to bring a discriminating eye to what we read and believe—especially when the conclusions pit us against a plant or animal in the Earth community. A 1997 study by a Brazilian allergy researcher found that the exoskeletons of cockroaches comprised only 2 or 3 percent of substances that could cause allergies, hardly a "major cause" as claimed.

Work on developing a vaccine based on substances found in cockroaches is also being conducted in Brazil. It is a line of research linked to the premises of homeopathy. Cockroaches, found to be therapeutic in stubborn cases of asthma, allergies, and other respiratory ailments, have long been used in homeopathic remedies. So a legitimate link exists between cockroaches and allergies—it's the homeopathic "signature" of these insects.

Regardless of our credentials, hostility influences what we observe and how we interpret what we find. Hating and killing cockroaches will not stop an allergic reaction to a world flooded with chemicals. Nor will it permit us to escape the consequences of enemy-making and the distortions of the propaganda that uphold it.

Phobic Reactions to Cockroaches

Reactions to cockroaches frequently border on hysteria. Irrational fears, in turn, often prompt people to use insecticides unnecessarily. A recent news item, for example, reported that a twenty-year-old Israeli woman sprayed an insecticide into her mouth when a flying cockroach landed on her tongue. The chemical burned her mouth, tongue, vocal cords, and larynx, and she needed hospitalization. All she could say afterward is that she hated cockroaches so much, she didn't think before grabbing the spray. And in Sue Hubbell's *Broadsides from the Other Orders: A Book of Bugs*, a college professor confesses to a lifelong terror of cockroaches. When he sees one he is literally paralyzed by his terror, unable to speak or move.

A phobic reaction has an intensity that marks it as a disorder. The strength of their feelings put the professor and the young woman in the phobic category, where they are far from alone. Phobias and related anxiety disorders are the most common psychological problems in modern society. They are treated by desensitizing the individual, pairing relaxation exercises with images of the object of the phobia. Yet the treatment only addresses the symptom. Depth psychologists tell us that the intensity of our response to a person or situation is a sure indication that something else is at work. What we refuse to look at in ourselves—the projections we cast out into the world—dominates us, directing our energies from behind the scenes. The source of this influence is no wizard behind a velvet curtain, but the now-familiar shadow. We must only draw back the curtain and bring awareness to projected material to strip it of its power and free ourselves to respond appropriately to another—even a cockroach.

For most of us, our responses to cockroaches aren't phobic but display an intensity beyond what we understand. Unexamined, these feelings are the reason we don't object to the barrage of negative propaganda about cockroaches. A case in point was an article from the garden section of a newspaper in my area, featuring an exterminator turned urban entomologist who writes about the "satisfaction" of spraying or stomping on cockroaches. Ironically it is also why a rap / heavy metal group called Papa Roach revels in identifying with an insect the mass culture hates.

Exterminating cockroaches may make some of us feel powerful and in control. With a them-against-us mentality, every cockroach killed moves the person closer to some imagined safety zone. But the satisfaction that comes from eliminating our perceived adversary is always short-lived. There is never enough safety for the individual who has made other creatures the enemy. And projections like these keep us fugitives on the planet, operating from our suspicions and killing what we don't like or understand.

Learning to Hate Cockroaches   Too often, negative feelings about cockroaches appear reasonable. After all, the creatures look and act very differently than we do and are maddeningly indifferent to our wants. Not only do they move too quickly, they go into places they shouldn't be—like on our bodies as we sleep (or so we fear) and in our homes. Blatantly ignoring property lines, they also ignore our psychological boundaries. Violations are invasions. When they opt to live with us, their presence serves as a judgment on our housekeeping, their numbers an assault to the eyes and imagination, and their indifference simply insolent. It appears natural and acceptable, then, to ridicule and kill them in return for these crimes.

The fact that not all cultures feel and act this way toward cockroaches is evidence that our responses are not innate, however, but learned. East Indian and Polynesian peoples created jewelry and ornaments in tribute to the cockroach, and Jamaican folklore frequently includes cockroaches cast in a positive role. The Nandi tribe of Africa has a cockroach totem, and in parts of Russia and France people think of this insect as a protecting spirit, and its presence in the house is viewed as fortunate. In fact, in these communities, if the cockroach leaves, its departure is taken as a sign of bad luck.

Since an aversion to cockroaches is not natural, we must somehow be learning it and passing it on to each generation. And that is exactly what we do. Studies show that even children who have never had contact with cockroaches learn to hate them when they are around adults who hate them. Up to the age of about four, children have absolutely no aversion to cockroaches.

The negative slant in many introductory books on cockroaches is one way we pass on the culture's hostility. A case in point is this opening line: "Cockroaches are really yucky but like them or not, they are truly amazing creatures."

Another way is to describe them in emotional terms and use images of assault when pointing out body parts or their abilities. A good example is one author's description of the Asian cockroach in a juvenile book as "disgustingly different" from other cockroaches. What disgusts her is its ability to fly. She compares them to locusts, which cluster on the ground so compactly "that a person can step on twenty-five or thirty at once."

Perhaps suspicion that the insects have joined together, portending some misdeed, is behind her decision to use the image of "stepping on them" to describe their behavior. If another animal were involved—kittens, perhaps or a gathering of songbirds—the inappropriateness of the statement might be more evident. If we reined in our misgivings about their intentions, the questions evoked by the clustering scene might follow this line: Is there an order and purpose to this insect assembly, a common mission that unites them? Do they move as one thought, synchronized like a swarm of bees? What do they sense as they congregate, individual insect boundaries abandoned? These questions reflect the spirit of scientific inquiry more than images of humans killing nonhumans indiscriminately.

More information could also ease our fears about flying species. For instance, cockroaches are strong fliers but poor navigators. In Hawaii, the males of some species often fly on warm nights and frequently collide with people and other objects. If we knew about their lack of navigational skills, we wouldn't interpret their bungling attempts at flight and frequent collisions with people as acts of aggression—as many Hawaiians do, calling them the "B-52 cockroach."

Cockroach Communities

As our awareness increases, it is easy to see that those with a vested interest in having us view cockroaches as the enemy want us to believe that these insects are life forms that respond to the environment robotically and live without purpose. A cockroach "combat" manual calls cockroaches survival machines that hide together in groups but share no outward affection for each other.

Others, who don't make their living on substances that kill cockroaches report that they appear to live in organized communities. Although few insects beyond social insects like ants actively care for their young, many cockroach species display some signs of having a family life. On occasion, active youngsters even return to the nest site to share a drop of food still remaining on the mouth parts of an adult.

When at rest, cockroaches lie close to each other, antennae touching and moving slightly as though sampling the air for danger, or to reassure each other, or perhaps even to communicate. Scientists say that cockroaches have a strong need to be touched on all sides, a predilection called thigmotaxix. It's a phenomenon that probably supports their love of community. But it doesn't explain why cockroaches groom each other. Their togetherness is an interesting oddity in the insect world, most of whose members either ignore or fight one another.

Contrary to the idea of cockroaches as machines, researchers often credit cockroaches with being "smart enough" to solve a maze. As early as 1912, C. H. Turner used electric shock to train cockroaches in a laboratory experiment. The same questionable technique was used by the special-effects technician for the cockroach invasion in *Creepshow.*

Positive incentives for learning, which have been shown to be more effective and more durable in humans and other animals, are also more effective for cockroaches. Ronald Rood reports that a classmate of his taught roaches to distinguish right from left in a simple maze—without electric shock. They passed each test with flying colors.

The Shadow of Scientific Research Cockroaches are frequently used as laboratory specimens. Neurobiologists claim the cockroaches' tactile sensitivity, combined with a nervous system built of exceptionally large cells, makes this insect an ideal experimental organism for studying how nerve cells work. I wonder if these same exceptionally large nerve cells indicate that cockroaches have an uncommon sensitivity to life.

Although empathy with cockroaches or any other animal is considered a contaminant in traditional research, hostility is not acknowledged as the contaminating factor it is. One researcher reports that a cockroach's head will live and respond for at least twelve hours after being severed from its body. He ends his report with a smug statement lauding the cockroach as an ideal experimental animal since few animal rights activists will disrupt a laboratory to defend cockroaches, no matter what is done to them.

Perhaps his satisfaction will be short-lived. When the results of a series of studies performed in the spring of 2000 at the University of Bristol become more widely known, insects may finally be included in the effort to secure humane treatment for laboratory animals. Research showed that contrary to common opinion, cockroaches and other insects do suffer pain. In fact, in one experimental situation insects reacted much like cats and dogs in their aversion to electric shocks.

That news is not likely to curb state-of-the-art research like that being conducted at Japan's Tsukuba University by biologists who have created what reporters call the "robo-roach." Researchers have surgically removed the wings of cockroaches and implanted micro-robotic backpacks into them to control their movements. They have also replaced their antennae with pulse-emitting electrodes. When a signal is sent to the backpacks, it stimulates the electrodes, and pain forces the cockroach to turn left or right or go forward or backward. The altered cockroach, targeted for spying, can survive for several months, although over time they become less sensitive to the electronic pulses. The scientist in charge is optimistic that even that can be overcome.

In his concluding comments, the mask of objective scientist slips and the shadow is evident when he confesses, "They are not very nice insects. They are a little bit smelly and there's something about the way they move their antennae. But they look nicer when you put a little circuit on their backs and remove their wings."

Celebrating Our Hostility

Outside scientific circles, the shadow is even more apparent because hostility toward cockroaches is the norm. Dead and captive roaches are a big draw at Purdue University's "All-American Trot." Since 1991, students and staff from the Department of Entomology have invited the public to a cockroach race and a tractor pull where three Madagascar cockroaches, a large exotic species, are forced to pull miniature tractors across a finish line. Dead roaches dressed up as fans and placed in miniature stands evoke great mirth from the thousands of people who come to enjoy the event and bet on the race.

Contests are another cultural event that are used in service of the hostile imagination, and creativity in this context also takes on a twisted expression, as it must. Several years ago the International Roach Finals in Florida awarded a prize for creativity to a man who displayed dead roaches dressed up as wind-surfers and sunbathers. Not an isolated incident, the Cockroach Hall of Fame, a Plano, Texas, enterprise, sponsors a contest for cockroach "art" where people are encouraged to find and kill cockroaches and then dress them up as human personalities for display in shoebox scenes.

A popular advertising stunt involves releasing one hundred cockroaches branded with a bar code. This is a twist on cockroach contests that award prizes to the person who brings in the largest cockroach. A pest control company in Dallas, Texas, started it in 1986 with a thousand-dollar prize. Orlando, Florida quickly followed suit. By 1989, other U.S. cities also had contests to find the largest cockroach, most of them sponsored by roach control manufacturers. Today the search is international in scope, with South Africa and Bermuda participating.

An Elder Sighting   Contrast these events to a scene shared by environmental psychologist James Swan in his book *Nature as Healer and Teacher*. Swan was driving along a dirt road in the Yukon Territory when he stopped by an Indian salmon-fishing camp.

He watched as the Indians took most of the fish from their trap. Then someone called out, "Look!" In the bottom of the trap was a giant salmon nearly four feet long. One of the older men looked at it briefly and said, "Let it go, it's an elder." They opened the gate, and the giant fish shot out and up the stream.

"You have to respect the elders in all the tribes," the older man told Swan. "The plants, the animals, the mountains, the birds—they all have many tribes. If you don't respect them, you'll pay later."[1]

Swan considered it a lesson in seeing truly. Tribal people understood the visit as an intentional meeting of human and nonhuman, engineered by forces our culture no longer acknowledges. Writer-attorney Vine Deloria, Jr., a member of the Standing Rock Sioux, calls these sightings "glimpses into another dimension of consciousness,"[2] where our kinship with Nature and other species has its roots.

Perhaps the bid to find the largest cockroach or the largest one of any species is a severely distorted attempt to glimpse the elder of a tribe and touch the bedrock of our most fundamental selves. The fact that we no longer understand the impulse and blindly follow the cultural pressure to hate and kill the largest—and not only kill them, but accept a reward for doing it—is a sad commentary on our profound alienation and general lack of respect for elders regardless of species.

Alien or Other?

It is common to call cockroaches (and other insects) aliens and monsters. Focusing on the obvious structural differences between us, we justify the separation between us, calling it natural. But are they aliens and monsters—which implies exclusion, opposition, and hostility—or just "Other"?

We're adept at making monsters, especially from creatures that look so different from ourselves. I wonder, though, if this monster-making propensity has its roots in something more life-serving than creating separation and fostering alienation.

The word *monster* comes from a Latin term for a portent of the gods. If cockroaches are monsters, then, it means their presence signals that something momentous is under way. Joseph Campbell said it is always the disgusting and rejected creature that calls us to some undertaking, some spiritual passage, which, when completed, amounts to a dying of what is familiar and outgrown, and a rebirth. The creature—whether frog, snake, or insect—represents the depths of the unconscious where all the rejected, unrecognized, unknown, and undeveloped elements of life reside. So the appearance of a creature we despise, like the cockroach, may be a call that informs us it is time to pass through a threshold—time to separate from what we know in order to move toward what we don't (but can) know. And all threshold crossings, all initiations— when we turn, or are turned, toward our soul or true nature—produce anxiety. Depending on the importance and duration of the change, an element of dread and the fear of the unknown also marks these times.

Boundary Inhabitants   The late ecopsychologist Paul Shepard believed that the creatures outside our orderly classification system signify chaos and threaten our efforts to create order and maintain control. It is easy to see how the presence of cockroaches in our homes would threaten us and thwart our desire for clear distinction, since they inhabit boundary places, like drains, the cracks under our refrigerators, and the spaces between our walls.

Boundaries, however, are the places where change is possible and new things emerge. In chaos theory, there is a domain called "the edge of chaos." It is the borderland between stability and chaos, and the place where a system or organization loses enough of its coherency and stability to be open to change, transformation, and reorganization—without collapsing into chaos. Philosopher David Spangler calls it the "essence of life," a place where the known and familiar come together in a co-creative way with the unknown and the unpredictable.

So maybe cockroaches are messengers of this spirit of the boundary, this push from inside to change—a call from our deepest nature that fills us with anxiety. By triggering in us an awareness of our shifting inner ground and introducing disorder and anxiety into our thoughts, they act as initiators, disrupting the quiet stability of the status quo. Maybe their presence nudges us toward this edge of chaos, so that we may touch a primal force of self-organization and unfolding, a force of newness and emergence.

Awakening   Seeing a cockroach nudged or perhaps catapulted a forty-three-year-old woman named Byron Katie into an enlightened way of seeing and being. It happened in February 1986. It was early morning, and Katie was lying on the floor in a locked attic room of a halfway house for women recovering from eating disorders. She had spent the preceding two weeks largely incoherent and consumed by terror and rage. As she describes it in Christin Lore Weber's *A Cry in the Desert: The Awakening of Byron Katie,* "A cockroach crawled over my foot—I was awake."[3] First she just felt the cockroach moving over her foot. Then she saw her foot but didn't know it was hers, and in the next instant she saw the cockroach and thought she was seeing herself. Suddenly joy and wonder replaced all the fear in her. The immense chaos of her old life dropped completely away, and she found herself in a heightened state of awareness that many call an enlightened state.

When she reflects on her turning point, on that moment when a cockroach crawled on her, she calls her awakening a resurrection. She awoke from pain that had become unbearable, to live the reality of joy.

If we consider that cockroaches are "Other," not alien, we could view Katie's experience of awakening as a moment of grace where the potent medicine of this species allowed her to finally see that all otherness emanates from an underlying and essential Oneness. And maybe we could move toward our own resurrection or awakening and invite grace into our lives by courting this quality of otherness in whatever form we find it.

We typically repress what is different or "Other" within us in order to fit in. Once repressed, we project it onto others and then view them suspiciously. Perhaps we have just lived too long afraid of the cockroaches' shadowing presence beneath the teetering scaffold of beliefs we have constructed to elevate us above the natural world. What unknown or despised aspect of ourselves do they (or any other insect) evoke? And how long can we afford not to invite them into our awareness and teach us what is required? How many times will we refuse the call to grow? When will we understand that we must entertain all kinds of otherness to discover our essential selves?

The Power of Empathy

Entertaining the quality of otherness can mean empathizing with a being that appears very different from ourselves. An ability to empathize with another is a characteristic in Daniel Goleman's model of "emotional intelligence." This ability to participate in another's worldview presupposes connection, and contrary to popular opinion, it requires participation and a blurring of the boundaries that separate and distinguish one from another—not structural similarity.

When learning to empathize with an insect, it also helps to remember that empathy is neither anthropomorphism nor behaviorism. The goal is not to make cockroaches into people, like journalist Don Marquis's poetry-writing cockroach, Archy, or Rodney Roach on the Internet. Neither is the goal to turn cockroaches into machines. They would resist both transformations. The real objective is to learn about them by participating in their world through the use of our imaginative faculties.

In traditional science, empathy is frowned upon and thought to distort reason because its influence often interferes with an expedient course of action. Empathy, however, is a critical element to understanding ourselves and others. Scientist-initiates, who are shamed and mocked when they empathize with other species and express concern for their lives, typically must dissociate from their feelings or leave the field.

The Intelligence of All Brains   Fortunately not all researchers succumb to the pressure of trying to appear totally objective. When biologist William Jordan was a graduate student, he was responsible for the department's cockroach cultures. His close observation of the activities of a variety of species triggered questions about their intelligence and similarities to humans. What he observed didn't line up with the official version of cockroaches as survival machines. He saw them as intelligent beings adapting to their life circumstances with flexibility and innovation.

He noticed that many common behaviors in cockroaches—like pursuing food, territory, social position, and mates—were also behaviors in people and he reasoned that since humans have evolved from animals, it was only logical that reason was driven by emotion.

Jordan decided that all brains were intelligent and generate behavior remarkably similar in dealing with the basic tasks of life. In human beings our conscious mind merely overlays our instincts and watches them operate, making connections among memories, emotions, urges, and the like—which we then experience as rational thought. The late Willis Harman would have agreed with Jordan. He said that goal-seeking and purpose in other species (dismissed in traditional biology as our tendency to project human traits onto Nature) appears to be a universal process through which Spirit contemplates and directs its own evolution.

For Jordan, the long hours he spent observing the university's cockroach communities made a profound impression on him. He decided that since evolution's basic objective is survival, the final goal of that process would be eternal existence. The ancient cockroach, around in recognizable form for eons, is approaching that eternal state. Add the fact that the basic purpose of the brain is to aid survival and, by that criterion, the cockroach is without doubt "divine genius."[4]

Master of Living

Most of us do not have or want opportunities to observe cockroaches to verify what Jordan saw in them. Stephanie Laland, the author of *Peaceful Kingdom,* didn't know anything about cockroaches other than that she didn't want them around. But they were in her house anyway. She tried the usual methods of getting rid of them, using boric acid and toxic Roach Motels with limited success. Apparently, she didn't want to buy a lizard, whose appetite for cockroaches is legendary, nor did she know that the stuff in ordinary catnip is a powerful insect repellent; so out of desperation she decided to try J. Allen Boone's method for communicating with another species. After all, he had had great success communicating with ants and with Freddie the fly.

The first step Boone recommends is to find something admirable about the species that you are trying to contact. Laland watched the cockroaches in her kitchen uneasily and could not see anything about them that she liked. Finally she told them that if they would leave, she would find *that* admirable, and she promised she would then say good things about them whenever someone asked her. Unsure about whether that was good enough, she wrote them a letter with the same message and put it in the garbage for them, hidden away from any friends who might deem her crazy. The next day, to her wonder, the cockroaches were gone. She lived there for two more years, but they never returned, and she kept her word and praised them to other people.

I like the story but am surprised that Laland didn't find anything about cockroaches to admire. I guess they don't look like the masters of living that they are, having evolved behaviors and survival strategies for all sorts of climates. Nor does the presence of a few species in our kitchens reveal that most live in the equatorial belt, where they pollinate plants, recycle wastes, and provide food for other species.

She must have known from her own experience, though, that it is nearly impossible to sneak up on a cockroach, regardless of the hour. And maybe she could see them stroking the air with their delicate and refined antennae, as though divining the news from molecules in the air. Those who study them know that they are superbly equipped to detect danger from all sides and even have sensors that can predict earthquakes.

Ironically, as we persist in hurting ourselves with toxic chemicals, the cockroaches' ability to resist pesticides continues to baffle and amaze scientists. It appears that the cockroach can dine on lethal substances without being harmed, a feat that may help us find a cure for cancer.

Those who study cockroaches agree that almost everything about these insects is a lesson in survival that goes far deeper than their adaptation to our presence on Earth. Instead of feeding cockroaches to the hostile imagination, cursing them for surviving and viewing them as adversaries, we would serve ourselves and them by cultivating a genuine admiration for these remarkable creatures. We might then say to one who has survived despite great odds: "You're a veritable cockroach!"

Relating to Giant Madagascar Hissing Cockroaches

One embodiment of divine genius is the three-inch-long giant Madagascar hissing cockroach. It has a calm presence, a shell the color of polished wood, and a hiss that punctuates the air and can startle predators from twelve feet away. People with private breeding colonies sell them as novelties. Many end up in colorful plastic houses entertaining humans for a few months—although their life span under better circumstances is about two years.

I became interested in this species after reading a true story that stretched my imagination in an entirely new direction. I found it in *Animal People*, a book written by Los Angeles psychiatrist Gale Cooper about people who have relationships of unusual intensity with animals.

One of these is Geoff Alison. Blind from infancy, Alison reports that he has always had a sense of connection with insects. As a child he was gradually introduced to the animal world in his backyard when his brother placed insects in his hand. Through an assortment of pets, his awareness and sensitivity to other species grew.

When he turned eighteen, a friend gave him four giant Madagascar hissing cockroaches. In time, he got to know them as individuals with distinct temperaments, each responding differently to the same situation. Some were born curious, others cautious. Another one was always fearful, while still another demonstrated a remarkable memory.

After close interaction with his cockroach community over many months, he also learned that they formed friendships outside the mating bond and passed the responsibilities of leadership from elder male to younger male in an orderly communication that lasted several days. But these behaviors are not exceptional to one who, like Alison, recognizes the intelligent awareness that permeates and directs all species.

The Death Pose   The death pose of cockroaches—on their back when death comes naturally—has long puzzled scientists. Alison discovered, however, that cockroaches die in stages, progressing into a gradual euphoria or death state reminiscent of a yogic state in which all involuntary body processes are controlled. In the first stage, the cockroach stops eating and moving. The insect appears completely relaxed yet totally unrelated to the world. As the gradual disengagement with the physical world proceeds, the cockroach voluntarily roles over on its back, legs limp. The cockroach may lie that way for several days before actually dying.

Communication with Cockroaches

Adversity often brings opportunities for relationships that otherwise might not occur as it did for Alison when a cockroach in his colony became disabled. She was an old female who had lost her feet to a fungus infection. Alison gave her special care. When he brought food for the others, for instance, he gave her the best of everything and put it next to her. He noticed that the other cockroaches were careful of her, giving her a place to sleep undisturbed by their activities. In time she learned to trust that her needs would be met. Alison could feel her calmness and a certain kind of "shared mutuality."

Alison also felt she rose above her essential instinctual responses to meet him. He would feel her pleasure intuitively when he brought her food she liked, but he also picked up thoughts and images, not his own, about less concrete things such as her welcoming his company and acknowledging his response to her situation.

When the time came for her to die, she signaled Alison. She was already on her back when he entered the room. He picked her up gently, and she conveyed through mental pictures that the time of death had arrived and that she was starting to vibrate or express through the whole of her being a pitch rising in volume. Before that compelling process drew her in further, she wanted to say goodbye to him. She conveyed that it had been good being together. It was her last communication. She became limp and died several days later at two years of age.

Although Alison's relationship to insects exists outside our cultural models, his is a story that could open the possibility of relationship—it is a story for the children of our time.

Another story with its own charm comes from Brenda Marshall, editor of *Light*, the journal of the College of Psychic Studies in England. When Marshall and her husband were in Brazil for a few weeks, they ran exceptionally hot water in the bathtub one morning, and a large cockroach popped out of the drain. After that, they were more careful about keeping the water tepid. One night not long after, they were sitting in the living room, which was separated from the bathroom by a long corridor, when a cockroach appeared at the doorway. It walked straight across the room to Marshall's husband, climbed up the chair, and stayed there. He fed the insect and discovered it liked tiny pieces of hard boiled eggs. During the rest of their visit, the insect would often join them on quiet evenings.

English-born Faith Maloney, director of Best Friends Animal Sanctuary in Kanab, Utah, communicated with animals telepathically when she lived on a coconut plantation in Mexico. Her first communications were with her dogs. From there she expanded her circle and communicated with other creatures, including cockroaches, whom she found to be "friendly creatures," who always accommodated her requests for them to leave. When she later lived in Chicago, a cockroach became a regular visitor to her bathroom. The insect would appear and then pause, as though waiting for her greeting. Once she gave her acknowledgment, the insect would move away again.

A Lesson from a Cockroach

In one of my classes on "Thinking Like a Bug," after a general orientation and discussion about how to enter a positive and respectful relationship with insects, I scheduled a young arthropod enthusiast that I had met at a local insect fair to come and bring a variety of creeping creatures. He brought a giant Madagascar hissing cockroach, among others. As he talked about the cockroach, my class clown Brian asked, with one eye toward me, "If I step on it, will its shell crack?" The class laughed, giving Brian the response he wanted. I interrupted the speaker to admonish Brian for the way he asked his question about the strength of the shell. Fully aware of what he had done, he just grinned sheepishly and assured me he was just kidding around.

After the presentation, I decided to take the cockroach, called Cedar because of his coloring, around the room while the guest speaker let some of the children hold his tarantula. Most of the children wanted to pick Cedar up, but I suggested that we could best demonstrate our respect for him by letting him choose to be held or not. I asked them to hold their hand palm up next to mine. Cedar, at ease in the palm of my hand, might choose to walk over to their hand, or not. They liked that idea and lined up for a turn.

Brian was first in line. I told him since he couched his question about the strength of Cedar's shell in an aggressive manner, Cedar might not go on his hand. Although I had shared the story of Freddie the fly with them, I could tell that Brian didn't really believe that the cockroach might have been aware of his attitude—just as Freddie the fly seemed to know that one of his visitors didn't like flies and routinely killed them.

Brian held his hand, palm out, next to mine. Cedar crawled to the edge of my open palm until his antennae briefly touched Brian's hand. Then Cedar withdrew and turned around, walking away. Brian was disappointed and suddenly not so sure that I hadn't been right. He stayed and watched as child after child came up and put his or her hand next to mine. The cockroach moved slowly, without hesitation, onto each child's hand, exploring.

After a short while, Brian was back in line, asking for another chance. I agreed, and again he put his hand next to mine. Again, Cedar walked to the edge of my hand, antennae moving. When he reached Brian's hand, he stopped and turned around, moving away. Brian was visibly upset now. I suggested that he make his peace with the insect by sending him his sincere apology and desire for connection.

More children lined up for a chance to have the cockroach on their hand. Each time, he obliged. Then one little girl approached, exclaiming: "Ooh! He's ugly, he's ugly!" Nothing I said got through to her or stopped her from reciting this shrill chant of distaste. Still, she held her hand next to mind. Cedar refused to go on it—wouldn't even move toward it. She left without absorbing the fact that the cockroach acted as though he knew she was insulting him, for the insect crawled without hesitation onto the hand of the next child in line. It was a powerful lesson for all of us.

When the class period was almost over, I told them we had to stop. Brian begged for one last chance to have Cedar walk on his hand. He said he had been really working on his thoughts and was ready. He held his hand next to mine. Cedar again moved to the edge of my hand and then crawled onto Brian's hand. Judging from the look of pleasure and triumph on the boy's face, you would have thought that he had just received a great gift—and he had. This discerning insect had honored his efforts and let him know that trust was restored.

Experiences like this one in the classroom raise more questions than they answer. Perhaps they merely serve to orient us correctly. A feeling for cockroaches is both the path into the mystery of our connection with other species and the lantern that lights the way. There is much to know about these creatures and the resiliency they embody—secrets accessible through intuition and empathy, delivered like pearls when least expected.

7. Go to the Ant

Go to the ant, consider her ways, and be wise.

—*Proverbs 6:6*

Anthony de Mello, a Jesuit priest, writes in *Taking Flight: A Book of Story Meditations* about a prisoner who lived in solitary confinement for many years. Taking his meals through an opening in the wall, he didn't see or speak to anyone in all that time. One day an ant found its way into his cell. It crawled around the room while the prisoner contemplated it. He was fascinated by the small creature and held it in the palm of his hand to observe it better. He gave it a grain or two of food, and at night he carefully placed a tin cup over it. One day the thought struck him that it had taken him ten long years of being utterly alone to open his eyes to an ant's loveliness.[1]

How many of us have opened our eyes to the loveliness of an ant? The author of *Kitchen Table Wisdom*, Rachel Naomi Remen, M.D., reminds us that Life asks of us the same thing we have been asked in every classroom situation: *Stay awake. Pay attention.* We don't pay attention to insects though, and we know very little about ants even though they cover our planet in unimaginable numbers. A conservative estimate is a million billion.

Native people studied ants, reflecting on their ways. We let our specialists do that, publishing their observations in books and articles for other specialists. Maybe we believe that the separation between ants and humans is too great and that the manner in which they live their lives has no correspondences to the way we live ours. But if we believe that, we've forgotten that every species has important lessons to share with our species, and that size and appearance are not valid criteria for assessing importance. Native people knew that even an ant could impart a revelation. Everything teaches, but not everyone learns.

Ants live everywhere except in the extreme Arctic regions, and not only do they outnumber us, their services are absolutely vital to the functioning of life on Earth: circulating nutrients in the soil, pollinating plants, preying on small species, and disposing of 90 percent of all small creature corpses. We would be in trouble if they disappeared, and species extinction would increase significantly over the current alarming rate. Not so if human beings were to disappear. Without people, the Earth would recover rapidly from its overburdened condition and flourish once again.

We are participants in an unequal partnership, but we don't have the knowledge or the good sense to appreciate the blessings of ants or our dependence on them. In fact, we rarely notice them unless they enter our homes or show up at our picnics, and then we're just annoyed by their appearance. What if, instead of being annoyed, we acted as though they were household spirits and made them an offering in a gesture of respect, to establish boundaries and promote harmonious coexistence?

Household Spirits   In *The Spell of the Sensuous*, David Abram tells of the time he was in Bali and a guest in the household of a magic practitioner, or balian. Each morning the balian's wife brought Abram a bowl of fruit. She also carried a tray containing many two- or three-inch boat-shaped platters woven from a section of palm frond and filled with white rice. After handing him his fruit, the woman disappeared from his view behind the other buildings. When she returned for his empty bowl, the other tray was always empty. He asked her what the rice platters were for, and she explained that they were offerings for the household spirits of the family compound.

Curious, one morning Abram followed her and saw her set one platter at each corner of the other buildings. Later that afternoon he walked back behind the building where she had set the platters down. The rice was gone. The next morning, after the woman picked up his empty bowl, he went back behind the buildings again. As he looked at the platters of rice that she had set out, he saw one of the rice kernels moving. He knelt down to look more closely and saw a line of tiny black ants winding through the dirt to the offering. At the second offering he saw another line of ants carrying away the kernels.

He returned to his building, amused, thinking the gifts of rice were stolen by ants. Then a strange thought slipped past his Western orientation and entered his mind. What if the ants were the household spirits? What if the offerings were made with them in mind? The family compound was constructed in the vicinity of several ant colonies and was, therefore, vulnerable to infestations by ants, especially where there was food. Maybe the daily gifts of rice prevented such an attack by keeping the ant colonies well fed. Perhaps the offerings also established a certain boundary between the ants and the humans since the platters were placed in regular locations at the corners of the compound's buildings. By marking and honoring this boundary with gifts, the balian's wife may have intended to enlist the cooperation of the insects to respect the boundary and not enter the building.

His encounter with ants was the first of many experiences suggesting that the "spirits" of an indigenous culture are those modes of intelligence or awareness that are in a nonhuman form. Instead of waging war on them, these people acted in ways that we would do well to emulate.

The Wisdom and Ingenuity of Ants

It has only been in the last three hundred years that ants have not been accorded respect. Ants were worshiped in ancient Thessaly, for example, and in the Harranian mysteries of ancient Mesopotamia, ants were grouped with dogs and ravens as the brothers and sisters of humanity. Hindu holy writings teach that ants are divine, the "firstborn" of the world. Ants were also examples of the transitory nature of existence, and Hindus fed ants on certain occasions associated with the dead.

The tribes of Benin, West Africa, believed that ants served as messengers for the Serpent God. Other African tribes related anthills and termite mounds to cosmogonic ideas and sometimes fertility, because if a woman sat on either, it was thought to make her fertile.

In the Middle East, medieval Arabs believed that ants embodied wisdom, and so astronomers placed them among the constellations as earthly teachers of Solomon. Besides wisdom, ants were linked in the minds and imaginations of ancient people with ingenuity—the often underestimated power of the small. Stories from many traditions tell of the ant that outwits the larger, stronger adversary.

Traditional Japanese culture also held ants in high esteem. In fact, the Japanese word for ant, *ari*, is represented by the character for insect combined with a character that signifies unselfishness, moral virtue, justice, and courtesy.

Ant Creators Ants appear in many creation stories. The Navajo creation myth speaks of Red Ant and Black Ant, who reside in the First World. In a legend of the aboriginal inhabitants of the Andaman Islands off India, the first man emerged from the root of a tree and cohabited directly with the inhabitants of an ants' nest.

The myths of the Pima Indians of South Arizona tell of an ant creator who divided the tribe into Red Ants, White Ants, and Black Ants. The Hopi tribe, like the followers of ancient Hinduism, believed that the first people were ants. These Ant People obeyed the laws of creation, providing shelter to a few pious humans when the Creator destroyed the first world.

The Hopi belief in ants as firstborn has parallels in ancient Greek myths, such as the famous legend recounting the origin of the Ant Men (originally "an Ant clan subject to the Goddess") called the Myrmidons, who were ants transformed into warriors by Zeus.

Becoming Antlike

Common to all cultures prior to our age was the belief that other species could transmit their qualities to humans. The transmission of attributes from other species to humans was most often accomplished by eating the creature, being near it, or by being bitten or stung by it. For example, in parts of Africa and India childless women ate termite queens to assume this insect's tremendous fertility. And the ancient Arabs, who saw wisdom and skill in ants, placed an ant in the hand of a newborn baby with a ritual prayer that the baby would be graced with antlike qualities.

The Arawak Indians of Guiana welcome the bite of the local black ant and place it on newborns, believing that the bite will stimulate the baby to walk early. And when a black ant unexpectedly bites a member of this tribe, the ant is not harmed, because its bite is thought to be an omen that something good and satisfying is being bestowed on the one bitten.

The ant is so much an integral part of the Arawak culture that part of the preparation for a hunt involves enduring the bite of these ants. A trial by ants is also part of the Arawak puberty initiation rites. Being bitten is a test of fortitude that bestows strength and a willingness to work on girls and makes the boy skillful, clever, and industrious.

These kinds of practices are foreign to us, yet their existence across diverse cultures suggests they emerge from a universal pattern that links human beings with other species in profound ways. In fact, in the domain of the shaman, the result of all trials presented by another species is the transmission of certain qualities.

If we look at this phenomenon from a psychological perspective, it is likely that these practices assist and mark the death of a certain aspect of self and the awakening of another, more expansive identity. This new identity in turn reflects the favorable attributes associated with the creature while giving the individual new rights and responsibilities.

Nightmares about Ants

We have little encouragement from modern culture for coexisting with ants, much less seeking them out for their bite in order to receive their admirable traits. In fact, most of us learn that being bitten by an ant is justification for retaliation.

Jim Nollman, a musician and pioneer in the art of communication with cetaceans, writes candidly about his struggles with ants and his nightmares of being overwhelmed by them. While wrestling with his fears, Nollman let anger get the best of him after his daughter was bitten. He poured gasoline down the anthill near his home and set it on fire, perpetrating "a waking nightmare holocaust" upon the unfortunate ants trying to go about their business.

Peaceful coexistence with other species is not always easy to accomplish when fears run wild and anger goes unchecked. If Nollman had been aware of the Arawak's beloved black ant, he might have comforted his daughter until the pain of the ant bite subsided and then celebrated the knowledge that the ant had favored his child, bestowing many fine qualities through its bite.

Nollman's reaction is not uncommon. The messages from our culture teach us that life should be pain-free. But it is not, nor has it ever been, without pain. Aboriginal people worked with pain and adversity and found it had its uses. Enduring pain, for example, was an integral part of becoming an adult. Pain matured an individual and prepared him or her for greater responsibility. Adults of the South American Orinoco tribe placed inch-long Bolla ants on the bodies of boys on the threshold of adulthood. To prove they were ready to be adults, the adolescents had to withstand several stings, each one powerful enough to temporarily disable a person.

In the West we brand any ant that stings a pest, including the imported red fire ant from South America. Yet the fire ants in their native habitat of Brazil are not considered pests but are looked on as helpful predators—the way we look on ladybugs. Their reputation as pests in the United States stems from alarmist news reports and not because they pose any real life threat to farmworkers, livestock, or crops. In fact, red ants appear reluctant to attack any large creature unless it ventures into their nest.

Our fear of being overrun and stung by large groups of ants has primed us to believe the worst about fire ants—especially when we hear reports from the U.S. Department of Agriculture, the culture's public information specialists. Capitalizing on our readiness to dislike any species that stings, a group of administrators in the 1950s (accused later of wanting to make a name for themselves) launched a massive eradication campaign against fire ants. Not only was the chemical war costly, it did great damage to other wildlife.

Ironically, our assaults and the fire ant's defenses only helped the species increase its range throughout the South. And since that time, many entomologists have changed their view about fire ants because whenever they (or any species of ant) are abundant and chemicals are restricted, cotton boll weevil populations, a threat to cotton crops, are checked.

Image-Making for Our Wilderness Selves

We would all benefit from studying ants. Within us is a natural curiosity about them, a part of our rejected wilderness self. A lack of interest in creatures like ants is a direct result of the fears and assumptions that keep us apart from many of our kin in the Earth community. By eliminating our biases and feeding information to our image-hungry minds, we invite the natural self back into our consciousness, letting it guide our responses to other kingdoms—and in this case to community-minded insects like ants.

Guardians of the Soil   Ants and termites were thought to be in touch with the secrets of the soil, and ants in particular were regarded as guardians of what was in the ground. An Australian aboriginal myth tells of a nest of luminous green eggs guarded by the Ant People. Any disturbance to this nest was believed to anger the Ant People and result in great changes to the planet as a whole. Today we know these luminous eggs as uranium. And as the activities of the uranium mining companies exploit and threaten the life of the Australian Martujarra people and their land, prophecies foretell a dire outcome.

Ants were also believed to know about items buried in the ground by people, so they have a long association with buried treasure. Legends from China, Persia, India, and Greece tell of giant ants that guard underground treasure. The Greeks believed the giant ants of India brought gold up out of the Earth and were the secret of India's great wealth. The search for giant ants continues and may underlie in some unmeasured way our modern fascination with giant ants in horror films.

The psychological significance of these ant legends has been lost today. From the perspective of depth psychology, these tales refer to the universal process of psychological growth. Ants and other insects that make appearances in our dreams are aligned with beneficial forces and come to assist the human being in this process of retrieving the inner gold. Gold in this context is an alchemical symbol of the soul within an individual.

Buried Wealth   Today only a small percentage of specialists are aware of the ants' historical connection to treasure or their symbolic link to the treasures buried in our psyches. Yet these industrious species are still turning over inner and outer soil. On the outer plane, ants were credited for the discovery of diamonds in South Africa's Botswana. In their search for water, ants brought kimberlite particles to the surface, the soft volcanic rock in which diamonds are found. And in Zimbabwe, geologists routinely analyze the mineral-rich soil of termite mounds to determine whether or not prospecting for gold and other valuable minerals is likely to be profitable.

Ants are also connected to turquoise, and in New Mexico certain ants harvest it. Some species have a definite affinity for blue and green stones, perhaps because of their thermal properties. The fragments found at the ant mounds in the area cover the outside of the structure's dome and may help regulate nest temperature.

For the Lakota tribe, the stones ants collect are sacred and used in traditional ceremonies. Healers like medicine man John (Fire) Lame Deer seek out these anthills for the tiny rocks and place 405 of these sacred stones in their gourds and rattles for ceremonial use. The stones represent the 405 tree species native to their ancestral land.

Messages from Ants

In keeping with their ancient ties to the ground, ants are credited with forecasting earthquakes. I found a contemporary account about this ability in *Spirits of the Earth,* a book on American Indian symbols. The author, Bobby Lake-Thom, tells of an occasion when he and his wife were in northern California to do a presentation and joined other speakers at an expensive restaurant in San Francisco. While they were engaged in a lively discussion about rituals and symbolism, a large black ant slowly walked across the white tablecloth. All conversation at the table stopped, and all eyes went to the ant as though directed by an unseen power. The ant walked over to where Lake-Thom was sitting and stopped in front of him. Then it "danced" in a circle four times and jumped two times as Lake-Thom talked to it in his native language. He thanked the ant, and the insect traveled south over the edge of the table and out of sight.

They all knew something unusual had happened. Insects were not usually seen in plush restaurants. Another visitor at the table voiced what they were all thinking: The ant had appeared out of nowhere and had communicated something deliberately to Lake-Thom.

Lake-Thom said the ant was a messenger of Nature and that it was a sign that a big earthquake was coming to southern San Francisco in four days. It would be preceded by two small warning quakes. The people at the table laughed, but Lake-Thom and his wife took the warning seriously. They canceled their plans to stay and do some sightseeing over the next few days and returned to Washington State. Four days later, a large earthquake hit Hayward, a city south of San Francisco, resulting in deaths, injuries, and damage to bridges and buildings.

Ants and the Harvest Mother

Since ants were frequently observed carrying grains and seeds, ancient people also linked them with the Harvest Mother, one of the many personifications of the goddess. This connection to grains and seeds is frequently seen in symbolic stories where ants appear, like flies and other insects, as helpers. These insects represent discriminating and organizing energies in the psyche that assist the process of growth by eliminating the barriers that block integration and expansion of the individual's identity. In one of the best-known tales, the Greek myth of Psyche and Eros, ants play the role of helper to Psyche (who symbolizes the feminine soul) during an archetypal rite of initiation.

In a Chinese folktale, a young man is faced with a series of impossible tasks by a witch trying to kill him. When he is told he must collect all the linseed he had sown in a field, thousands of ants perform the deed for him. In another version a swarm of ants is being swept by floodwaters past a boat carrying the young man and his mother. The mother uses a sieve and manages to get the ants safely into the boat. Later, when the witch commands the young man to perform an impossible task, the grateful ants do it for him.

In both tales—master teachings of the dynamics of the psyche—ants represent energies aligned with the innate push toward wholeness. They come during these periodic rites of passage to assist those who are ready to advance to the next level of consciousness, helping them outwit the forces that guard the gates to these zones.

The link between ants and the Harvest Mother is also played out on the physical level, where relationships between ants and plants takes many forms. Many ants are in mutually beneficial alliances (called symbiotic) with plants that secrete a sweet solution they love. Ants guard these plants from plant-eating insects in return for a supply of this sweet substance.

Ants are also in symbiotic relationships with animals. In fact, according to a recent tally, ants have this type of "farming" relationship with over 580 different kinds of creatures—the best-known example occurring between ants and aphids, a relationship that invokes many a gardener's wrath.

Plant-Insect Relationships in Native Myth

Native people knew of these plant-insect relationships because they lived in intimate relationship with the natural world and observed them closely. They also learned about these relationships from their shamans. Shamanic visions frequently revealed intricate connections between certain plants and certain insects. Among the Peruvian plant-inspired shamans, for instance, certain plants brought insect spirit helpers. One such shaman under the influence of two hallucinogenic plants—ayahuasca and chakruna—not only communicated with a large "ant of knowledge"[2] but was invited by the ant to ride home on its back (being helped by an animal or riding on it was a way to assume that animal's qualities). When the shaman reached his home, a tiny chakruna plant emerged from the abdomen of the ant, and the dust and pollen that clung to a sticky substance secreted by the ant's body turned into the ayahuasca vine.

Deep Bonds of Friendship Myths of indigenous people contain a wealth of information about relationships between plants and animals encoded in story form. In *Wisdom of the Elders*, a collection of indigenous visions of Nature, authors David Suzuki and Peter Knudtson include a myth that describes the relationship between the women of the Amazon Kayapo tribe and the tropical red ants they consider guardians of their fields, friends, and relatives.

In Kayapo myth, both ants and people share a reverence for and a responsibility to the manioc plant, a sought-after source of nectar for

100

the ants and a precious source of food for the Kayapo. The ant and the manioc plant are in a symbiotic relationship or, as Kayapo myth describes it, bound by deep bonds of friendship. Drawn by the promise of the manioc's nectar, these ants frequent vegetable gardens where Kayapo women cultivate manioc and other domestic food plants. To reach the young plants, the insects cut trails through the tangle of bean vines that might otherwise choke the manioc plants. This activity encourages the bean vines to redirect themselves to nearby corn plants. So ant, manioc, and Kayapo women exist in a mutually satisfying relationship. Their shared responsibility for the plant unites the women and the ants, and to honor the connection, they care for one another.

What is striking about this relationship is the feelings the Kayapo women have toward these ants. They cherish them and seek to be more antlike. Each symbiotic relationship in their lives is evidence of all relatedness in a sacred world in which they know themselves to be an integral part.

Our specialists don't lack for information about symbiotic relationships, but neither expert nor layperson holds dear what is known. The information published on this phenomenon exists outside our daily lives and speaks of a world we no longer know from direct experience. As a consequence, it has lost its power to inform and enrich us. Complicating the situation, we're discouraged from translating the wealth of available facts into anything real and immediate for fear of anthropomorphizing. Risking it now, consider that anthropomorphizing allows us to relate to other species. We can understand symbiotic relationships because we have many of our own, and healthy relationships cross species lines. They're the ones that are mutually beneficial to both parties—you help me and I'll help you.

Looking Out for the Community

Since most of us don't observe ants closely, our contact with them is infrequent—unless they enter our homes. Their ability to protect scale insects is largely responsible for their ranking on California's pest list as third in the state. Small- and large-scale gardeners consider them pests because of their "bonds of friendship" with other insects like aphids that suck plant juices and secrete a sweet substance called honeydew. With the ants' protection from predators, these insects flourish, to the dismay of growers.

Since most of us are unaware of ant guards, our reasons for calling them pests revolve around their periodic "invasions" into our living spaces. When annual rains flood their nests, for example, many ants seek refuge in dry places like our kitchens. A recent Stanford study concluded that the movements of ants are tied to weather conditions, and there isn't much humans can do about it, so we might as well forgo spraying our homes with deadly pesticides and just try to operate around the ants until they leave on their own.

The Individuality of Ants

A kitchen full of ants is undoubtedly inconvenient, but it is also an opportunity to observe a species that rivals our own in complexity. To prepare, you could read *Empire of the Ants*, the 1998 best-selling novel by Bernard Werber (not to be confused with the movie of the same title). He takes the reader into an ant colony for a glimpse into the lives and struggles of individual ants. Yes, ants are individuals, and they communicate and cooperate with one another as we do.

Studies show that ants (and termites) use many modes of communication including tapping, stroking, nudging, and streaking chemicals called pheromones from their abdomens. Interestingly, individual ants interpret the meaning of a pheromone differently and respond accordingly. How much of the chemical is present and whether it is alone or part of other odors, for example, influences what it means. Contrary to popular opinion and horror movie theatrics, chemical communication is not an exact mechanical science as much as it is an expressive art, and there is surprising room for individual interpretation and response.

It is old news in research circles that ants cooperate with other members of the colony and behave sensibly and individually in the context of their lives. Sometimes personality differences are great even within a group, within a species. Consider that different ants will perform the same task at different speeds, with some worker ants consistently fast and others consistently slow. A telling study showed that when a group of worker ants was presented with a caterpillar, the individual ants reacted differently. Some of them attacked the caterpillar and fought it until they killed it. Some didn't attack at all but stayed on the sidelines as though wringing their hands in a flurry of anxiety and indecision. Others fought the caterpillar but left before it was dead, and the remaining ants retreated from it as if afraid. It would seem that evolution has produced and maintained individual variations within each species—even those known for their devotion to the good of the community above individual desires.

Besides individuality, ants can learn, and they routinely alter their environment to reach their goals. In fact, they demonstrate great innovation and flexibility when put in a new or different situation. And, like many birds, they learn to use the sun as a compass by making connections between its position in the sky, geographic directions, and the passage of time. In short, the ways in which an ant meets and overcomes new difficulties and adapts itself to new conditions show a considerable amount of independent thinking.

All these abilities, however, haven't been translated into the mainstream culture in any positive way. Popular stories and films continued to capitalize on our fears by portraying ants as a robotic mass of bodies ruled by a ravenous hunger. The 1954 classic film *Them*, for example, features ants exposed to radiation from an atomic bomb site. The radiation transforms them into giants with humanoid eyes, a bellowing war cry, and an insatiable appetite for humans.

With the later discovery of communication through chemicals emitted by the colony's queen (with each colony having its own odor), filmmakers used the knowledge in another classic film, *Empire of the Ants*. They endow the same mutated ants from *Them* with an intelligence superior to humans. The colossal insects capture people and expose them to the queen's pheromones. Under the influence of this chemical, the terrified prisoners become servants, without personal will or the energy to resist.

Without reflection, we are destined to remain uncomfortable with the strange appearance of ants, their vast numbers, and their devotion to the colony. When on occasion we notice ant life and sense the colony's unified purpose, for example, we are at best confused by it. Its solidarity exists in sharp contrast to the "looking out for number one" mentality that permeates our society. In fact, *Antz,* a wildly popular 1998 animated movie, features an ant that wants to be an individual and leads a revolution against the colony.

The Altruistic Society

A persistent bid for individual success and recognition in Western culture leaves us, as its citizens, without a context for understanding the evolution of a species whose service to the colony and self-interest are one and the same. We typically assume an oppressive, even despotic arrangement is involved that prevents all individuality.

That ants display many so-called human emotions and engage in altruism has long been known. Ants display a range of emotions including anger, fear, depression, elation, and affection. They also demonstrate empathy when they help crippled and distressed sister ants. A remarkable piece of film produced in 1973 by a Russian entomologist, for example, showed an ant of a South American species extracting a splinter from the side of another ant. Other ants in the community formed a circle around the "patient" and "doctor" ants, preserving a clear space for the two until the procedure was completed. What we think of as distinctively human qualities are actually rooted in animal instinct. It is not that ants have human emotions but that all of us animals display certain common responses.

What is not, however, a predominant human behavior is the suppression of the sex drive in the majority of ants. In certain advanced forms of ant life, sex totally disappears in the majority of individuals— a fact sure to evoke ambivalence in us. More startling than that is the fact that this practical suppression or regulation of the sex drive appears to be voluntary. Ants have learned how to develop or arrest the development of sex in their young by nutrition.

Rigidly restraining all sex to within the limits necessary to ensure survival is one of many vital practices of ant species. The female worker does not associate with males. Her femininity is expressed in every way but sexually, for she has all the tenderness, patience, and foresight that we consider maternal.

Ants don't seem to have any individuality that is purely selfish. The life of an ant is entirely devoted to altruistic ends. That fact has led some scientists to conclude that ants have advanced beyond us in regard to social evolution. Scientist Herbert Spencer goes further, maintaining that ants are ethically as well as economically ahead of human beings.

In ant society, the will of the individual and the well-being of the community are a seamless whole, so that the only possible pleasure is the pleasure of unselfish action—a stance similar to some native cultures like the altruistic Hodi of south-central Venezuela, who look after themselves by looking after one another.

Ants attend to their individual life only so far as it is necessary for the life of their society. In other words, the individual takes only the food and rest that are needed to maintain its vigor. No ant takes more, and no ant sleeps longer than necessary to keep its nervous system in good order. Each ant works without stopping, and workers keep themselves and their inner living areas neat. By modifying their physiology, they have apparently repressed every capacity for individual pleasure except when that pleasure directly or indirectly helps the community.

It is not that ants (or bees or termites) have a sense of duty or constantly sacrifice themselves for the colony. In fact, the concept of duty is meaningless. Instinctive morality replaces any need for an ethical code—it is simply the nature of these insects. They have a biological disposition to pursue altruistic ends, and as their relations we have a biological basis for community as well.

If we turn our imaginations in the right direction, we might entertain the idea of a global society in which a regard for other beings produces so much pleasure that it overrides the pleasure derived from gratifying our personal desires. Spiritual traditions acknowledge the rewards of service, in which, by taking care of others, we are actually taking care of ourselves. Eventually, there may come a time in humanity's evolution when egoism and altruism are so in agreement that they become one and the same.

Living on the Edge of Chaos

The ways of ants invite our inspection and reflection. Our innate, and perhaps surprising, emotional affinity with these creatures is part of Wilson's idea of biophilia. Not only do we depend on Nature for food and shelter, says Wilson, but we also depend on it for aesthetic, intellectual, emotional, and spiritual meaning.[3]

Part of the draw is connected to the timeless and universal patterns encoded within each species that illuminate our human nature. The macrocosm is in the microcosm. This is also the central message of indigenous wisdom: human nature is a reflection of the nature of the universe, and we can learn about ourselves by paying attention to the natural world.

Perhaps we can learn to live more fully by attuning to a universal pattern revealed recently in studies on ant colonies. Ants live on the edge of chaos. What's more, they seek it out. Remember how household cockroaches, who instinctively seek out the cracks and crevices in our homes, can signify the spirit of boundaries, those potent transition places between stability and chaos where change is possible—in both systems and in people? And remember how in this boundary place, enough coherency and stability are lost to permit change, transformation, and reorganization—without falling into complete chaos? Well, this borderland is where ants hang out.

The finding comes out of new research that demonstrates how the behavior of individual ants is chaotic (as opposed to rhythmic or random) until there are enough ants interacting or communicating with each other to shift them all into a rhythmic, orderly state of being. This shift to the "superorganism" state, a unified state long sensed by ant aficionados, depends on density, that is, on the size of the territory the colony inhabits in relation to the number of ants in the colony. Ants purposively regulate the density in order to live near this transition point— between order and stability on the one side and chaos on the other.

Biologist Brian Goodwin believes that if we knew why ants always try to live near the edge of chaos, we might have a theorem about everything that is complex and nonlinear (which is nearly everything). Complex systems (economics, high-temperature superconductors, brains, beehives, and ant and termite colonies) are more than the simple sum of their parts, and can evolve. Within such systems the next evolutionary phase is always waiting to emerge—given enough complexity or numbers and level of interaction. And ant colonies, by adjusting their density, know intuitively to how to find this edge of chaos and stay there. They know somehow that this is where the best life for the colony is possible.

So it appears that optimal life is at the edge of chaos in all open complex systems, and that an ability to shift, to advance creatively, is an essential requirement for the emergence of new levels of evolutions. It means we could emulate the ants and also live on this edge, in readiness for that next creative step into a new order. This model, anchored as it is in biology, points to new possibilities in the functioning of human open systems.

Margaret Wheatley has applied this idea of optimal life at the edge of chaos to organizations and discusses its implications in her book *Leadership and the New Science.* She believes that generating enough information and interaction between people (and weathering the state of confusion that it brings initially) is the place to be if the members of an organization want to be open to new thoughts. The period of chaos is an essential part of a deep ordering process that, given time and enough interaction, can arise from a stew of ideas and people.

The Global Brain   What the ants are demonstrating is also evident in the vision of physicist and futurist Peter Russell. Drawing on chaos theory, quantum physics (which says that at the quantum level all is relationship), and the science of living systems, Russell proposes that humanity as a complex living system is moving toward an evolutionary shift into the next level of complexity and order. He sees each person as a nerve cell in the "global brain." In this model (described in detail in Russell's book *The Global Brain Awakens*), as our population increases to stabilize at 10^{10} in the year 2020, and as communication technology permits us to interact more frequently with one another, conditions are right (as ant colonies also illustrate) for a new order to emerge and shift us into the next evolutionary phase.

Although some might find this vision of how the information revolution is shifting consciousness and fostering planetary citizenship an overly optimistic perspective, the fact that it is deeply established in the world of ants and other social insects lends it strength. The pattern already exists. And moving toward a more rhythmic and more integrated society would ease our sense of isolation and alienation. Individual activity, held within such a stable matrix, would increase, and new patterns of order and creative energy would be available to the individual.

And there is still more to be gleaned by looking at the ants. Not only does the superorganism reflect the principles of emergent order in evolution, but ant species like the previously mentioned Argentina ant (a rapidly spreading species that authorities consider a pest) indicate the possibility of a "super-superorganism." Consider that although most ants will fight any strange ant—even one of the same species that lives in a nest a few hundred yards away—the Argentina ant recognizes as family all others of its species, even across international boundaries. Consequently, this ant will move from nest to nest, joining forces without conflict. As human beings increasingly identify themselves as planetary citizens, perhaps humanity will follow the biological model provided by the Argentina ants and move from nation to nation, joining together without fighting.

Relating to Ants

Observing ants is the first step toward seeing correspondences between them and us and eventually relating to them with compassion. The fourteenth-century ruler Tamerlane was said to be inspired by watching an ant trying to climb a wall carrying something heavy. The ant failed sixty-nine times before succeeding on its seventieth attempt. Afterward, Tamerlane resolved to go out and conquer Asia—which he did with all the persistence of the ant he observed.

Those who study ants find fresh insights into human society and a vision beyond the subject of their observations. A Jesuit scholar from the Netherlands, Father Wasmann, made many studies of ants and their parasites and was able to see in them manifestations of divine power. The best contemporary example of an individual who, focusing on ants, found all the mysteries of life and stimuli for many insights is Edward Wilson, whose contributions appear throughout this book and beyond these topics.

Compassion for ants is found in the stories of religions that placed great emphasis on cultivating harmlessness and right relations with other species. A Sufi legend tells of a man who traveled several hundred miles every month or so to purchase supplies in the nearest city. When he returned home, he discovered a colony of ants in the cardamom seeds he had purchased. He carefully packed the seeds up again and walked back across the desert, intent on returning the ants to their home.

A relationship with ants often springs from their appearance in our homes. When ants invaded his kitchen, J. Allen Boone felt angry and wanted to eliminate them. Guilt stopped him from doing so, however, and he decided to try to contact them. He couldn't find the queen, so he sought to broadcast a message to all of them. When he began his communication by reprimanding them for spoiling his dinner and questioning their right to be in his house, they ignored him completely. Then he remembered that in his other attempts at interspecies communication, he had discovered that all creatures like to be appreciated.

He sent the ants his admiration for their keen intelligence, their energy, their focused attention on their tasks, and their harmonious relationships with each other. He asked for their understanding and cooperation. Then he left the room, feeling like he hadn't made contact. Later, he went out for the evening, and when he returned, there wasn't an ant in sight even though the food that had attracted them earlier was still there. He was never bothered again in his home, or when he traveled, although ants lived outside his door in great numbers and regularly invaded his neighbors' homes, much to their annoyance.

A Swiss businesswoman, Kathia Haug, also had success in communicating with the ants that visited her home each summer. Although in previous summers she had tried to solve her "ant problem" by killing them, she had never been completely successful. One year, she embraced a new spiritual discipline that brought a change of heart and prompted her to try talking to the ants mentally. She told them that she wished them a long and happy life but that she wanted them to stay out of her house. In one day, the ants were gone from the house, although they still passed across the doorstep from her kitchen into the garden.

Those who practice this kind of communication agree that it requires a combination of compassion, positive expectation, and the ability to hold a visual picture in your mind, since animals communicate with images, not words. When the effort fails, it is usually because the person attempting it is in some kind of mental turmoil or is feeling ill-at-ease or impatient. In *Animals Are Equal,* British author Rebecca Hall tells of one woman who wanted to get ants out of her kitchen and lectured them crossly, saying, "Get out, you load of little communists." The ants ignored her until she took a more respectful approach.

Feng-shui practitioner and dowser Kerry Louise Gillett owns a "pest" control company in San Francisco called Dances with Ants. She works with ants using a series of techniques gleaned from her energy work before contacting their overlighting spirit. That her business is thriving is testament to the fact that her methods work, although she cautions her clients that they must be patient. It takes several days to a week for the ants to leave a residence.

Only once did she fail. Her client was a commercial grower who was desperate to rid his plants of ants and the aphids they were protecting. Two days after her initial contact with the ants, the grower panicked, his mistrust of the process feeding his fear, so without telling her, he saturated his plants with toxic chemicals. Gillett knew something was wrong, however, when her second communication with the ants was garbled. When he admitted that he had not followed her instructions, she tried to contact them a third time, concerned about their welfare. She didn't know that the grower, in a knee-jerk act of desperation, had hit them again with a massive dose of insecticide, but she suspected it when all she could pick up was chaos and despair. "When a colony is under siege, there is—like a human city that has been bombed—so much death and destruction that, in this extreme state of emergency, constructive action is almost impossible to achieve. All one can do is mourn."[4]

If Larry Dossey's theory of the nonlocal mind is indeed operating to connect every species, it is only logical that contacting the overlighting spirit of a species could result in an agreement beneficial to both parties. And many esoteric sources affirm the wisdom of this methodology. In *Awakening to the Animal Kingdom*, for instance, trance channeler Robert Shapiro and his assistant, Julie Rapkin, received the following message from the insects about how to make contact and requests.

> Respect us if you would, for we are in fact an idea of God/Goddess/All That Is. Be willing to come outside . . . and speak to us where we live. If we are inside your dwellings, speak to us there, out loud or in your thoughts. Speak to us with honor and respect and ask us if we would be willing to live outside of your dwelling space. Be willing to share your foods with us, for at times we do require it.[5]

The insect spirit also asks that people bring gifts of food outside to a safe location for three days to ensure the prosperity and continuance of local species. And it directs us to be respectful and thank the insects for their willingness to cooperate with our lessons.

The suggestions are in deep accord with the ways of traditional native people, who always brought gifts to other species to show respect and enlist their cooperation. Respect is a necessary condition for harmonious coexistence. Without it, the channel for communication is closed and we stand outside our own community, looking in from the outside and unable to participate.

Returning to the ground of science, we find that Wilson also encourages us to respect the ants. The most frequent question Wilson is asked is what to do about ants in the kitchen. He answers: "Watch where you step. Be careful of little lives. Feed them crumbs of coffeecake. They also like bits of tuna and whipped cream." Kindness is always appropriate and the springboard from which we can best observe and learn from ants.

Into the Light

In her book *Proud Spirit,* healer Rosemary Altea tells of the time a friend once asked with some regret (but not enough to stop her) as she stepped on an ant, "Rosemary, what happens to it now? Does it go to the spirit world?"

Even as she asked the question, Rosemary heard and then repeated her spiritual guide Grey Eagle's answer, "It becomes light."

Acknowledging ants and other insects as spiritual beings is not an exercise in logic or a leap of faith as much as it is an acknowledgment that life is sacred and all species emanate from the same unfathomable light. As another healer, Rachel Naomi Remen, reminds us, "We are all more than we seem. Many things do not wear their true nature on their sleeve." Every species has intrinsic value apart from its usefulness in the world. And all are worthy of respect, love, compassion, and entering into communion with them.

Seeing in the ant colony a level of synergy and cooperation that we might want for our own species and a unifying spirit that makes each member a part of a cohesive whole—greater than the sum of its individuals—we might return to our human community inspired. We have gone to the ant, considered her ways, and gained insight and wisdom.

8. LORDS of the SUN

Maybe if we love them, they will not have the need to
be aggressive.

—*(Roc) Ogilvie Crombie*

In "Family Circle," a syndicated cartoon by Bill Keane, young Billy
comes across a beetle scurrying along on the sidewalk. As he goes to
step on it, he hesitates, wondering suddenly whether the beetle has a
wife and kids eagerly awaiting his return. That imaginative thought not
only stops Billy from killing the insect but lets him wish it well and a
safe return home.

When children use their imaginations to put themselves in the
place of another creature, they are expressing their natural affinity for
other species. Right relationship and right action follow from the use of
right imagination.

Adults can also exercise their imagination in a way that encourages
connection. David Hyde Pierce, best known for his television role as
Frasier's brother, says he had little difficulty in finding his "inner bug"
to voice the character of Slim, a walking stick featured in the movie *A
Bug's Life*. "I guess you need to have an active imagination," he explained to a *People* magazine reporter. He also shared that his role as

Slim has made him more familiar and friendly toward individual bugs and more sympathetic to insects in general.

Most adults have not gained a sympathetic view of insects by using their imagination in the way Pierce did for his role. An us-versus-them mentality has prevailed, dictating a diet of hostile images for our imagination, including Marvel comics' villainous Beetleman and Franz Kafka's "monstrous vermin" in "Metamorphosis," a existentialist classic in which a young man turns into a beetle (although the debate continues about whether the insect was a beetle or a cockroach).

In a recent seminar in New York, His Holiness the fourteenth Dalai Lama was asked what he thought was the most important thing to teach children. He replied, "Teach them to love the insects." I wonder whether the participants were puzzled or realized that his advice, if followed, would cultivate in the young a capacity for tolerance and a respect for differences that we desperately need as a culture. We could start by teaching them to love beetles, which comprise two-thirds of the total number of insect species and 80 percent of all animal species.

God must have "an inordinate fondness for beetles," said biologist J.B.S. Haldane to a group of English theologians who wanted to know what one could infer about the Creator from a study of creation. Indeed, what kind of God or Goddess would love beetles so much that he or she would populate the Earth with more of them than any other animal?

In a delightful essay published in *Orion Nature Quarterly*, Edith Pearlman decides that one possible Creator with a preference for beetles would be a wise and compassionate deity who loved beetles for their flexibility and humility. A second kind of deity might love beetles because of their variety and beauty, believing that "God is in the details." Perhaps it is this deity's love of beetles that inspired the proverb "The beetle is a thing of beauty in its mother's eye."

And finally Pearlman decides there could be a Creator who *is* a beetle. This omnipotent one would have created beetles in his or her image 250 million years ago. And perhaps as this almighty beetle looked over creation with antennae finely tuned to detect beetles in rotting tree trunks and stored grain, buried in dung, wood, and under leaves, nibbling on plants and crunching on insects, he or she would also noticed how other creatures were faring—admitting, however, that it was the beetle for whom the universe was made.

There is precedence for such a god in many cultures, including the South American Lengua or Chaco tribe, which had a beetle god called

Aksak. The Sumatran Toba also had a beetle creator, who brought a ball of matter from the sky to form the world. And then there is the famous beetle god of the ancient Egyptians. Modeled after the dung beetle, this insect was a symbol of the body's strength, the soul's resurrection, and the omnificent and unknowable Creator. And in its Lord of the Sun aspect, the scarab deity represented light, truth, and regeneration.

The ancient Egyptians also revered other beetles. A wood-boring beetle, for example, signified transformation and rebirth. Its symbolism arose from an actual beetle that feeds on the tamarisk tree. Just as this beetle emerges from the trunk of the tree through small holes bored by beetle larvae, so Egyptians believed the imprisoned Osiris, lord of the afterlife, emerged from the confines of the tamarisk, freed by Isis.

A wood-boring beetle may also be the species referred to in one of the most picturesque images of transformation. The image comes from an old story retold by Henry David Thoreau in *Walden*. In it a "strong and beautiful" insect emerges out of an old table made from apple tree wood that had been in the farmer's kitchen for sixty years. The insect came from an egg deposited in the living tree many years earlier. Its emergence was due to a hot urn placed on the table that warmed the spot above the egg. Thoreau writes:

> Who does not feel his faith in a resurrection and immortality strengthened by hearing of this? Who knows what beautiful and winged life, whose egg has been buried for ages under many concentric layers of woodenness in the dead dry life of society, . . . may unexpectedly come forth from amidst society's most trivial . . . furniture, to enjoy its perfect summer life at last![1]

The idea of a hidden life inspires and gives us hope. Like countless numbers of larvae that live underground or in trees and are buried for months or years before emerging for their transformation, perhaps our potential is also hidden inside us, waiting—buried under layers of societal and familial beliefs. And perhaps our thoughts and actions can help create the welcoming conditions they need to emerge.

Teaching the Children

In the state of California where I reside, a teaching unit on Egyptian mythology is part of the middle-school curriculum, although the connections the Egyptians made between beetles and matters of life and death don't make much sense to the teachers, much less to the students. The seed ideas underlying ancient philosophies conflict with our current way of looking at the world. The former are based on an animated, interdependent world, whereas a bid to control life underlies our contemporary mythologies, with economic values guiding the process.

What if we told children that, just like the beetle that has wings concealed under its glossy shell, we too have a hidden life tucked away within our physical bodies, a hidden spirit with wings? If we helped them make that single comparison, the beliefs of the Egyptians and other cultures might make more sense. Perhaps they could see then that the beetle's astonishing transformation from a wormlike larva called a grub to a winged creature has always made it a powerful and appropriate symbol for rebirth and eternal life.

For psychologist Sam Keen, a visit from a beetle in a dream provided unexpected help. It was in the months before his sixtieth birthday and he was preoccupied with death. Although he had explored the Buddhist beliefs in karma and reincarnation, he still struggled with a recurring nightmare of disappearing completely when he died.

One night he dreamed about a silver beetle that could detach part of itself and then come back together. The dream insect walked into a piece of wood, disappeared, and then reappeared on the other side. Then it vanished into stone and once again reemerged. Finally it entered a transparent gemlike substance and disappeared from sight, but Keen knew that it would reemerge whole from that journey too. He awoke with a profound sense of relief, comforted without knowing the meaning of the dream.

In the following days, the dream worked quietly inside him until in a flash of insight he remembered that in the religion of ancient Egypt the scarab beetle was a symbol of immortality. He thought perhaps the dream was telling him that he too would disappear into death and then reemerge. He still had his doubts, but the dream gave him a "momentary peace that passes understanding."

An Inordinate Degree of Beetleness   There are points of kinship between beetles and human beings. From the perspective of deep ecology—which maintains that our identities don't stop at our skin but extend outward to encompass the world—the fact that there are more beetles in the world than any other species means our true identities have an inordinate degree of beetleness. Or to use James Swan's metaphor, we have more beetles in our "inner zoo" than any other creature. But if we have so much "beetleness" in our makeup, why are our current relationships with beetles based only on whether or not they serve or thwart our agricultural and gardening objectives?

Children, unsullied by our views, are quick to feel a connection to insects and ready to be inspired by the presence of all beetles. Any hesitation about beetles they might have is easily diminished (or exacerbated) by how the adults in their lives react to them. A few years ago I took my niece Laura, then five years old, on a walk to look for bugs, a favorite pastime. As we wandered down a country lane in rural Michigan, she noticed a large number of insects on the green thickets that lined the path. I told her they were beetles. Since I always encourage her to name the insects she sees, she told me she was going to call them "Christmas beetles," because they were red and green and beautiful. I didn't tell her that adults call them Japanese beetles, an imported species that has received the full weight of our chemical arsenal and still breeds and eats furiously in our fields.

Beetle as Messengers

Beetles, like other insects, are messengers, often conveying information simply by their presence as in synchronistic events like the beetle that showed up at Carl Jung's window when his patient was telling him her dream of the Egyptian scarab.

When beetles are out of balance—that is, when their populations are greater than normal— their number and presence also convey a message, telling us that either a natural cycle of transformation and growth is at work—as when masses of beetles emerge in the spring—or a problem exists.

In growing fields we are quick to judge large numbers of insects a problem, not knowing that they are merely a sign that a problem exists. Agricultural experts have demonstrated that in a balanced environment insects attack only weak and dying plants. It is one of the tenets supported by science that gave rise to organic gardening. Insects appear when declining soil fertility produces crops that lack vitality. So insects and disease are not the cause of a failing crop but the symptom that something is wrong.

Insects communicate with other insects and with plants using a variety of different-shaped antennae tuned to the infrared band of the electromagnetic spectrum (much as we communicate with radar and radio wavelengths) and by sensing radiation from oscillating molecules. In other words, they "smell" odors emitted by their own kind and by plants. If a plant is sick, it signals its impending death to the insects. The sicker the plant, the more powerful the scent it emits, and the easier for the insect to hone in on it. So when large numbers of insects "attack" crop plants, we would do well to ask whether these plants, often modern hybrids that need excessive fertilization and irrigation to grow, have signaled the insects, "telling" them that they are declining.

Another message communicated by large numbers of beetles or other insects ravaging our crops is that the pesticides routinely applied to the fields have killed off their predators—those insects that keep their populations in check. Without them, their numbers mushroom. What's more, with the insect predators out of the way, other insects that were once in balance, and thus harmless, also multiply rapidly, so that secondary insect infestations arise.

Killing the insect messengers continues to be standard operating procedure for the farmers and the agricultural conglomerates that control how they farm—what seeds, fertilizer, heavy equipment, and pesticides they buy. As a result of this approach, which has replaced natural systems with totally alien systems that pit us against Nature's processes, they have created more serious problems. And many of these problems—like the degradation of the soil and our chemically soaked environment—are becoming too big to ignore.

Our Complicity

Rather than taking a simplistic approach and separating ourselves from advocates of current practices, we'll accept our complicity in creating or allowing these kinds of enterprises to operate as they do. Our lack of knowledge and interest in this area have been costly. We have bought the idea, for example, that insects compete with us for our food and so necessitate the use of insecticides. It seems straightforward enough, and few of us outside the arena of agriculture question it. Yet, in many instances, the rationale for having to combat insects is merely a cover-up for selling more insecticides or selling a particular genetically modified seed.

We have also insisted on cosmetically pleasing food, so growers use heavy applications of pesticides to ensure that we won't have to see insect body parts on our produce or see holes made by insects. Perhaps if we were more willing to allow surface imperfections, we could send a different message to those who grow our food. We could demand a more wholesome and nutritious fruit or vegetable instead of just one that looks good. It would foil the plan of agrichemical companies to maximize yields by restructuring and altering DNA in our produce to produce a counterfeit appearance of freshness and desirability long after the product's natural shelf life.

The cosmetic issue is only one of many. Behind a variety of new approaches and techniques, we see a now-familiar military and profit-hungry mentality driving the agricultural industry. It is the same mind-set underlying the war against the mosquito, and we will see the parallels when we delve into that area in the next chapter. Even the Green Revolution, touted as a movement by developed countries to supply food to Third World countries by introducing them to modern agricultural methods, is little more than colonialism colored green.

The War against the Cotton Boll Weevil

Space considerations require that we limit our investigation and keep our sights on beetles as we briefly examine current agricultural practices, which is a big topic; but the message from the beetles, who in this chapter represent all insects branded crop pests, is short and to the point: We are not the problem, nor are we your enemies.

In the United States, the hostilities toward plant-eating insects soared when farmers began large-scale planting of one kind of crop, referred to as monoculture. Although inherently unbalanced, monocultures promised high yields, and therefore high profits, so the government funded farmers who agreed to specialize in one crop. Unlike a balanced ecosystem, which keeps populations in check by predators, limited food supplies, and even diseases, monocultures destroy natural population suppressors. And without them they are vulnerable to the slightest disturbance.

The monoculture of cotton was responsible for the war waged by the United States against a beetle called the cotton boll weevil. Those favoring the war (and most felt that there wasn't any choice) are quick to point out that damage by the cotton boll weevil has been estimated in the tens of millions of dollars annually. Those who question the hostilities point out that the problem is not the insect; it is the monoculture.

The Cotton Boll Weevil   The cotton boll weevil is a specialist. Of the forty thousand weevil species, each likes a specific plant, and most common trees and shrubs are host to one weevil species. For cotton, it is the cotton boll weevil.

We branded this insect our enemy when it took advantage of the monoculture of cotton, perhaps thinking when it saw the fields of its favorite plant that it had died and gone to weevil heaven. It couldn't know, and wouldn't care, that the United States was preparing to enter the world of international trade in cotton. Predictably, the weevil multiplied rapidly. After all, its remarkable reproduction abilities, like those of most insects, were designed for a balanced environment with natural population suppressors in place. As the weevil spread, those aiming to make their fortunes in cotton could see their dreams disappearing. They used insecticides to contain the weevil, but with limited success.

When DDT was invented and its production exceeded the amount the military needed to protect World War II troops from malaria, the U.S. government okayed it for civilian use. The public was easily convinced that they didn't have to settle for cohabitation with fiendish insects when an insect-free world was now within reach. And to emphasize the demonic character of insects during this time period, a political cartoon showed a beetle with Adolf Hitler's head—a far cry from the ancient Egyptian Lord of the Morning Sun, Khepri, a god who was often depicted as a beetle with a human body.

We believed the advertisements about DDT that said it was harmless to all but insects, for we were righteously indignant that a mere beetle could threaten a promising enterprise like cotton. Every authority recommended its use. In fact, farmers were urged to spray their fields every week as insurance against hunger and disease. But as Frank Graham points out in *The Dragon Hunters*, a book on biological control, most of the insecticide use had nothing to do with preventing hunger or disease. It was directed to cotton and a bid by the United States to lead the world in its production.

The power of pesticides and the belief in the eventual subordination of Nature and its creatures prevented any serious consideration of changing the practice of monoculture to polyculture or using any other methods, like crop rotation, to introduce balance back into the growing fields. We thought we didn't have to. Monocultures were the road to great yields and greater profits. Most people thought hybrid seeds and the chemical fertilizers and pesticides they depend on could override natural laws and counteract the inherent imbalances of monocultures. So the boll weevil's large numbers and devastating effect on cotton crops—clear messages of imbalance—were ignored.

Fortune Disguised as Misfortune   In at least one town, however, the boll weevil did win the fight, with surprising results. After the weevil's activities resulted in a 60 percent loss in yield on Alabama's cotton crops, the farmers in Enterprise surrendered. Forced to diversify, they planted peanuts, corn, and potatoes. The results of this change of direction were wholly unexpected. From the new crops, they realized substantially greater profits than they had in their best years of cotton, and their economy began to thrive. Better yet, the citizens of Enterprise knew they were indebted to the boll weevil and erected a monument in its honor with the inscription:

> In profound appreciation of the Boll Weevil and what it has
> done to the Herald of Prosperity. This Monument was erected
> by the Citizens of Coffee County, Alabama.

Today cotton is still being grown in the region, and the crops and boll weevils continue to thrive. The rest of the country didn't follow Enterprise's example and instead kept their faith in technology's promises of better chemicals and practices that would allow them to keep their cotton monocultures. And it seemed to have worked. No one in power is pointing out the hidden costs of our practices.

Resistance to Pesticides Ignored   So driven were we as a nation to become and remain an international power in cotton that data showing the resistance to pesticides in boll weevils was ignored by the industry and hidden from the public. They knew as early as 1954 that pesticides didn't work, that no matter how many insects were initially killed, some always survived and passed along their immunity to the next generation. They also knew that eliminating insect predators and parasites always led to secondary insect infestations.

Spraying, however, let them survive for the short term and produced great yields and profits. The cost of this "success" has not been widely publicized, although in the area of human health the links between pesticides and various kinds of cancers, including breast, bladder, and prostate tumors, are being exposed in well-researched books like Sandra Steingraber's *Living Downstream: An Ecologist Looks at Cancer and the Environment.* Steingraber points out that since Rachel Carson's *Silent Spring* was published in 1962, pesticide use has doubled in the United States, and women born here between 1947 and 1958 have almost three times more breast cancer than did their great-grandmothers at the same age. And a 1988 study showed a significant association between agricultural chemical use and cancer mortality in at least 1,500 rural counties in the United States.

As a woman diagnosed with bladder cancer, Steingraber is concerned that the uncertainty about relatively minor details has been used to throw doubt on the real connections that exist between human health and the environment. And the effect on human health is only one of the costs of our success in producing great yields. Other authors have documented the declining soil fertility and the loss of plant and animal health and biodiversity.

As laypeople, what we hear about current practices makes us vaguely anxious—and not only anxious but confused about the issues. Glossy brochures created by chemical companies and biogenetic enterprises still talk about hope, satisfaction, and partnership. They show happy families with good-looking children playing against a backdrop of green fields. Their advertisements justify the chemicals (or genetically altered seeds) they sell to farmers. They boil it down to a war between insects competing for our food and the valiant farmers with their allies—entomologists and chemical companies—trying to prevent them. We tend to believe the propaganda, our own misgivings about insects confirmed. Even after many exposés have revealed widespread corruption in chemical and now biotechnology companies who are trying to make a profit by downplaying the danger of their products, our doubts about insects are so great, our beliefs in insects as the enemy so firm, that they overrule our reason and common sense.[2]

Although we're concerned about pesticide safety, we still believe that to have enough food we have to keep fighting crop-eating insects with chemicals. But we don't. Consider that in 1945, when corn was grown in rotation with other crops, few insects fed on it. In fact, corn lost to insect damage was only 3.8 percent. In the 1990s, after forty years of chemicals, it was 12 percent.

Today the subterfuge is still going on. The battles against cotton-loving (and corn-, soybean-, and potato-loving) beetles and other insects continue, as do the monocultures and chemical use that led to and sustain the imbalances. Keeping our war mentality, the only real change we've made in response to the threat of pesticides is that we've added biological control and genetic engineering tactics to our arsenal under an umbrella called "integrated pest management."

Biological Control and Genetic Engineering

The primary tactic of biological control is to import and introduce insect predators to eat insects damaging our crop plants. It's a widely praised environmentally friendly solution, but for the record, in the West it is still fueled by a war mentality and aimed primarily at shoring up monocultures. On the plus side, biological control mimics Nature to a certain degree and decreases pesticide use. It has to in order to allow the new predator to do its work. On the minus side, it sometimes backfires when complexities in the ecosystem are not known or are ignored. And when a mistake occurs—as in Arizona when an introduced beetle displaced a native species—no one knows what the end result will be.

Still another downside of biological control concerns the exploitation of predator insects like the ladybug. Ladybug prospectors are rapidly wiping out the hibernation sites of these creatures, capturing millions at a time. Those that survive being collected and transported (the mortality rate is 20 to 40 percent) are distributed to orchards and garden shops by the millions.

Ancient Roots of Biological Control   Although ladybugs first demonstrated the potential of biological control to farmers when they effectively controlled scale insects on crops, it's not a new tactic. The use of natural predators to control insects has been going on since ancient times.

In many countries, biological control was carried out by humans. In Thailand, for instance, people ate the beetles and caterpillars that fed on their crops. The strategy also worked for locust swarms. In fact, African natives looked upon great plagues of locusts (a survival strategy for the species when facing starvation) with delight and gratitude, a gift from their gods.

Eating boll weevils or locusts is not an option in the United States. Instead we continue to search for a boll weevil predator and have harnessed insect hormones (helpful at one stage of an insect's development and disruptive at another), pheromones (chemical signals conveying information to others of the same species), and sterilization and radiation techniques to the war effort.

If we returned to the premise that insects are messengers, aligned with the environment and natural forces, consider how different our approach would be. What would we discover if we were looking for information that would allow us to coexist with insects? What insights into the nature of life would reveal themselves if we were looking to create balance and sustainability and willing to change our methods of growing food just to end the war?

Genetic Engineering   We are not at that point yet. In the last ten years, biological control strategies have been augmented by genetic manipulations. Genetic engineering (GE), also called genetic modification (GM), is a process by which genetic material is transferred from one species to another. Artificial breeding across species lines produces a "transgenic" plant or animal species. Genetic engineering of a plant or animal so that it can be a more effective weapon is almost commonplace today. A standard practice is to alter a predatory insect so that it can control other insects more efficiently, withstand new climactic conditions, or "self-destruct" at a particular age. Release of some of these altered creatures has prompted lawsuits to stop further releases until ecological risks have been determined.

Another major genetic alteration to crops involves inserting a gene that allows the plant to produce a natural insecticide and so—advocates claim—reduce the need for pesticides. A little-touted fact, however, is that many of these genetically altered plants (GM hybrids) now have toxic substance levels that could reclassify them as pesticides instead of vegetables. The toxin in these altered plants comes from *Bacillus thuringiensis* (Bt), a soil microbe that produces a natural insecticide best known for its effect on caterpillars. Bt exists in countless natural strains, each fatal to a specific insect. Its natural precision, however, is seen as inefficient and therefore a handicap compared with synthetic poisons that kill insects indiscriminately. Yet its limitations are the very traits that make it sustainable and environmentally friendly, and a tool for organic gardeners when used in spray form.

As insects adapt and resist Bt in hybrid crops, (and they are already doing so), all Bt varieties will soon be rendered obsolete, and Bt hybrids will be scrapped before legal battles against it have been settled. The few years it will take for the insects to develop a resistance to Bt is apparently enough time for a few corporations to reap large profits. It is also enough time for other consequences.[3] Recent studies showed that several kinds of Bt-corn pollen naturally deposited on milkweeds in and near cornfields kill monarch butterfly caterpillars. And Bt potato plants designed to kill aphids may inadvertently harm the ladybugs that feed on them.

The Tyranny of Efficiency   Interestingly and tragically, in all these attempts, most of which have had disastrous impact on the health of beetles and other species, no significant attempt has been made to sacrifice the efficiency of monoculture and chemicals. In *Kinds of Power,* James Hillman says that "efficiency is a primary mode of denial." It elevates the job being done—in this case, agricultural productivity— above all other considerations. The Nazis killed people efficiently, Hillman points out, and now we are raising food efficiently, supposedly to end world hunger—at a cost we have yet to comprehend.

It is not science and technology themselves that are to blame for our present critical situation but rather the way in which we have allowed them to be used. Efficiency favors short-term thinking because time is its enemy. Poisons are efficient. Spraying and dusting methods currently used in our agricultural fields to efficiently kill insects and weeds were adapted from methods developed to kill people efficiently in concentration camps during World War II.

A panel of members of the American Association for the Advancement of Science has said publicly that if current trends continue, the United States will no longer be able to export food in the near future. It will have exhausted its resources, and productivity will drop until we undertake a major revamping of mainstream agriculture.

Any long-term solution can only emerge out of a radically changed identity. If we change our ideas of who we are individually and as citizens of Earth and return to what we already understand about the functioning of the natural world, we may discover sustainable technologies that honor our extended identities. Perhaps embracing our inordinate degree of beetleness can also help lead us to regenerative methods of growing food. A perspective that recognizes the individual, the society, the Earth, and all its inhabitants will automatically gravitate toward holistic, nonexploitive, and ecologically sound long-term practices.

Sustainable Agricultural Technologies

If we look to the beetle for guidance, we can see that its food preferences and ability to multiply indicate the need for checks and balances in the growing environment—specifically, a diversity of plants and a variety of natural population suppressors. Taking our lead from them, we could start by replacing narrow-focused genetic manipulation with seed-stock diversity to balance life in the fields, in the soils, and in the environment at large. Maintaining diversity, says scientist and activist against corporate agricultural practices Vandana Shiva in her book *Biopiracy*, is our "cosmic obligation to keep a larger balance in place."

We can also read the beetle's symbolic association with rebirth and regeneration as a sign to return to the soil what has been taken out in the process of growing food plants. All sustainable agricultural techniques return nutrients to the soil while conserving topsoil, water, and energy. Mixed planting, crop rotation, trickle irrigation, and nitrogen-fixing crops are just a few techniques that reintroduce balance back into the fields.

Alternatives like permaculture and biointensive and biodynamic agriculture—which demonstrate the ability to produce equal or higher yields of more nutritious food—also build soil fertility while conserving natural resources. And there are sustainable agricultural technologies that could replace conventional methods right now with only a brief transitional drop in yields.[4]

As sustainable practices of growing food are reintroduced back into the culture, we might also stay alert to the assumption of insect as adversary. Some methods, although proposed as environmentally friendly, are still insect-hostile. True environmental friendliness, deeply rooted in a belief in the divinity of the natural world, will also include a respect—and even a fondness—for insects. The gardens of Scotland's Findhorn Community and Machaelle Small Wright's Perelandra in Virginia, for example, are uncommonly friendly to insects, and their founders have eliminated the influence of aggressiveness in the gardens, with surprising results.

Findhorn Garden

Few gardeners are unfamiliar with Findhorn, a small gardening community in Scotland that gained world attention in the 1960s for its unusually large fruits and vegetables. When pestered by reporters to reveal their "secret," the founders of Findhorn, Peter and Eileen Caddy and Dorothy McClean, attributed their success to a cooperative effort by people and plant "devas"—angelic presences or energies that oversee the growth of all plants.

For the Findhorn community, gardening was a way to experience, work with, and learn about the essential oneness behind Nature's diverse forms. Cultivating a state of attunement and love, the members of the community sensed, articulated, and met the needs of the garden.

In *The Findhorn Garden: Pioneering a New Vision of Man and Nature in Cooperation,* the community suggests approaching insects with "an attitude of love to reach a solution that is for the highest good of all concerned." They have discovered, as has science, that it is normal for plants to live with a balanced population of insects around them and that "healthy plants are not harmed by the insects they attract, just as healthy bodies are not infected by the germs they come in contact with."

Interestingly, in yet another instance of institutional science catching up with intuitive wisdom, a recent study published in the journal *Science* supports this idea that healthy plants are not harmed by the insects they attract. In fact, plants that had been "attacked" by caterpillar larvae had fewer problems with predators later and actually did better. Interaction with insects makes a plant strong and hardy.

At Findhorn, when a clear imbalance in the insect population did occur, it prompted members of Findhorn to examine their thoughts and behavior (reminiscent of the response invoked in native people when bitten by an insect). Sometimes they discovered that the plants had not been receiving what they needed physically for their optimal development. Other times, the imbalance occurred when certain offensive methods of gardening were practiced—methods contrary to the spirit of cooperation that was necessary for balance. And still other times, the problem originated from the general use of insecticides in the country, a use that often ruptured the web of interrelationship and balance between species.

To discover why a particular insect was out of balance in the garden, Findhorn gardeners would usually contact the deva or overlighting spirit of the insect species. These communications revealed that the emotional climate of the community had a great effect on the balance of the garden and the health of the individual plants and animals. And when insects appeared out of balance, the devas suggested visualizing the plants as strong and healthy, an action, they said, that adds to the plants' life force and helps them withstand the attack. Removing the insects by hand or using an organic repellent spray on the insects was also an acceptable course of action, as long as the insects were warned beforehand and disposed of with love and respect. Insects don't mind being killed—they are always killing and eating each other. They do, however, mind being hated. It is the energy of hate that is so destructive to them and to us.

Perelandra

For small communities and individuals with a penchant for gardening, working with the forces of Nature has always been the primary method for growing food. In the wooded foothills of Virginia's Blue Ridge Mountains, Machaelle Small Wright has also followed a method of gardening based on collaborating with Nature spirits.

Wright believes that a willingness to cooperate with these natural forces is the only way we will be able to reverse the damage done to the planet. It is a message that has been preached by many others from many different disciplines.

Wright has discovered firsthand that insects are messengers promptly directing her attention to problem areas. When she sees a plant or a row of plants overwhelmed by insects, she opens to the appropriate deva and asks whether the plant balance is off. Infinitely practical, the overlighting spirit of the plant often just communicates that the plant needs more mulch or water. Sometimes what is "off" and in need of correction is Wright's thoughts or intentions or those of the community connected to the garden. Sudden shifts in the emotional climate of nearby people affect the garden and its balance.

Giving Back   Wright also believes in giving back in gratitude to the Earth community and the soil what has been given in food plants. It's an ancient idea in accord with the beetle's message of regeneration and it is also a central principle guiding sustainable societies. And one of many forms of regeneration that Wright practices is tithing 10 percent of the garden back to Nature—although she says Nature has never fully taken that much.

Wright's nonmanipulative approach to gardening also gives us an alternative to buying ladybugs at our local nurseries. One season she was guided to plant costmary in the herb garden, although it was an herb she didn't use. Each spring, as she tended the herb, she saw it become completely covered with aphids—thousands of them. About a week later, almost the same number of ladybugs appeared on the costmary. They ate all the aphids and then scattered throughout the garden. Wright decided that the costmary in the Perelandra garden was obviously meant to be a breeding ground for the ladybugs, issuing an invitation and a welcoming feast.

Beetles and Roses   One of her most memorable stories involves the time Japanese beetles ravaged her corn crop. Wright decided to contact the overlighting spirit of the beetle and request that the beetles leave most of the corn plants alone. To her amazement, she touched into an energy that felt like an abused and battered child. She says, "It was an energy of defeat, of being beaten into submission. Yet it still had anger mixed in with it and a manic desire to fight for its life."[5]

Sobered by the contact, when Wright again tried to contact the deva of the beetle, this time she made contact and was informed that her original connection had been made with the consciousness of an individual Japanese beetle. She was permitted to sense its consciousness so that she would better appreciate what people's hatred had already done to it before she made any requests concerning her corn plants.

Wright was aware that the beetle, introduced accidently into the United States by an insect collector, had multiplied rapidly. It not only liked a wide variety of plants, but it also had no natural predators in the country. Consequently, Japanese beetles, like other exotic insects imported unintentionally, have been on the receiving end of a massive chemical attack that continues to this day.

Under the circumstances and still sensing its pain, Wright didn't feel it was appropriate to ask anything of it. She decided instead to ask the species to recognize Perelandra as a sanctuary, inviting it to join the rest of the garden community so that it could begin its own healing journey. To reinforce her message, she left an area of tall grass adjacent to the garden unmowed, a favorite haunt of the beetle.

In the years that have followed since making the agreement with the Japanese beetle, Wright has noticed that the beetles have grown more calm. For a couple of years they only damaged the roses. Although tempted to knock them off the plants, she refrained. Eventually she adjusted her thinking so that she could actually invite them to enjoy the roses. In time, they no longer clustered on the roses, although occasionally she sees one or two of them on the flowers. Wright says, "Because of their shifts and changes, I've found that I have not had reasons to request anything special from them. Their presence here is in balance."[6]

The thought of the blind anger and incalculable pain of the Japanese beetle—my niece's Christmas beetle—has always touched me deeply. What would our imagined god of beetles think of our war against its chosen ones? And what aspect of our beetleness have we battered and abused in our inability to accord them messenger status and understand that we cannot declare war on any member of the Earth community as though we were separate and outside the circle of life?

When we can acknowledge our role as abuser and the damage our hatred has wrought on certain species, we have tackled part of the required shadow work that in turn will help us reconnect to the assaulted parts inside ourselves. And if we can forgo the denial and justifications and undertake this work, we might be able to touch our greatly imperiled natural identity and coax our wounded "insect self" out of the dark corners of our inner zoo, reassuring it that its long exile is over. Reunited with our beetleness and infused with its vital energies, we might gain access to the power and the will that is necessary to end the silence and subvert those who would hold us to our current self-destructive path.

The Chinese solar calendar designates a day in February as Jing-zhe or "Waking of the Insects," which tells the farmer that spring is coming. Maybe we can designate a day to celebrate the Waking of the Humans—the day we can see beetles once again as Lords of the Sun, symbols of light, truth, and regeneration—and be reborn, emerging at last with the wisdom to create a sustainable life and transmit our love of insects to our young.

9. Telling *the* Bees

Last night, as I was sleeping, I dreamt—marvelous error!
that I had a beehive here inside my heart. And the golden bees
were making white combs and sweet honey from my old failures.

—*Antonio Machado (translation by Robert Bly)*

The affinity of beekeepers for their bees is called "bee fever." Its onset might be slow or fast, but the end result is the same. You fall in love with honeybees and get your first hive. Later, as puzzled friends and relatives ask you why, you try to explain, calling the malady a blessing.

The history of beekeeping contains many accounts of individuals stricken by bee fever. One is the Englishman Daniel Wildman, known as the Bee Man (although he also tamed wasps and hornets). Around the time of the American Revolution, Wildman traveled through Europe exhibiting his mastery over swarms of bees. He could command his bees to settle on his head, his beard, or any other part of his body he designated. Once he was even carried through London in a chair, his body almost completely covered with bees.

A contemporary Bee Man is the son of author Victoria Covell. In her wise and uplifting book *Spirit Animals,* Covell describes her own efforts as a young girl to save bees from drowning in the nearby pond and her belief that when she went to heaven she would be greeted by hundreds of bee souls whom she had saved, all speaking on her behalf.

Still, she was surprised when she saw the same behavior in her youngest son, Seth. At the age of four he began saving bees and was soon known as the "Bee Man of Pine Island." The islanders would see Seth paddling around in the water with fingers spread and hands raised above the surface—a water-soaked insect clinging to each fingertip. Or he would whiz by his neighbors on his bike with training wheels, pedaling toward home as fast as his legs could go, with a bee on an upraised finger.

"He took my care of the bees to a new level," said Covell. "He loved each and every one with a tender heart that would even cause him to cry if any of them died." And although occasionally people would reproach her for letting her son handle bees, she would assure them that the bees never stung him. And they didn't.

If we kept company with bees, we would know that there are correspondences between our species and a community of bees. Those who do spend time with bees report that they are calming to be around and invoke peacefulness. The bees' contentment is apparently contagious. Imagine a world where doctors prescribe bees, not drugs, to help us live with greater ease.

The strong sense of order and purpose that dominates a hive and the hum of confident industry has long inspired beekeepers. Before the industrialized age, people all over the world linked bees to peace, harmony, propriety, renewal, fertility, and eloquence. Bees' association with these qualities was so strong that people believed that bees would sicken and die in times of war and that a hive would not thrive if it were stolen. Apparently, deceit, anger, and strife were so contrary to the bees' intrinsic nature that their occurrence affected the health of the hive.

Few today are drawn to read about bees, although more has been written about these insects and the life of the hive than about any other insect. Ancient cave paintings depict strange beelike creatures, epiphanies of the Goddess, and Chinese legends speak of a giant race of bees. A Brazilian tribe considered bees enchanted creatures protected from human exploitation by the guardian spirits of plants and animals.

Would that they were protected from human exploitation! Our culture views bees primarily as resources, commodities of commerce. After all, the honey that bees produce each year is worth millions of dollars, and their pollination services are a $10 billion enterprise.

Bee products like venom, pollen, royal jelly, and beeswax are also sought-after commodities. Bee venom, for one, is valuable because of its reputed effectiveness in treating arthritis and other ailments, including multiple sclerosis and inflamed tissues from wounds or burns. And taken internally, bee venom is a natural antihistamine.

Venom is therapeutic because, as a natural stimulant, it mobilizes the immune system. Although many believe that they are allergic to bee venom, their reactions are often due to a protein hypersensitivity and not to the bee venom itself. Beekeepers who suffer regular stings actually have better than average immunization and a resistance to certain sicknesses.

Collecting venom for any kind of "sting therapy" is a process where our view of bees as commodities only, without rights or privileges, is clearly evident. A charged grid in or near the hive is typically used, with a thin synthetic material stretched beneath. When bees land on the grid, they get a mild shock that makes them sting through the material. The venom collects on the underside of the material. It takes ten thousand bees to produce one gram of pure venom. Happily, bees' stingers rarely get caught in the material, and so 99 percent of the insects survive the process.

In the Company of Bees

When we consider a species only as a resource—whether for honey, pollination, or bee products—it hinders our ability to care deeply for them, regardless of their importance. Dollars don't add up to meaning. If we aren't beekeepers, we're left outside the circle of bee and human, a circle that has fed the imaginations of people since recorded history began.

A contemporary beekeeper, William Longgood, drew his knowledge of bees from his feelings and intuition and what his long intimacy with the insects has taught him. In *The Queen Must Die,* he tells of bees grieving over the loss of a queen, making war cries, or humming with contentment. He describes them as angry, fierce, calm, playful, and aggressive, and distinguishes their happy sounds from their distressed ones. We can relate to what he says. We know about grief and distress calls. We might hum too when we are content, and we emit all manner of grunts and groans and sighs and whistles to express how we feel as we go about our day.

Living outside the circle of beekeepers, we know too little about bees to reflect on what traits we have in common or to be inspired by them. The division between humans and bees is part of the culture and too wide for us to bridge unless some incident with a bee forces us to reconsider them.

A dream was the first of a series of events that prompted Alison Yahna to not only reconsider bees but to accept them into her life as spiritual directors. It started with a dream in which she was told to make her spirit like honey. Around the same time she began to meditate, using the sound *hum* and literally buzzing like the sound of a hive. In her meditations, she began to visualize a hive of bees in her womb, and within a few days a swarm of honeybees arrived at her house. Although words fail to fully describe her experience, with the swarm outside, inside Yahna was undergoing an initiation in which the energy of the bees entered her and filled her with a vibration of laughter and joy that was illuminating. She understood that they were messengers of the Goddess and that their primary message was that "We are all one."[1] Feeling chosen or "claimed" by the bees in some mysterious way, Yahna purchased a hive the following day and placed it outside her meditation room for the swarm to occupy. They accepted the new home, and through meditation, trance, and shamanic journeying, she has been in communication with them ever since.

Although an uncommon story in today's world, Yahna is following a long line of spiritual traditions where bees and honey figure prominently in the alchemic symbolism of transformation. Bulgarian spiritual teacher Omraam Mikhael Aivanhov says that, "the only thing that the great Initiates, those true alchemists, teach is how to become a bee." Highly advanced disciples or initiates are bees because they extract the pure and divine elements from the people around them, like nectar from flowers, and prepare a food in their hearts for the angels.

The Sacred Bee

The bee has appeared in sacred books of many traditions, from the ancient Sanskrit scripture the Rig-Veda, to the Koran and the Book of Mormon. The Prophet Muhammad taught that the bee is the only creature ever spoken to directly by God.

Long linked to the mystery of death, the bee was believed by many cultures to be a human soul. The Aztecs refer frequently to a Bee God, and in ancient Egypt the bee as a human soul was associated with the solar cult of Ra. Myths say that when Ra wept, his tears were honeybees—a symbolic image of the ability to transform compassion into something beneficial and greater than itself.

In India, Vishnu—one of the great nectar-born trinity that includes Brahma and Shiva—is represented as a blue bee on a lotus blossom. Krishna and Indra are also frequently portrayed as a bee on a lotus flower, and Krishna wears a blue bee on his forehead. The Indian god of love, Kama, carries a bow with a string formed by a chain of bees, and the deity Prana, who personifies the universal life force, is sometimes portrayed encircled by bees.

Bees have also been linked to fertility and its seasonal cycles. Wild hives tucked away in the hollows of ancient trees or in rock crevices linked the bee to the secretiveness of generation in the womb and the mysteries of life before incarnation. The fact that bees disappeared in the winter and reappeared in the spring tied them specifically to annual fertility rites.

Christian bee symbolism followed that of the Earth Mother religions. The bees' three-month disappearance into the hive at the onset of winter is compared to the three days that Christ's body was hidden in the tomb. And their reappearance in the spring symbolizes his resurrection and immortality.

Christian saints associated with bees have strong parallels with the ancient gods and goddess, perhaps assigned to older legends to legitimize the stories and cancel out the Earth Mother images. Saint Sossima, for example, the patron saint of beekeeping in the Ukraine, resembles Zosim, a pre-Christian Russian bee god. And a Brittany legend that corresponds to the myth of the Egyptian sun god Ra tells how bees were created from the tears Christ shed on the cross.

Birds of the Muses In Asia bees were called the Birds of the Muses. The idea that bees have the power to impart eloquence to a child of their choosing has a long history in many parts of the world. For example, bees were believed to have swarmed on the mouths of great teachers like Plato when they were babies, giving them their eloquent style. And bees were said to have fed their finest nectar to the poet Pindar when he was born.

Among the Jews, the bee was also related to language and its name, *dbure*, and the Hebraic root of which means word or speech. In Christianity, Saint John Chrysostom, known for the sweetness of his preaching, was called Golden-Mouthed. His eloquence was believed to have come from a swarm of bees hovering around his mouth at birth. The same story was told about the famous preachers Saint Bernard of Clairvaux and Saint Ambrose.

The Symbolism of Honey

Honey has as long and as complex a history as the creatures who create it. Rock paintings dating from the earliest era of human life show people stealing honey from wild bees. Myths of the Greek deity Zeus tell how he was hidden in a cave as an infant and guarded by bees that nourished him with honey. The Incas of Peru offered honey as a sacrifice to the sun. And the Sumerians erected their temples on ground consecrated with honey.

Honey was a substance that all ancient mythologies considered sacred. Like the sacrament of the Christian tradition, in which bread and wine are believed to be transubstantiated into the living flesh and blood of Jesus Christ, honey was believed to change into a mystical substance after being consumed. This substance of spirit, then, carried a beneficial power for the person eating it. Symbolically, honey was both wisdom and the sweetness that comes from the mouths of the wise and the strong.

Interestingly, when interspecies communicator Sharon Callahan was asked by a beekeeper friend to contact the overlighting spirit of the bees, she discovered (without knowing anything about honey's ancient role) that, as the bees tell it, honey still should be regarded as a sacrament, a holy communication between the partaker and God. She learned from the bees that honey is transformed into an energetic pattern inside the body of those who eat it. Once digested, its properties act upon the DNA structure, and honey created from pollen gathered in different regions carries different patterns or information—so we would do well to eat honey produced in our own region.

The Spirit of the Hive

Like ant and termite colonies, a hive of bees has long been thought of as a single living organism, inspiring many analogies. The Desnan, a

Colombian tribe, conceived of a sophisticated and detailed comparison between the meticulously organized beehive and the human brain—a comparison that those inspired by the possibility of a global brain will appreciate.[2] Others have compared the hive to the human body with the queen serving as the brain and the individual bees performing like cells.

From the start, beekeepers have found the colony's unity and division of labor extraordinary and not a little mysterious. Some of these mysteries are tied to their language and others perhaps to the influence of a unifying morphic field, an invisible, evolving blueprint that organizes the life of the hive. Whatever its source, beekeepers almost universally are moved to admiration by the insects' organizational genius and ability to work together to accomplish their goal.

The Dance Language of Bees

When we reduced bees to resources, we assumed they were mechanically programmed to find and pollinate vegetation and produce honey. But science has since verified what ancient people knew intuitively: honeybees, like other social insects, respond flexibly to their environment, communicate with each other, and have a great deal of intelligent awareness. Consider that honeybee scouts don't proceed robotically to report their new food discoveries. They report them only when the colony needs more food, when the new source is close by, and when its quality and quantity are worth mentioning. That's discernment by anyone's standard.

Dancers, passionate about their art, may have an affinity for bees without knowing it. Bee dancing is part of a complex social communication system that goes on continuously in a community of bees. Austrian zoologist Karl von Frisch, who discovered the phenomenon, said that a bee communicates by dancing and only does so when there is an audience of other bees.

When the dance is performed in the darkness of a hive, the dancer makes faint sounds. The audience responds with its own sound, a kind of signal begging the dancer to stop and regurgitate food samples. It is like asking for proof that the food source is as good as the dancer is indicating by her movements.

A bee performs a "round dance" when she has discovered food close to the hive. "Waggle dances" are performed to communicate information about things at a greater distance from the hive. Both convey the direction and distance to the food source using a kind of geometrical symbolism. And the intensity of the dance indicates the quality of the food.

Although much energy has been spent trying to disprove that an insect is capable of symbolic communication—out of insistence that it is a unique human capability—Princeton professor James Gould has demonstrated that bees really do use the information coded in the dance. Gould says that the dances of bees is definitely language, and it accomplishes what human language does—it describes something removed in time and space.

Swarming A lot of communication goes on among bees when a part of the colony breaks off from the main group with a new queen to look for another home. It is called swarming. Since swarming involves a lot of preparation, including gorging on honey to sustain them while they search for a new home, honeybees must plan their swarm.

A swarm often clusters on a tree branch close to its old home. From there, scouts venture forth to look for a suitable location for a new hive, reporting back periodically to the other bees. Waggle dances performed in front of a swarm lead to a group decision about where to establish a new colony. After many hours of exchanges of information, when, finally, all of the scouts indicate by their dance that they favor the same hive site, the swarm flies off to its new home. This consensus depends wholly on the "speaking" and "listening" interactions between bees.

Bees and Quarks One of the most interesting and most far-reaching research involving bees, reported in *Discover* magazine, has been conducted by Barbara Shipman, a mathematician at the University of Rochester. Shipman grew up with a beekeeper father and never forgot the round and waggle dance of bees that had captivated her as a child. When she was performing a series of routine mathematical exercises, she noticed a pattern emerging and followed that thread.

Shipman has described all the different forms of the honeybee dance using a single coherent mathematical or geometric structure (the flag manifold). This structure is also the one that is used in the geometry of quarks, those tiny building blocks of protons and neutrons.

From technical evidence too complex to present for our purposes, Shipman speculates that the bees are sensitive to or interacting with quantum fields of quarks.

It has already been established that bees are sensitive to the planet's magnetic field, but this sensitivity has always been attributed to the presence of a mineral in the bee's abdomen. Shipman's research indicates that the bees perceive these fields through some kind of quantum mechanical interaction between the quantum fields and the atoms in the membranes of certain cells. Shipman says simply, "The mathematics implies that bees are doing something with quarks." If Shipman is correct and bees can "touch" the quantum world of quarks (without "breaking" it as we do when we try to detect a quark), it would revolutionize biology and physicists would have to reinterpret quantum mechanics as well.

The Intelligent Awareness of Bees

The more James Gould works with bees, the more he is convinced that they have a great deal of intelligent awareness, including a "head" for navigation that surpasses ours. For example, bees know when an experiment is going on, and many anticipate what the researcher is going to do next. In one typical experiment, Gould was moving food at regularly increasing distances from the hive, and some of the bees flew past the training station to wait for him at the next food location.

Gould has discovered in his long, intimate association with these insects that bees have both distinctive characteristics that make them individuals and predictable traits that are common to them all. He is always impressed by the chaos in the hive because the behavior of bees is not reliable statistically except when they are taken as a group—a fact that suggests that bees, like ants, live at the edge of chaos where life and new possibilities abound.

The bees are so individual in the way each approaches her duties that Gould and his colleagues can recognize them by their differences. One, for example, is brief and goal-oriented at the food dish while another appears to feed at leisure, even taking time to fly around the dish looking for drips. Sometimes, just for fun, Gould closes his eyes and predicts which insect is coming to the food dish: the one who always circles twice or the one with the very "throaty" buzz. New recruits are even easier to identify, he says. They fly in to the food source low to the ground, hovering and hesitant, buzzing in a different tone.

Since bees only live six weeks, Gould has even watched them grow old. Suddenly they are not quite as good at foraging, and they are apt to be blown off the feeder by the wind, indicating to Gould that his "old friend" is not long for this world.

Talking to Bees

The intelligent awareness of bees was recognized long before experiments confirmed it. This observed awareness in bees is probably one of the reasons that "telling the bees" is still a time-honored custom in some areas.

Throughout Europe it was generally believed that bees wouldn't thrive if important news was withheld from them—especially the news of when their keeper died. The custom has deep roots in the bees' association with the human soul and their habit of frequenting caves. Caves were thought of as semisacred entrances to the underworld, and bees were seen as the souls of the dead either returning to Earth or en route to the next world.

So when bees were told of important events like births, deaths, and marriages, it was a way of conveying news to souls no longer in a human body. Telling the bees also arose from the typically close relationship between the bees and the beekeeper and the fear that if the bees weren't told, they would take offense and leave.

Diane Skafte shares a story in her original and provocative book *When Oracles Speak* about an English beekeeper, Annie Burt, who lived on a farm in Upton. Annie was seen frequently sitting by her hives and talking to her bees. She told them all the family news and also brought her personal problems to the bees. After explaining a troublesome situation, she would lean toward them, listening carefully. Her family remembered that when she returned from her counseling sessions with the bees, she always had a different manner about her. She had obviously found relief and peace.

Sam Rodgers's Bees   Telling the bees that their keeper had died was done in different ways. Sometimes relatives of the deceased would place black crepe or a small black piece of wood on the hive for the period of mourning. In other places they turned the hives as the coffin left the house.

Today, telling the bees is still done and has given rise to at least one recorded mysterious event. It occurred in Shropshire, England, in the mid-1960s. In the small county of Myddle lived a beekeeper named Sam Rodgers, who was also a postman, cobbler, and handyman. Although he liked his work and had many friends, his great love was for his bees. Each day he would go to the hives and care for them. He would always talk tenderly to them, as if they could understand his every word and affectionate gesture. People say that Rodgers would sit in a chair in front of his hive and ring a small bell. The bees would swarm out and cluster all over him. Then one day the benevolent eighty-three-year-old beekeeper died.

His family, aware of the old customs of the area, knew that someone must tell the bees of his death. Two of Sam's children walked down the path to the hives and solemnly told the bees of Sam's passing.

Sam was buried a few days later in the local cemetery behind the town's church. The Sunday after the funeral, parishioners called the parson outside to witness what was happening. The Reverend John Ayling reported later that he saw a long line of bees heading straight for Sam's grave. They came from the direction of his hives a mile or so away. It resembled a funeral procession. Once the bees had circled Sam's gravestone, they flew directly back to their hives. Friends and members of Sam Rodgers's family were mystified by the strange behavior of his bees; so were bee experts in the area. No one could explain logically what they had witnessed, for it seemed as if the bees had gone to the grave site to pay their last respects and bid Sam goodbye.

Building Bridges

Contemporary beekeepers, if they feel "known" by their bees, are likely to keep it a secret or dismiss it as fancy. Subjective experiences carry no weight in scientific bee circles. Still, they form much of what keeps a beekeeper devoted to his or her hive. A New York beekeeper wrote in *Bee Culture* that people always ask him whether his bees recognize him. Although he admits that it would seem so—since he can move about his bee yard at certain times of the year without a veil, while a stranger who suddenly appears in the yard is likely to be stung—he answers no, that his bees have no idea who he is. It only seems as though they do, he decides, because he has learned how to move among them.

Although this beekeeper would receive an approving nod from traditional scientists for avoiding the trap of anthropomorphizing, bee specialist James Gould and others would argue with his conclusion. Gould discovered that just as he and his research team could tell the bees apart, the bees soon learned to tell the humans apart. Gould thinks they do it by smell. If, for example, an observer who had been watching the bees at a feeding station walked off into the bushes to relieve himself, the bees, noticing his absence, would usually come to him in the bushes. And foraging bees that Gould had been working with would come looking for him first thing in the morning as if to say, "Let's get started." If a stranger or other researcher came out onto the field instead of Gould, however, the bees would fly to him or her, hover for a moment (as though taking a sniff), and then leave.

The desire to be known, recognized, even loved by another species is great within us. It emerges out of the needs and hunger of our inner wilderness self, the instinctive, intuitive, natural self that we have abandoned.

As we learned in our look at other insects, what we see is shaped by our assumptions and unexamined biases. Common evaluation of other species involves only two questions: Do they serve us, and can they hurt us? With bees, the answer to both is yes, throwing us into a state of ambivalence. Bees so obviously serve us and all creation, yet we don't know how to be in relationship to those who can also hurt us. And to complicate the situation, in the past few years we have been put on the alert about Africanized bees, popularly called "killer bees." The media's portrayal of killer bees more than satisfies our unconscious need to find and fight insects as enemies.

Killer Bees

Sensational news reporting about killer bees has left us panicky about all bees, and Hollywood has lost little time in adding to our fears by depicting killer bees as creatures that maliciously seek out victims to kill. So great is the uproar about them that I feel compelled to investigate the charges.

The thought of killer bees frightens us. Although the sting of a killer bee is no more toxic than the sting of the normal honeybee, these bees are reputed to be easily agitated, and their "angry nature" makes multiple stings more likely. We are not accustomed to being careful around other creatures. We are used to seeing them at a safe distance—on television or in zoos.

Killer bees are a relatively new strain created by crossing two subspecies: the European honeybee and an African honeybee. The result of the crossing has been a more aggressive bee that is harder to manage and promises a rapid genetic takeover of our domesticated honeybee— a phenomenon that has already occurred in South America.

To understand the issues involved and separate media invention from fact, we need to know more.

Of some twenty to thirty thousand bee species, only six are honeybees. Our familiar honeybee is actually one of several subspecies ranging from the gentle and easy-to-manage Italian bee to the larger, more aggressive German bee. Another subspecies is the bee that comes from eastern and southern Africa. Since all these honeybees are of the same species, bees from one subspecies can mate with bees from another subspecies and create even more variation within the honeybee tribe.

Bees are shaped by their environment. The temperament and habits of the bee we brought to the Americas from Europe, for instance, were affected by its adaptation to a change of season. During the warm months, abundant foraging opportunities, plentiful water, and a dearth of predators let them maximize their honey storage to make it through the winter.

African honeybees had different challenges. They had a warm climate year round, with frequent droughts that diminished the surrounding vegetation. They also had to contend with a large number and variety of predators, who would attack and destroy any colony that was not fiercely defended. When faced with drought or when their nest was threatened, they were forced to flee and find a new nest, a survival tactic called absconding.

Knowing even this little bit about African bees, it is easier to see how the current situation evolved. To survive, they have had to respond to any perceived threat to their colony with quick and efficient aggressive tactics, and, to the dismay of those who would "manage" them, they don't stay around when threatened by lack of food or predators. Their behavior, overstated and exaggerated in the news, emerges from their will to survive.

The African Bee Comes to Brazil   The killer bee scare originated in Brazil in 1956 when Professor Warren E. Kerr brought the African bee to Brazil, acting under the authority of the Brazilian Ministry of Agriculture, which wanted to strengthen Brazilian beekeeping. Since the African species was already used successfully for commercial honey production in South Africa, Kerr believed it would be valuable for Brazil.

The trouble began in 1964 when military forces took over the government and Kerr, an outspoken human-rights advocate, criticized the new regime. He was jailed twice. Military leaders are suspected to have played upon people's general fear of stinging insects in an attempt to discredit him. News leaked out about a few African queen bees escaping from the school's hives and taking over established colonies. From that point on, when anyone was stung, whether by wasps or bees, government officials blamed the incidence on Kerr's "killer bees."

For the detailed story, turn to beekeeper Sue Hubbell's illuminating account in *Broadsides from the Other Orders*. She is one of many who believe that the term "killer bees" was a government-instigated media invention. The original name for these bees was "assassin bees" because on rare occasions they would raid the hives of other bees and kill the queen. The term "killer bees," however, went deep into our imaginations. Our fear of all stinging insects had already prepared a place for it.

Controlling Killer Bees   In 1986, the U.S. government joined forces with scientists in Mexico to stop Africanized bees from moving north, killing the first natural swarm of killer bees that crossed the Rio Grande into Texas in 1990. It didn't stop them though. They showed up in Arizona in 1993. Two fatalities from killer bees were subsequently reported in Texas (although one thousand deaths have been attributed to killer bees throughout South America). Both were elderly men. The first was stung when he tried to eradicate a colony with a flaming torch. He had an allergic reaction to the stings and died. The second man, ninety-six years old, was sitting on his porch when a nearby gardener disturbed a colony. The bees mistook him for the threat and stung him repeatedly. In 1995 a pair of tree trimmers were stung in the small California river town of Blythe. One man received twenty-five stings and the other fifteen—unpleasant but not life-threatening by any stretch of the imagination. Healthy adults can sustain as many as fifteen hundred stings and survive, and they can outrun a swarm (which flies at between ten and fifteen miles per hour) and usually find safety in an enclosed space.

About forty people die each year in the United States from the stings of venomous insects. European honeybees are responsible for about half the deaths, and usually from an allergic reaction. Since killer bees are hard for laypeople to identify, any bee that stings a lot is assumed to be an Africanized bee.

Bravo Bees

The caution that we need to exercise around Africanized bees is matched by the caution we need to bring to what we read and hear about them or any species the public has decided is an unqualified threat to human life. Most of the stories about killer bees are products of the active imaginations of journalists unfamiliar with bees. Journalists are looking for action, or better yet, threatening behavior. Sometimes, Hubbell reports, they even offer to pay beekeepers to stir their bees up for a better story.

One step we could take toward promoting coexistence is getting rid of the term "killer bees." I like Hubbell's name for them—"bravo bees," following the example of some South American beekeepers who have learned to work with the bees' natural inclinations—so we'll adopt the term for the rest of this chapter.

Opinions differ, but some beekeepers think the bravo bees' aggressiveness has been overstated. They are preferred by many Central American beekeepers because they are more productive and disease-resistant than other honeybees. Consider that the takeover of bravo bees in Brazil has catapulted its ranking as a honey producer from forty-seventh in the world to seventh.

Living with Bravo Bees To assume the role of beekeeper to bravo bees requires returning caution to beekeeping activities. Bravo bees will defend an area up to two or three city blocks in size, so beekeepers must move the beehives away from houses, barns, and farm animals that might inadvertently bump their hive and be attacked for the action. Beekeepers must also contend with the tendency of bravo bees to abscond when the blossoms in one area cease flowering or when the hive is threatened. Minimizing threats and feeding them sugar syrup when flowers disappear has already persuaded many hives to stay put.

Balk as we may at the idea of living with bravo bees, we have no choice. We can't destroy bravo bees without destroying all bees. The key to sorting out irrational fears from reasonable concerns is knowledge. If we are afraid of bees or any stinging insects, it behooves us to learn something about them. For example, the best defense is not to swat at the bees—which makes them more likely to attack—but to run for shelter. Bees don't look for trouble, nor do they attack without provocation. And any bee, even a bravo bee, will not sting while happily collecting pollen or nectar unless she is stepped on or otherwise threatened. She can only sting once and dies afterward, so she will save that action for the defense of her hive, its honey, and her sister bees.

Knowledge about swarming bees also prevents undue panic. A swarm may look dangerous to us, but they actually may be more docile than normal because they don't have a home to defend and are busy "discussing" new possible nesting sites. What's more, they are usually so full of honey that they can't bend their abdominal area to insert their stinger even if they wanted to.

Learning the likes and dislikes of bees can also help us choose an appropriate response when we are near them. Experts advise that we not breathe directly on them, for instance. Honeybees are sometimes aroused by human breath. And as James Gould noticed, bees seem to distinguish people by their smell. This sensitivity extends to a variety of smells. People who wear colognes and perfumes outdoors, for instance, will find themselves under close scrutiny by bees. Be aware, too, that bees become agitated in the presence of body odors that come from uncleanliness, so good hygiene is important.

Bees are sensitive to bright colors and have excellent color vision, so when we wear clothes that simulate the bright hues of flowers, we must expect bees to notice us and find us attractive. They also like sweets, so when drinking from a soda can or bottle outside, examine it before taking a swig.

Replacing myths with facts will help gardeners coexist with bees safely, for all bees are beneficial to gardens. What is not a good idea, however, is providing bees with appealing nesting sites in our gardens like empty boxes, cans, buckets, upturned flowerpots, tires, open pipes, or overgrown shrubs and trees.

As we become more comfortable with the idea of coexisting with bees—even bravo bees—and as beekeepers adapt their management techniques to the ways of these bees, I suspect that we are going to have an opportunity to learn that there are always unexpected benefits in situations where our customary manipulations have led us to believe that we are in control of the forces of Nature. Consider that the same life force that allowed African bees to survive in an environment with many dangers appears to make bravo bees more productive and resistant to disease. Their hardiness may prove to be the single most important reason to welcome them into the United States, for our wild and domestic honeybee populations are facing extinction.

Our Declining Honeybee Populations

Since the 1980s, two varieties of mites have been wiping out honeybee populations here and abroad. A 1997 report says that an alarming 95 percent of the United State's wild honeybees have died during the past two or three years. The domesticated honeybee is dying out too, resulting in soaring rental costs for agricultural pollination and prompting entomologists to study other pollinators. An unexpected benefit is that protection has increased for wild pollinators. The downside is that many are writing off honeybees rather than investigating the reasons why our honeybees are so vulnerable to the mites.

If we consider the possibility that the mites are not the real problem but are messengers, what might their overwhelming presence be telling us about honeybees or the larger environmental picture? A growing number of beekeepers believe that honeybees have been so weakened by years of manipulation that they cannot ward off the parasites as a healthy hive could.

Authorities such as Gunther Hauk, beekeeper and director of the Pfeiffer Center, a New York biodynamic gardening and environmental program, believe that the mites and other diseases that plague our honeybees are all symptoms of the bees' weakened immune system and overall degenerated state of health. According to Hauk, one of the most serious factors in our manipulative management of bee colonies is the way we breed queens. We have turned an emergency situation in a colony where, upon the loss of a queen, the workers raise a new queen out of the egg or larvae of a worker bee, into a standard method of propagation.

To understand why this practice has been so detrimental to bees requires an understanding of the impact of form on the development of embryonic life—for in Nature queens are raised naturally in round cells and workers and drones are raised in hexagonal cells. Those unfamiliar with the influence of form upon life—what is called "sacred geometry" in esoteric traditions—have not recognized that our modern technique of raising queens with artificial insemination is one of the reasons for the weakened health of our bees.[3]

Hauk points out that when Rudolf Steiner warned people in 1923 that the honeybee might not survive the end of the century, he was referring to the way we raise bees and how our best methods contradict the requirements of Nature to create and sustain a healthy hive. As the plight of the bee grows more serious each season, more beekeepers are willing to explore what those requirements might be. Beekeeper Ron Breland of West Nyack, New York, believes that we have to turn beekeeping back into a sacred art. He has been working on a new hive prototype, "an artistic receptacle in which the spirit can manifest."[4]

Hidden Killers The saturation of our environment with pesticides has also contributed to the ill health of bees and has led, in many circumstances, to the death of both wild and domesticated bees. So has transgenic crops. Early studies have shown that rapeseed oil plants, for example, engineered to produce the insecticide Bt, not only killed the caterpillars and the beetles it was engineered to exterminate, it killed bees as well. So did more than 30 percent of bees who visited a new Bt cotton hybrid. And honey produced by bees that take pollen from plants with this insecticide gene may also be poisonous or cause severe allergic reactions in humans.

If we consider all the factors contributing to the plight of our honeybees, we might want to not just put up with bravo bees, but start welcoming them into North America. They are hardier and more efficient than our European bees.

At this point the threat (or promise) of bravo bees has not materialized. Although bravo bees are in North America, they tend to confine themselves to a year-round existence in southern Texas. The grim possibility that honeybees will be extinct *in the near future,* however, is the more pressing threat, and if that happens, many believe that the consequences would be dire and far-reaching, for agriculture as well as for Nature's intricate interrelationships.

In Sharon Callahan's 1998 communication with the overlighting spirit of the honeybee (in which she was told about the potency of honey), she also learned that bees play a critical part in the repatterning of the Earth and planetary grids as well as struggling to hold in place a new "pulse" of energy from the Creator—struggling because of their weakened constitution. Within this energy is all the information needed for all species and the Earth to move in harmony into the new millennium. "Natural selection, comb shape, the speed of vibration of the bees themselves are all vital to the bees' ability to keep up with instructions from the Creator [on how] . . . to build the vibrational matrix necessary for . . . [all to move] into the next phase of becoming or spiritual evolution."[5]

Perhaps it is these energetic instructions that the honeybees are receiving from their mysterious interaction with quarks in quantum fields. And perhaps in this area science is meeting the insights provided by "spiritual sight." Both are needed if we are to help restore the bee to health, enlist its continued cooperation in pollinating our food plants, and help all bees—if only by not interfering—hold the new energetic pattern emerging in our midst.

Communicating with Bees

For the nonbeekeeper, contact with bees may be limited to watching them visit our flower beds and gardens. But for the adventuresome, and for those times when there are no other options, communicating with bees is also a possibility. A classic story of communicating with these insects is found in Doug Boyd's account of intertribal medicine man Rolling Thunder, who teaches that all fear comes from misunderstanding. When a friend of his was gathering herbs, she reached for some horehound but drew back suddenly when she saw that bees were swarming all over the plants. She stood up abruptly, pale with fright. Rolling Thunder told her that she wasn't really afraid of any living thing; she only believed she was. He reminded her of the loving experiences she had had as a child with other species and urged her to talk to the bees, telling them that she wouldn't hurt them and asking them to share the plants with her. She did what he suggested and to her wonder all the bees flew to the back of the plant. When we can move past our fears and self-consciousness, we open ancient pathways that have always linked us to other species.

Chiquinho of the Bees The link between people and other species, even potentially dangerous ones, is sometimes revealed in special human beings, people who have a "gift" so unusual and outside the norm that their behavior is rarely thought of as a latent human potential. One such person is a young man named Francisco Vicente Duarte, called "Chiquinho of the Bees," who was born in a small Brazilian city of farmworker parents and grew up in the company of nine siblings. Since the age of three, Chiquinho has demonstrated a rare ability to understand other species. Poisonous snakes don't bite him, dangerous spiders become his friends and confidants, and bees (no doubt bravo bees) and wasps land amiably on his face.

Chiquinho's affinity with other species and his preference for dangerous invertebrates have given him quite a following in the city where he lives. Born with an affliction that makes him look more like a twelve-year-old than the thirty-plus-year-old man that he is, Chiquinho is also believed to be slightly retarded. Perhaps these disabilities have provided the permission he needed to explore his other gifts, instead of spending all of his time laboring in the fields. Today he sometimes helps his family by responding to calls from people having trouble with bees or wasps in their homes. He goes to the home and calls the insects. They land on his body and stay with him as he heads for his home and an improvised bee yard.

Parapsychologist Alvaro Fernandes, who investigated Chinquinho as a boy of twelve, says that Chiquinho can indeed talk to animals and they respond. Although skeptical at first, American parapsychologist Gary D. Richman accompanied Chiquinho on his excursions into nearby farms to catch animals and was amazed at what he observed. No creature, fish, spider, or snake appeared to be scared when the boy approached them. They remained quiet, as though waiting for him to catch them.

Chiquinho says of his rapport with other species that the animals have always understood him. He doesn't analyze his affinity with animals but simply accepts it. "I talk to the animals and they talk to me. I can understand everything they say. My talent is a gift from God."

A friend of mine, Silvia Jorge, had an opportunity to speak with

Chiquinho at his home and to film him. Jorge said Chiquinho's mother told her that when he was about three years old, she found her son in their backyard intertwined with a large poisonous snake. She feared greatly for his life before realizing suddenly that the boy was playing with the snake. She says that is when the gift emerged.

The day Jorge visited Chiquinho in the summer of 1997, she found him personable and eager to demonstrate his ability. She watched as he talked softly and patiently to the poisonous snakes that live with him. Then she snapped pictures as Chiquinho lifted his hand to a large wasp nest hanging from a nearby building and called the wasps to his hand. Finally the neighborhood boys located a wild beehive, and Chiquinho and Jorge went to have a look. Demonstrating his affinity with bees, he talked to them in a soft, affectionate tone as he put his hand into the hive. During his demonstration, a few bees flew over to Jorge, landing on her as she was videotaping. She called out to Chiquinho and told him that she was very nervous. He called to the bees telling them not to sting Jorge. He told them that she only wanted to take their picture because they were "very great beings" and to fly back to him. The bees left Jorge and went to Chiquinho.

After witnessing Chiquinho, it was apparent to Jorge that his communication with these species is a natural, even casual, behavior on his part. Fernandes didn't view Chiquinho's abilities as paranormal either, because Chiquinho's accomplishments are not achieved through any great power of mental concentration. Rather, it seems that what occurs between Chiquinho and the animals happens at an instinctive level, a body-to-body exchange of energy. Barbara Brennan, former NASA scientist and pioneer in the exploration of the human energy field, says that the communication of feeling between people and other species is an energy field interaction and that our intentionality influences our human energy field. So Chiquinho could be broadcasting to other species, via his energy field, his deep accord and intention not to harm long before he interacts with them physically.

A Brazilian professor, Dino Vissoto, believes that Chiquinho doesn't pose a threat to other species because he isn't afraid. When people are afraid, he explains, they produce and give off some kind of secretion. Rolling Thunder talks about this scent of fear in terms of vibrations (perhaps Brennan's energy field interaction) and teaches that we can learn to control our vibrations and so affect the way we interact with other species.

J. Allen Boone believes that when we are taught to despise a creature, our feelings are a kind of mental poison that is somehow communicated to the creature, who then reacts against it. Chiquinho loves and trusts other creatures—including sometimes dangerous invertebrates like bees. That in itself sets him apart from most other people raised in industrialized society. Whatever the mechanism, these feelings appear to be communicated to the creature as he approaches them, for they display great trust in him.

Special people like Chiquinho hint at the great latent potential within all of us to communicate with other species. Interspecies communicators Sharon Callahan and Penelope Smith maintain that these abilities are our heritage. We have only to pay attention and cultivate them to enter the community of other species where we belong. In *Life Song*, Dr. Bill Schul says communication with other creatures may not only be important, it may be critical to our survival. "Interspecies communication becomes a matter of the parts recognizing their kinship with the other parts and the whole . . . all life is a creation of and with God, the All-Conscious."

10. BLOOD RELATIONS

There is nothing in life too terrible or too sad that will not be your friend when you find the right name to call it by, and calling it by its own name, hastening it will come up right to your side.

—*Koba in* A Far Off Place *by Laurens van der Post*

Bloodsucking insects anger people. In the ten years I have been lecturing on the insect-human connection, only twice have tempers flared (not mine), both times over the mosquito. One was a caller to a radio show on which I was being interviewed after the publication of the first edition of this book. He demanded to know who was more important: mosquitoes or people? I told him that I thought it was the wrong question (which, judging by the tone of his voice, made his blood pressure rise). Again he demanded that I answer him. Again I refused, telling him it was like the question "Have you stopped beating your wife?" When he finally realized I was not going to go in that direction, he demanded to know my religion. At that point the host interrupted him, admonishing him for the personal turn in the conversation, and he hung up.

What religion, indeed, supports caring about the mosquito? We have already entertained the idea of a God with a fondness for beetles, but what kind of deity would create a creature prone to being hijacked by smaller creatures that sicken it and block its feeding apparatus? What kind of a master plan is this that then allows the parasite to be transmitted to a new host, tumbling out of the feeding tube when the dying mosquito, starving now, tries to feed? That's the territory awaiting us if we are to look clearly at our blood-needing relatives.

"People who have not been in Narnia sometimes think that a thing cannot be good and terrible at the same time," wrote C. S. Lewis in his famous trilogy. In this line Lewis could well have been talking about mosquitoes and other biting and blood-dependent insects. Our ability to find and hold the good as well as the terrible about them—insect-transmitted diseases like malaria kill thousands of people every year—is the only way through a landscape that is overwhelmingly complex and requires that we stay in the tension of uncertainty and not succumb to fear or enemy-making.

Life as a Battlefield   One reason it is hard to be neutral about mosquitoes is that we don't want to be bitten or share our blood with them. We view the pain or discomfort of being bitten as an assault and an act of war. Our interpretation comes from seeing life as a battlefield—a struggle between the forces of good and evil. In fact, this perspective provides the context for all wars between human beings and all wars against other species. It is also the infrastructure underneath the attempt of industrial societies to eradicate, albeit unsuccessfully, the mosquito. When this view is dominant, enemy-making is supported in all its variations.

If we operate out of this view of life as a battlefield, the pain or itching of the bite makes us angry. We are likely to feel victimized and want to retaliate against what we perceive as unprovoked aggression. Since this interpretation is congruent with our belief that insects are our adversaries, we don't question our feelings. And projecting malice into a creature lets us feel justified in countering its attempt to bite us with an equal or greater violence.

The now-familiar heroic and aggressive stance, so common in our culture, benefits from our readiness to divide all other species into good ones or bad, friend or foe. Once we've determined just who the bad ones are, we can pursue them with a reactive vengeance. And so we have.

This culturally sanctioned position of seeking revenge was the basis of an award-winning television commercial promoting Tabasco sauce and aired during the 1998 Super Bowl. A man who has just smothered his sandwich with the condiment savors the intensity of heat in his mouth and watches without concern as a mosquito lands on him and takes a blood meal. When the mosquito is finished, it takes to the air. A few seconds later the insect explodes while the man smiles wryly and applies more sauce. Cleverness harnessed to the hostile imagination is a common approach in marketing.

Vengeance is not limited to commercials, however, but is also found in journalism. A case in point is an article published in *Discover* magazine on why mosquitoes suck blood. The author concludes the straightforward, factual piece by advising the reader that if a mosquito "picks on us" we can always "get even" by using a trick she learned from a research scientist (who asked not to be quoted by name). It involves stretching our skin taut around a feeding mosquito so that it traps the mosquito's feeding instrument, or proboscis. When it can't withdraw, it is forced to suck until it pops.

These are typical responses from individuals raised in a society that has embraced the myth of superiority and dominance, and has cast its repressed hostilities over the natural world. They are also responses that have dire physiological consequences.

Carolyn Myss, a new voice in the field of energy medicine, says that vengeance, or "getting even," is an emotional poison that is highly toxic to our bodies and causes afflictions ranging from impotence to cancer of the genital area. Many clinical studies support Myss's contention that toxic emotions threaten our health. Evidence is growing for a direct physical pathway that allows emotions to impact the immune system. Chronic, intense, negative emotions cause stress hormones to flood the body. And when our dominant approach to life is antagonistic—that is, when hostility in the form of mistrust, cynicism, temper flare-ups, and rage is our personal style—Myss says, we "double the risk of getting a disease including asthma, arthritis, headaches, peptic ulcers, and heart disease."

The Myth of Objectivity   A second context for translating the experience of being bitten is closely related to the "world as battlefield" view. Its roots grow, however, from the paradigm that has separated us from Nature and then fashioned a lifeless world of creatures wired to respond to particular stimuli. It includes the illusion of absolute objectivity and the belief that everything can be explained in terms of linear cause and effect and understood by our rational faculties. This context strips intentionality and intelligence, however defined, from insects and reduces them to mindless (and soulless) life forms programmed to pursue goals regardless of circumstances, other forces, or human behavior. So it is just unfortunate to be bitten or stung. The act does not invoke a particular response or invite the recipient of the bite or sting into deeper reflective waters. To kill or curse them is fine, but basically irrelevant.

This context also denies the possibility of a consciousness-directed universe, an inspirited world, noncausal symbolic connections, and all paradoxical and seemingly illogical relationships and observations that lend depth, meaning, and mystery to our lives. If we operate from this framework of beliefs, we must ignore a lot of evidence that contradicts it, including recent discoveries in quantum physics, synchronicities, an increasing number of people who report experiences of interspecies communication, and our own feelings and intuition.

The Bite as Punishment   A third context has benign roots and arises out of a genuine desire to live authentically. The growing minority who hold this view cultivate harmlessness and try to live on the Earth lightly. They may also seek, to one degree or another, communication and kinship with other species. So, being stung or bitten feels like a betrayal—or a judgment. Perhaps the insect perpetrator has judged the human victim and found him or her lacking. The pain is punitive, then, some unknown transgression having been noted and punished. "But I always liked insects," people will exclaim, confused and upset by such an encounter.

Many native tribes also viewed the sting or bite as a judgment—usually evidence of a transgression or a warning; but they didn't collapse in remorse or self-blame. They took it as a call to reflect on the situation and correct what needed to be corrected. They might ask themselves whether there had been a violation of right relationship and, if so, what needed to be done to rectify the situation. This kind of reflection would move them from confused victim to someone willing to take responsibility for upholding his or her end of the relationship. We will return to this idea of the bite as feedback shortly when we look at "big biter," a fly believed by some tribes to be a guardian of fish.

Still another way to look at being bitten or stung is to view it as part of a larger process. We can't assume that if we just act right, we will not be bitten—that is too simplistic. Our conscious intention and behavior are only part of the equation—and not always the final determinant of an encounter with another species. To think otherwise is to indulge in a type of wishful thinking that many popular self-help programs propagate. In this view, if you are not prosperous, healthy, and happy (and free of mosquito bites), you have done something wrong. But ignoring or denying pain and death does not make them go away. And growth does not occur in comfort. Carl Jung was known to remind his clients and students that "there is no birth of consciousness without pain."

Given the limitations of the three contexts through which we typically interpret being bitten, it is fairly obvious that we need a new one. The first two views of other creatures as malevolent or robotic simply impede understanding and cooperation between our species and others and prevent goodwill. Even the third context, which is a big step away from overt abuse of other species, still leaves us feeling victimized, our willingness to coexist peacefully negated by the bite—or so it feels. A new context must emerge from our understanding of the interdependence of all species that includes a recognition and acceptance that we are food for some other species, and that some pain and discomfort is a necessary part of living. It must also come out of an evolving maturity and psychological sophistication that help us acknowledge the elusive forces that move into our lives and push us to grow (a topic that we will return to in the chapter "The Language of the Sting").

Other Views

Saint Rose of Lima, a seventeenth-century Peruvian recluse, chose mosquitoes as her favorite animals and enjoyed having them "sing" to her while she prayed. The Buddha suggested that if we realize that all living beings have been our mother in a previous life, we will be more likely to generate love and compassion toward them. So if a hungry mosquito comes for us, we are advised to consider the kin relationship and act accordingly.

In accord with this perspective is an anecdote about bedbugs (another blood-loving, biting species) from a letter written to the editor of the *Pakistan Times* in 1985. The irate writer had been a passenger on an express train during which he was bitten by bedbugs that had infested the train:

On being tortured by the bug's bite, I started killing the insects. A shrewd passenger said to me, "Why are you killing these bugs?" I retorted: "They have sucked my blood." The man said, "Well, human blood is an object of love for these bugs and they are thus, our kids." I was constrained to deduce that this very idea is, perhaps, preventing the Railway authorities from taking any remedial measure to eliminate the bug menace.[1]

We are apt to agree with the exasperated letter writer. Viewing the hum of mosquitoes as song or thinking of them as our mothers from a previous life and bedbugs as our offspring are not acceptable points of view today. We don't trust the compassionate view, perhaps thinking that insects will take advantage of us if we give them any latitude at all.

Native Views   When we look at how indigenous people understood and dealt with being bitten, we uncover a more compassionate view. In many native stories, for instance, mosquitoes originally helped humans, but when the people forgot their responsibility to assist other species and use the earth's resources in a balanced way, mosquitoes were given the ability to bite us to remind us of the imbalance.

In tribes like the Kwakiutl of British Columbia, creatures like the bee, wasp, midge, mosquito, and gnat played a role in creation, and the Kwakiutl carved wooden masks and engaged in ceremonies to invoke the spirit of each insect.

To be bitten or stung by your ancestral kin was viewed as a transmission of power, a warning, or a call to action. Thus pain didn't prompt a counterassault, nor was it treated as a random act or as a judgment. It served to alert the person and initiate a thoughtful reflective process.

Stories like the "Old Woman Who Was Kind to Insects," shared in the first chapter, emphasize our kinship with biting creatures and the rewards of treating them with compassion. A Miwok story tells how the biting talents of a local fly species were enlisted in times past. In the creation story of this California tribe, Fly helped the people defeat a cannibal giant by biting the giant all over his body while he slept—until Fly found his vulnerable spot and revealed it to the Miwok so they could set a trap for him. A story like this created good feelings. When someone from this tribe is bitten by a fly, the experience is tempered by the knowledge that the creature once saved the entire tribe.

Contrast this attitude with naturalist Steward Edward White's view of blood-loving black flies. In his 1903 book *The Forest*, he calls killing black flies a "heartlifting . . . unholy joy . . . [that] leaves the spirit ecstatic. . . . The satisfaction of murdering the beast that has had the nerve to light on you . . . almost counterbalances the pain. . . ."[2]

In his statement, White upholds the dominant viewpoint of the last three hundred years. The vindictiveness of this stance and the tinge of self-righteousness identify it as a reaction emerging from the belief in the world as a battlefield, and we saw the same kind of reaction in the Tabasco commercial and the recent *Discover* article.

Big Biter   To the Eastern Canadian Montagnais, the overlord of fish, particularly of salmon and cod, was a fly known as Big Biter. This species of fly would appear whenever fish were being taken from the water and hover over the fishermen to see how their subjects, the fish, were being treated. Occasionally, Big Biter would bite a fisherman to remind him that the fish were in his custody and to warn him against wastefulness.

Indigenous people were willing to be held accountable for their interactions with the natural world. It was a necessary component to survive and continue to receive the benefits of their plant and animal kin. Today, Big Biter is likely to be sprayed or swatted if it comes near fishermen. Our culture doesn't require accountability, unless it is economic accountability. As a result of overfishing, coho salmon was placed on the threatened species list in 1996. The legendary steelhead trout is also an endangered species because we have damaged the streams where this fish spawns.

If we were to adopt the native practice of holding ourselves accountable, it would help return accord to the web of relationships of which we are a part. For the Miwok and Montagnais tribes, biting flies were understood and accepted in a nonadversarial context. They would recoil at White's words and actions and consider his behavior and attitude a horrendous act of disrespect, punishable by having the fish avoid his hook. We scoff at those notions. We are too sophisticated to believe that the natural world can hold us accountable. Our science is too advanced. Yet the same science has finally evolved enough to verify that we are interdependent with all other life forms and that insects are the stream keepers, the messengers of the level of biotic integrity. We have also learned time and again that mistreatment of any part of the community will, in time, adversely affect us.

161

It doesn't really matter whether the current decline of salmon and other staple species like the sturgeon is related to our overwhelming disrespect toward the insect species that still may serve as guardians or the result of polluting the streams and overfishing. The tie to insects is an imaginative truth, a way of acknowledging our interdependence and the insect's role of messenger. Letting them prompt us into self-reflection, we might become our own critics, evaluating and righting our relationships to the finned creatures before our disregard results in further imbalances and the demise of still other species.

Our conditional reverence for life continues to hurt us. And the Endangered Species Act upholds our ecocentric view of who is valuable and who is not, allowing companies and individuals to eliminate pieces of the natural world that compete with us for our food and for our blood. It is not surprising to find that among those condemned are mosquitoes.

The War against the Mosquito

Mosquitoes are on the receiving end of our hostilities—most of it, if not all, never questioned. Over one thousand agencies in North America spend more than $150 million each year on mosquito controls, including the use of pesticides that harm mosquitoes' natural predators and other nontarget species. Thousands of acres of swamps, drained and filled in the name of mosquito control, sentence the creatures that live in the water, like dragonfly larvae, to death along with those that depend on mosquitoes for sustenance.

In the past, the mosquito control effort in the United States was not initiated to curb the kind of mosquitoes that carry malaria or other insect-transmitted diseases—a topic to be discussed in a later section. We allowed regulatory agencies to poison our streams and wetlands because we feared being bitten.

We also target them because they impede what has been called progress. It's a viewpoint that we teach to each generation. The author of a juvenile book on these creatures, for instance, presents the cultural view:

> Mosquito bites alone are reason enough for constant war on
> these pesky insects. Great swarms of them have delayed
> agricultural or industrial developments until the swamps and

bogs where they were breeding were drained. Areas that would otherwise make ideal vacation spots have been abandoned or left underdeveloped just because of the mosquitoes' itching bites. . . .[3]

The assumptions that human-centered plans have supremacy above all else and that to be bitten is an outrage that justifies war are behind this narrow line of thinking. Anything that interferes with human activities is dismissed as an irritant, a pest, and an obstacle to be eliminated.

Justifying the War

Each year the war against the mosquito is justified in newspaper and magazine articles, whose propaganda-like strategies warn us of the potential danger of a burgeoning population of mosquitoes. After arousing us with sensational headlines and copy, they assure us that vector control agents have everything under control and our best interests at heart. And we believe them.

Ironically, the primary source of large numbers of biting mosquitoes (at least in California, and no doubt elsewhere) has not been addressed publicly. Entomologist Richard Garcia points out that agricultural practices have created most of the mosquito breeding sites. For example, the 600,000 acres of rice fields in California are the source of two or three species of biting mosquitoes considered pests. In these fields where hybrid crop plants require intensive irrigation, the water doesn't drain off but collects in small pools. The pools aren't permanent enough to support aquatic predators, but they can and do breed tremendous numbers of mosquitoes.

Florida's Mosquito Control Program   California's news reports on mosquitoes are not so different from those in other states where mosquitoes thrive. A Florida newspaper warns its readers that with the advent of rain, mosquitoes are thriving and "almost as big as alligators and ten times as ferocious." Maybe these kinds of descriptions are why Florida residents allow authorities to spray 222,000 to 333,600 pounds of fenthion—a pesticide similar to DDT and banned in most states— over two million acres each year. Environmental groups including the American Bird Conservancy and Defenders of Wildlife cite this chemical as the reason thousands of migratory birds were dropping dead in Florida in late 2000 and have recently filed a notice of intent to pursue litigation with the EPA to stop the spraying.

At the Florida Mosquito Control center, scientists are exploring solutions other than pesticides. They have finally learned that insecticides can't be sprayed in sensitive environments like the Everglades where most of the mosquitoes breed, because the chemicals kill too many beneficial insects. What authorities still seem unable to grasp is that mosquitoes are essential for the health and continuance of the Everglades. They are food for the fish of the Everglades, which in turn feed the alligators, whose activities keep channels through the marshes open. Without mosquitoes the Everglades would grow over.

One strategy gaining acceptance involves importing giant mosquitoes ten times the size of the local variety. Researchers released a test group of these insects in an area close to Miami, expecting them to eat several species of freshwater mosquitoes. It didn't work. The big mosquitoes have no appetite for the mosquitoes that inhabit the region. What they do like to eat and how that will impact other species are not known.

Other Strategies Mosquito control agencies have also turned to the mosquitofish, a minnow that feeds on mosquito larvae, as an alternative to pesticides. It sounds like a great solution, yet in an early trial in Hawaii, it ate not only mosquito larvae but harmless insect larvae and the young of commercial and game fish. In India an experiment using mosquitofish to control mosquitoes also failed when this predator consumed the local fish that also consumed millions of mosquito larvae. And the history of its use shows that where predatory fish or birds are scarce, the mosquitofish overpopulates new habitats.

Another strategy currently in the news is euphemistically called a "diet pill" for mosquitoes. It is a formula that alters the mosquito's digestion so that it can't feed. When the concoction is placed in water where mosquitoes breed, the larvae eat it, starving to death within seventy-two hours. Again the role of mosquitoes in the food chain is ignored, dimmed by the clamor of the public for elimination of whatever might cause them discomfort.

The Price of Fear Today the fear of being bitten is augmented by our fear of insect-transmitted diseases and bacteria in general. News of the rise of infectious diseases throughout the world and microorganisms resistant to our antibiotics keeps us agitated and battle-ready. So does the threat of biological warfare with viruses like anthrax. But making decisions out of fear has always proved to be dangerous. Consider the widespread use of antibacterial products that kill bacteria indiscriminately. Experts are warning us that this practice pushes benign forms of microbes into mutating. And since bacteria share a common gene pool, once any form has developed a resistance, all bacteria can use it to survive.

In 1999 outbreaks of the West Nile virus, a form of encephalitis virus spread by both birds and mosquitoes, generated fear at a level that exceeded the actual threat. In fact, according to mosquito authority Andrew Spielman, the risk of new infections in New York City was approaching zero (since mosquitoes head for shelter as daylight recedes in the fall) when the announcement was made that the West Nile virus was present in the city. Fear took over the city. Events were canceled and people slathered themselves with repellents. When a few mosquitoes carrying the virus were found in Central Park, foggers covered every acre of the park with insecticides. The drama was as intense as the hysteria over killer bees. New Yorkers put themselves in danger of chemical poisoning because they allowed fear to dictate a solution that only appeared to counter the threat.

Granted that West Nile virus can be fatal (although most infected people only experience flu symptoms for a few days), but we are "dead-end hosts." We can be infected, but our immune systems almost always prevent the virus from multiplying enough to be passed back to mosquitoes and then to other hosts.

Learning about Mosquitoes

We can't make educated decisions about mosquito control if we rely on those who make money from the control programs or others gripped by fear to tell us the facts of either the species or the situation. We need unbiased information, but this isn't a subject that people want to learn about. A few years ago when *Natural History* magazine devoted an issue to the mosquito, one outraged subscriber wrote to the editor and canceled his subscription, proclaiming hotly that the issue was an absolute waste of effort and of no interest to anyone.

By learning something about mosquitoes, however, we leave the black-and-white opinions of the culture and restore a desperately needed complexity to the relationship between us and these species. Facts can also feed the nonhostile imagination and help us relate to mosquitoes with empathy and compassion.

To start with, let us consider the good. Like other flies, mosquitoes are pollinators. In fact, in the Arctic, bog orchids depend exclusively on mosquitoes for pollination. Mosquito researcher Lewis Nielsen believes mosquitoes are more important as pollinators of wildflowers than anyone has previously realized. He has identified pollen grains from more than thirty species of flowering plants on their bodies. If you consider that each plant species supports ten to thirty animal species, eliminating the insect that pollinates it not only destroys the plant, it destroys all the other insects who depend on the plant and who may be parasites of still other insects. The web is intricate.

Mosquitoes begin life in eggs floating on the surface of water. After the egg stage, they live as "wrigglers," feeding many other species like dragonflies, fish, warblers, swallows, and bats. Many trap bacteria in stagnant water, and some catch and kill other mosquitoes.

In a week to ten days, the mosquito wriggler becomes a pupa. Looking like a tadpole with a jointed tail, the pupa tumbles through the water for a few more days before turning into an adult. Biologist Ronald Rood likens the metamorphosis from tumbler to adult to the transformation of a jeep into a jet plane in two days while driving the jeep at sixty miles an hour. In short, it's an astonishing feat worthy of admiration.

Although we always associate mosquitoes with their blood-sucking habits, plant sugar is their main food for flight and survival. And many exist only on fruit juices, nectar, and tree sap.

Wraparound, compound eyes let mosquitoes see in almost all directions at once, and tiny ears found at the base of their antennae provide them with good hearing. They are guided to us even on the darkest of nights by a sophisticated sensory system that lets them detect the carbon dioxide that we exhale. We know they are near when we hear their hum—a sound caused by wings whirling at an amazing six hundred beats per second.

Mosquitoes also locate us by the chemicals our skin exudes, and those chemicals are affected by our diet. One substance that attracts them is octenol, which was first detected in the breath of oxen and was later found to be produced by grass fermenting in the stomachs of these mammals. One theory says that an individual who eats a lot of greens produces excess octenol, which in turn attracts mosquitoes to them. If this is true, greens-lovers might counter their attractiveness by eating garlic—a strategy that has worked for the natives of Tanzania. Recent studies also confirm that garlic, which is exuded in sweat, repels malaria-carrying mosquitoes in particular (although other species are not necessarily repelled by it).

Mosquitoes are particular about where they bite a host. Some species like feet and ankles, while others prefer our heads and shoulders. The ones that like feet favor smelly feet and locate their feeding site by tracking foot aromas. Those smells are in turn linked to odor-producing bacteria (the same bacteria that give strong cheese its flavor).

The Female Mosquito

In most mosquito species, blood is needed to produce eggs (although what it is about the blood specifically that mosquitoes need is still a mystery). Without it, though, egg production goes from one hundred eggs to fewer than ten. If we imagine ourselves a female mosquito, then, we might appreciate that the need for blood stems from an instinctual push to gather the resources to start a family and perpetuate the species.

In the interest of fairness and to help us throw off our victim stance in regard to being the blood bank for these creatures, it is important to accept our complicity in creating the current situation. Consider that the handful of species that has developed a preference for human blood has only done so in the last couple of hundred years as their natural hosts—other warm-blooded animals—have diminished. With the destruction of wildlife and the corresponding increase in the human population, we have become, of necessity, a primary host for some species. The mosquito has fewer and fewer options as we continue to wipe out much of its ancestral forest habitat and the animals that it once depended on for blood.

That said, if we could remember that the intent and behavior of any species, even when it is threatening or disconcerting to humans, arises out of its "worldview," we could tailor our responses accordingly. In those places where mosquitoes may carry the malarial parasite or West

Nile virus, we could then choose, without undue anger or vindictiveness, to eat garlic, use netting, and otherwise prevent a mosquito from feeding on us. And in our own neighborhoods we could share our blood with an occasional mosquito or two without feeling victimized or angry—or, if surrounded by many of them, use a topical treatment or extra clothing to dissuade them.

A primary long-term survival strategy to reduce the risk of getting an infectious disease is to preserve biodiversity. New studies indicate that the roots of disease lie in disrupted interactions between other species and land changes wrought by human beings. In fact, vector blood-needing creatures like the mosquito and the tick thrive best in disturbed environments. So to protect ourselves, we need only keep Nature's rich ecosystems intact and healthy. The incidence of tick-transmitted Lyme disease, for instance, drops dramatically in areas with a greater diversity of small mammals. And in the West, a lizard that ticks feed on actually neutralizes the Lyme microbe and renders it harmless. It seems that the interactions between other species buffer us from diseases in ways we have only begun to explore.

The Malarial Parasite

We haven't protected biodiversity. We haven't realized its importance or the need to temper our ambitions and move beyond the desire to control and master our environment. One consequence of our ignorance and misplaced superiority is that malaria is on the rise. Our schemes to eradicate the malarial parasite and its carrier, one species of mosquito, have failed. In fact, overall, despite advances in biotechnology, the health of tropical people has gotten worse in the past twenty years, and in many places malaria is more prevalent, less treatable, and less controllable than it was thirty years ago because of intensive spraying with DDT and overuse and improper use of antimalarial drugs. And worse, before our chemical intervention, many adults in tropical regions were clinically immune to malaria. Today they have lost that hard-earned protection and are frequent victims of malaria's intermittent fever. The threat to young children from acute, life-threatening malaria has also grown because of the recent appearance of drug-resistant strains.

In 1972, the World Health Organization (WHO) formally declared the war to eradicate the mosquito a failure, and many involved feel a sense of defeat. An entomologist employed by WHO and author of a recent book on the mosquito believes that DDT itself was not the problem, but merely its overuse. He advises that it still be used on a limited basis, a regressive move and a disturbing recommendation considering the long-term damage that this chemical has already inflicted on other species and the environment.

A small minority realize that defeat can be instructive. Political historian Gordon Harrison suggests that such widespread and pronounced failure is trying to tell us something—either "we have proved ourselves incompetent warriors [or] . . . we have misconstrued the problem."[4]

The Bid for Land and Supremacy

The facts indicate that we have misconstrued the problem. If we look at the history of the first all-out war against another species—the mosquito—we encounter not a humanitarian crusade, as some propagandists would have us believe, but a chain of events motivated by greed and riddled with widespread corruption.

The war against the mosquito begins at the peak of colonialism. Historians of this period report that its roots are grounded not in an altruistic concern for the well-being of tribal people but in racism and a common desire among colonists to dominate land and people. The colonists viewed every land conquered as empty (of people with value), and so they didn't feel a need to respect anyone's rights—human or mosquito.

Equatorial Africa resisted settlement by the white colonists, as did tropical Asia and Central and South America. Heat and diseases like malaria took their toll on the foreigners. The number of colonist victims was so high that many believed that the hostile and "savage possessors"[5] of the tropics—that is, the native people of those lands—had put a spell or curse on them.

This belief that Caucasians had somehow been bewitched was supported by the observation that native people seemed immune to malaria. In 1870, an Italian doctor speculated that these "inferior races"[6] shared the immunity to malaria of the lower animals. The apparent immunity of indigenous people then was used as evidence of the hierarchy of species and races, in which the colonists believed the Caucasians were first and would be master over all others.

Although the self-deceptions and theories about the cause of malaria continued until the malarial parasite and its carrier, the mosquito, were identified, the threat to colonialism from malaria was the primary motivation for scientists at that time to focus on the disease and then try to eliminate the mosquito. Concern centered on keeping tropic-based administrative, military, and economic rulers alive and healthy. Concern for the native population was limited to maintaining a healthy work force for commercial enterprises.

Battling the Mosquito and Malaria   World War II renewed the motivation to eradicate the mosquito and find a malaria vaccine because the military needed protection from malaria. When DDT was developed in the 1940s, it looked like a gift from the gods. We now know that it was not.

The failure of DDT to eliminate the mosquito shifted the focus from prevention to treatment. People once again turned to chloroquine—although today, due to its overuse, it is no longer effective against many new resistant strains of malaria. A two-thousand-year-old antimalarial drug called *qinghaosu* (artemisinin) has also been found to cure certain deadly strains of malaria in humans more rapidly and with less toxicity than chloroquine. It has even been effective against chloroquine-resistant strains. Now chemically analyzed, it could be synthesized for large-scale production, and it may be shortly, now that global warming has expanded the malarial parasite's territory and international travel has brought the likelihood of contracting malaria closer to those in a position to fund this kind of research.

Susceptibility and Malaria

Some people are immune to some strains of malaria because of an abnormality of hemoglobin (the "working" constituent of red blood cells). What the colonists interpreted as an immunity to malaria based on racial inferiority was actually strain-specific, naturally acquired immunities, all of which involve genetic modifications that make the red cells less appetizing to the parasite.[7]

Besides naturally acquired immunities to particular malaria strains, susceptibility is the single most critical factor as to whether a person gets sick or not. Susceptibility factors also determine why one mosquito succumbs to the malarial parasite and another does not.

Few people appreciate the fact that a mosquito carrying the malarial parasite may suffer as much as the person or creature she bites. When a mosquito takes in a blood meal containing the malarial parasite, the microscopic invader penetrates the insect's stomach. Once in the mosquito's stomach, the parasite multiplies, forming cysts on the stomach wall. Sometimes it even kills its mosquito host at this stage. If the mosquito survives, the cysts break and release hundreds of new parasites. Some of these make their way to the salivary glands, where they are transmitted when the mosquito tries to get a blood meal. If this doesn't rouse your empathy for mosquitoes, at least let it be noted that mosquitoes are as much or more a victim of malaria as humans. We have that much in common.

As we saw with houseflies and disease, conventional Western medicine has fostered dangerous delusions about cause-and-effect relationships between diseases and agents of disease. We are taught, for example, that the malarial parasite is an agent of disease and therefore the cause of the set of symptoms known as malaria. But when the malarial parasite is injected by a mosquito into the blood of a susceptible person, the key word in the equation is not mosquito or malarial parasite; it is susceptible. Not everyone exposed to the parasite gets sick with malaria. In some individuals, the illness fails to develop, either because it is checked by the immune system or for reasons yet unknown. As discussed in the fly chapter, an increasing number of people in health-related fields believe natural fluctuations in our state of health (or balance) may allow an agent of disease to find fertile ground in which to develop, or not.

New Battle Strategies

Although we claim to have renounced the war against the mosquito and settled for control, our war mentality keeps us ever on the lookout for weapons. U.S. scientists discovered a bacterium in the Negev Desert in 1976, for instance, that is now sprayed over vast areas in Africa, Asia, and South America to kill malaria-bearing mosquitoes. Although this discovery was lauded as a humanitarian milestone, it is just a matter of time as to when the mosquito or the parasite will mutate to survive the attack or whether the bacteria will take advantage of its new territory and harm other species as well.

A recent undertaking involves turning the fruit fly, the first insect to have its DNA mapped, into a carrier for the malarial parasite so that researchers can look for a weakness in the parasite's genetic armor. And altering the mosquito genetically so that it cannot inject the malarial parasite into a person or so that it is resistant to the parasite offers two other lines of research. How the malarial parasite or mosquito will adapt to such manipulations has not been explored, and those concerns get buried or dismissed in the overwhelming enthusiasm that greets the announcement of this kind of research.

Still another solution, a personal favorite, involves administering a "benevolent vaccine" to people that will not prevent them from getting malaria but will help keep them from transmitting it back to a mosquito taking a blood meal. It works this way: When a mosquito takes a blood meal from a person with malaria who has been vaccinated, the insect will not only take in the infected blood, but she will take in the antibodies that will protect her from becoming infected. This in turn, it is reasoned, will prevent small malaria outbreaks from reaching epidemic proportions.

Although this vaccine research is not motivated by concern for the well-being of mosquitoes—quite the contrary, as those involved were quick to reassure the public—one wonders, if our objective had been to keep the mosquito from harm, as well as protect people from malaria's deadliest strains, would a solution have been forthcoming? Even more radical would be an all-inclusive reverence that would honor the balance among mosquito, parasite, and human beings, working on behalf of all three to maintain a balance where all thrive and none lives at the expense of another.

Ending the War

The relationship between mosquitoes and certain parasites is a fairly stable one. Successful parasitism is based on both sides keeping the other in check. Ecologically, the human-mosquito-parasite relationship is also a stable and balanced system we have tried to eliminate, and can't.

Evolutionary medicine proponent Marc Lappé argues that part of our inability to find appropriate strategies for the treatment of malaria has to do with the pervasive belief that we are somehow apart from the forces of evolution. But we are not. "Diseases do not arise fully armed to strike unsuspecting hosts," Lappé reminds us. "Patterns of disease and illness have millennial roots." Modern medicine has not understood the complex interplay of disease, human and microbial coevolution, and modern therapeutics. We can no longer define progress and civilization as conquests over Nature's diseases. Progress can come only when we understand and cooperate with the forces of Nature, realizing that both we and mosquitoes are molded by the same forces.

This new perspective on disease results in radically different treatment approaches. Sometimes a "cure" may mean yielding control measures altogether and focusing on strengthening innate resistance. In large populations, the best prevention is to stop the transmission of deadly forms. As noted before, lethal parasites will evolve to milder forms if they cannot spread easily from host to host. They must, or risk dying out quickly. This finding, translated in terms of the mosquito and the malarial parasite (or any microbe that it unwittingly carries), simply means that we can help the parasite evolve into a milder strain by making sure that mosquitoes don't get to people who have malaria—using netting, isolation, or any other practical method.

Protectors of Habitat

In *The Fruitful Darkness*, Joan Halifax proposes that certain creatures and plants are protectors of place, allies to their habitats. In this view, the mosquito and other biting insects are animal guardians of the planet's rich resources.

We have been destroying the protectors of the wild regions for a long time, justifying our actions and insisting that we are only defending ourselves from harm. Intimidated and perhaps outraged by their power to hurt us, we have made such species the enemy and tried to destroy them, eliminating whoever or whatever requires us to change our ways. And whenever we have been successful, we have lost the integrity of the ecologies these protectors guarded on behalf of all species.

Mosquitoes and other blood-sucking insects have been viewed by some as heroes of the ecology because for decades they made tropical rainforests almost uninhabitable for human beings, delaying the great destruction of these forests that are home to an abundance of wildlife.

The tsetse fly is one such protector. This creature, which needs blood to lay eggs and sometimes carries a parasite that results in African sleeping sickness (to which cattle, horses, and donkeys are particularly susceptible but wild animals are not), stopped the settlement of Botswana's lush Okavango Delta for years. A paradise for wildlife, the central swamp of the Delta is the tsetse fly's kingdom. Attempts to eradicate these flies are fueled by the desire to open the central wilderness area to the cattle industry—a questionable objective. Making the Delta safe for cattle and humans would allow towns to get the water they need to thrive, but it would destroy wildlife habitats in the process. And in certain areas where this protector of wildlife has been wiped out, that is exactly what has happened.

The Myth of Progress

Most of us don't consider biting insects to be guardians of habitats. We assume that we have a right of access to the entire planet, that no place by right of its own nature is off limits to humans (including native and nonindustrial societies). If an area resists human settlement and our technologies, it becomes even more desirable because it challenges our sense of superiority and dominance. Attempts to conquer and subdue wild places are framed in heroic terms. When environmentalists suggest that humans respect the integrity of inhospitable lands, the idea is met with anger. The suggestion questions some deeply held beliefs about our status on Earth and who has rights of access to the planet.

Those beliefs, that misplaced superiority, must go if we are to work undivided and with renewed focus on restoring disrupted habitats and thereby reducing the risk of infectious disease. The task of educating those who still believe that their best interests are served by unchecked development falls to people who understand how intact environments buffer us from disease.

The Queen Mosquito

Whoever knows and loves the land tends to live in harmony with its cycles, respecting and accepting the protectors of place with a give-and-take attitude that acknowledges the right of every species to live on Earth, and the right of certain insects to occupy and even dominate the woods during certain seasons.

Indigenous tribes like the Sandy Lake Cree of Ontario, Canada, acknowledged ties to local creatures like the mosquito. It was a practical way to promote harmonious coexistence with the ones who inhabited the same territory. One of their stories that supports coexistence with mosquitoes is the tale of a Cree warrior called Mama-gee-sic who is forever down on his luck. One day he goes into the forest and is beset by hungry mosquitoes. Unable to protect himself, he finally submits, removing his shirt and lying down, prepared to die, as the swarm covers his body. When he is close to death, he hears a loud humming voice telling the other mosquitoes to leave him alone, that he has had more than enough trouble in his life. Hearing this, all the mosquitoes fly away. When Mama-gee-sic opens his eyes, he sees a huge mosquito hovering over him. The insect descends, touching him gently with her wings. An amazed Mama-gee-sic finds his wounds healed instantly and his strength returned. And from that day forward he is successful in his endeavors because the Queen mosquito had become his protector. The storyteller ends the tale by explaining to the children that the Queen mosquito has befriended the tribe and never harms them. And so of course they must respect and honor the mosquito.

We could use a Queen mosquito heroine, a protector of place that prevents us from disrupting the balance between species in an ecosystem. And if we could allow mosquitoes guardianship of our remaining wild places without resentment, we too might realize uncommon success in stopping the rise of infectious disease. It depends in large part on whether we can protect ourselves from deadly viruses without resorting to enemy-making and fear-driven eradication strategies.

As far as coexistence is concerned, in areas where the chances of getting malaria (or other mosquito-transmitted diseases) are great, it would behoove us to take protective measures to avoid being bitten and to keep mosquitoes away from people who have already contracted the disease. We could also step up our efforts to reintroduce wildlife back into our environments so that mosquitoes have more choices. And in the West, where the chances of mosquitoes carrying the malarial parasite are still slim, we might accept that we are food for some species and find practical strategies to balance their need against our ease. We might, for instance, decide to avoid areas at times when black flies or mosquitoes are abundant or use a topical solution to dissuade them when we are unable to leave the area—both effective strategies. For the more adventuresome individual, communicating with mosquitoes might also be an option.

Communicating with Mosquitoes

Most communications with mosquitoes are triggered by a desire to stop them from feeding on us. In Jim Nollman's book *Dolphin Dreamtime*, he introduces us to Nicholas, an old man, half Native American. Long after mosquitoes would drive his family and friends indoors, he could stay outside and the mosquitoes wouldn't bother him. When questioned, he held out his arm in front of Nollman's face and clenched his fist three times, explaining that this got the blood to flow through the body in a certain controlled way. "The mosquitoes," he said, "they know the language of the blood better than anyone else. I've spent forty years here, so I've had a lot of time to learn that language too. Now I know how to tell the mosquitoes to stay away."

Rolling Thunder had another, more benign method. He teaches that the emotions that produce good feelings are vibrations with a smell to them that in turn repels mosquitoes. Those vibrations may be what the New Age community has latched onto as the ideal stance in dealing with mosquitoes. They may also be similar to the vibrations produced by the young Brazilian man we met in the chapter on bees when he communicates with insects. Such accounts certainly warrant further investigation and experimentation. But there is still another alternative—sharing our blood.

Feeding a Mosquito After my first speaking engagement on the insect-human connection in 1991, I fielded questions from the conference audience. A young man asked what I thought he should do about being bitten by mosquitoes. I suggested applying a topical solution to discourage them if there were many and if he couldn't avoid being in the area. But if there was only one, I added, he might consider feeding it. Then I told him what had occurred to me a few days before the conference.

I was home alone working at my desk when I heard the familiar sound of a mosquito around me. I looked up and saw the tiny creature flying in front of me. I knew she needed blood to start a family, and given my focus and intention to speak on behalf of insects, I thought I should offer my arm. So I extended my bare arm, and she promptly lit on it. Within a few seconds the incessant itching began, and I blew gently on her until she flew off my arm. Sheepishly, I offered my apologies, explaining how hard it was to be still because it itched so terribly. Then I asked her to try again while I braced my arm and willed myself to stay still, offering my arm once again. This time she landed on my palm and stayed there. I didn't feel anything so I brought my hand up close to my face to see if she was just resting. But I saw her body full with my blood and her proboscis (used for bloodsucking) still penetrating my skin. Still I felt nothing.

It didn't make sense. I knew from my reading that the properties of a mosquito's saliva affect how fast it can tap and take up blood. The speed is correlated with its antigenic activity. In other words, when the intake is slow, there is a compensatory delay in what the host feels—it gives the mosquito time to complete the act before alerting the host and putting itself in danger.

But in this case, the mosquito's first attempt to feed on me (the host) triggered major itching right away and the second attempt nothing. It couldn't be related to the properties of her saliva. And the discomfort wasn't just delayed, as I didn't feel any sensation at the moment or later. It was as though she had purposively, mysteriously, fed this way in deference to me. I recognized the gift and gave thanks.

When I finished the story, the young man thanked me. The next day he pulled me aside, excitement written on his face. He had sat outside after dinner the night before, and a mosquito had come humming around him. Remembering my story, he had extended his arm, offering her the blood meal that she sought. She had descended on his arm and taken her fill without causing him any discomfort then or later. He was filled with the wonder that always arises when we encounter the mystery of our interconnection. The experience brought up new questions about his relationship to this kingdom. Like the Cree warrior who was befriended by the Queen mosquito, perhaps this young man had found his affinity and entered the territory of rejoicing in mosquitoes.

The life-serving forces of growth move toward us in many disguises, asking us for our best. Emmanuel, a wise and loving being channeled by Pat Rodegast, says that animals are one of the most compelling packages of Love on this planet; and that "sometimes, believe it or not, Love is a mosquito, alighting upon your hand and asking you for generosity."

When we position ourselves in accord with the other inhabitants on this Earth, when we view the world through another creature's eyes and understand their motivation, we can move in compassionate response to that awareness. Doing so, we open ourselves up to the powers that support this planet and to the unexpected response of a gracious mosquito, realizing that the world, at heart, is more benevolent and friendlier than we have perhaps recently supposed. Give thanks.

11. Spinners of Fate

Man did not weave the web of life, he is merely a strand in it. Whatever he does to the web, he does to himself.

—*Chief Seattle*

In the memoir *Life and Death in Shanghai*, Nien Cheng, a former political prisoner in Communist China, tells of her six-and-a-half-year imprisonment. Isolated as she was in a small cell, her worry and depression concerning the fate of herself and her daughter threatened to erode her resolve to stay strong and confident. One day she saw a pea-sized spider climbing on one of the window bars. When it reached the top, the small spider descended on a silken thread and with a leap and a swing outward secured the end of the thread to another bar. Once the anchor threads were in place, the spider proceeded to weave an intricately beautiful web.

The spider's confidence and obvious mastery of web weaving filled Cheng with questions about this creature that she couldn't answer. The only thing she knew for sure was that she had just witnessed something extraordinarily beautiful and uplifting. She thanked God, feeling her hope and confidence renewed. She realized that God was in control and not the menacing Mao Zedong and his revolutionaries.

Sometimes adverse circumstances provide a background for attending to an event not ordinarily noticed, and insight and revelation follow, making the moment memorable.

And sometimes the spider does something unusual that captures our attention. For example, in his memoirs, the composer André Grétry described a spider that would descend from a single thread and hang suspended above his harpsichord when he sat down to play. Grétry rather liked the attention and took it as a sign that the spider had exceptional taste in music.

There are points of kinship between us and spiders that only observation and intuition can reveal. In *The Spell of the Sensuous*, magician David Abram describes how spiders and insects were his introduction to the spirits while traveling in Indonesia. From them he first learned of the intelligence within the nature of nonhumans, the correspondences between their form of awareness and his own, and their ability to "instill a reverberation in oneself" that moved him past his usual ways of seeing and feeling and opened him to an awake and alive world.

As he sat one day watching a spider climbing a thin thread that was stretched across the opening of a cave, he saw how it constructed each knot of silk in the web, and he marveled at its skill and surety. Out of the corner of his eye, his vision then caught another thread from another web and on a different plane than the first web. It was complete, with its own center and its own weaver. Although the two spiders spun independently of each other, to Abram's eyes they wove a single pattern with intersecting threads. Then he realized that there were many webs being constructed, all radiating out from different centers— patterns upon patterns. He felt as though he were watching the universe being born, one galaxy at a time.

Abram tapped into a way of perceiving that is common to indigenous people. The Hopi tribes of North America have a legend of a Spider Man whose web connected Heaven and Earth. And the revered gray spider of the Pima Indians of southern Arizona was said to have spun a web around the unconnected edges of both Earth and sky to help the Earth grow firm and solid.

In the cosmology of Vedanta, the mystical philosophy of ancient India, the spider is likened to Brahman (God in the absolute state) because just as it spins its web out of its own body yet remains independent of it, so does the self-existent Brahman create the world out of Itself, yet remains unchanged. And at the end of a world cycle, the Absolute draws the universe back into Itself, just as the spider draws its threads back into its body.

Other people of a philosophical or religious orientation who have watched spiders constructing their webs also report feeling they were witnessing the act of creation—the microcosm revealing the macrocosm. Spiritual teacher Omraam Mikhael Aivanhov taught that we can learn from the spider how God created the world because its web is a mathematically perfect construction of the universe.

Spider Webs

Spider webs come in all sizes, shapes, and orientations. Tropical orb weavers work through the night using touch alone to create aerial webs sometimes an astonishing eighteen feet in circumference. The orb weaver begins by spinning a single "bridge thread." Perched on a twig or branch, it releases this silk thread from one of its spinnerets on the underside of its abdomen and lets the wind carry it away. It is an act of faith. When the bridge thread connects to a surface, usually a branch or tree trunk, the spider tightens the connection and then travels along the thread, reinforcing it with additional threads. Then the work of constructing the web begins in earnest.

Some spider silks reflect ultraviolet light, which is visible to insects. Since many flowers reflect ultraviolet light to attract pollinating insects, these reflective silk threads may be designed to mimic blossoms and fool unsuspecting insects.

Spiders whose webs do not reflect ultraviolet light often weave designs into their webs using a special thread that has reflective properties. Perhaps the design is an encoded message, an invitation to insects, for these decorated webs capture 58 percent more insects than do plain webs. Some indigenous tribes believed that the geometric patterns and angles in spider webs were evidence that spiders created the first alphabet, overseeing the art of language and writing.

The Art of Weaving

Although Abram acknowledged the role of genetic instructions enfolded in the skill set of a spider, he also noted the intelligent awareness that makes the spider receptive to its environment.

Web spinning is not a mechanical endeavor but an art that requires the spider's attention, resourcefulness, and ingenuity. The average garden spider constructs a web using three or four kinds of silk and up to 1,500 connecting points—in less than an hour. Even when spiders were sent into space by NASA to test the effect of zero gravity on web building, it took them a mere three days to spin a near-perfect web.

The symbolism of weaving and woven cloth has complex and ancient roots associated with the feminine principle and creation. The spider's connection with fate is also an ancient one. In the oldest myths, the spider is associated with the triune Great Goddess, as spinner, measurer, and cutter of the threads of life. Spider Woman and Grandmother Spider, both weavers of the fate of humans and animals, plants, and rocks, are portrayed with a wise and knowing nature and figure prominently in many mythologies. The Three Fates of Greek myth—Clotho, Lachesis, and Atropos—also control the fate of others by their weaving. Jungian analyst Clarissa Pinkola Estés says that these female deities embody the essence of the wild instinctual self. They are the Life/Death/Life mothers, weaving in and carding out who lives and who dies.

The belief that fate could enter and influence one's life is one of the reasons the intelligent and cunning spider had a duel role in many mythologies—both helpful and deadly. The web of protection, for instance, under certain circumstances could be viewed as a spinning illusion, a web of entrapment, or a poisonous plot.

The most famous myth about spiders and weaving is that of Athene and Arachne. In pre-Hellenic myths, the goddess Athene, also a spinner of fate, could incarnate as a spider, and when she did she was called Arachne. But the myth that most of us are familiar with is a reinterpretation of the Athene/Arachne unity by later Hellenic mythographers. This later version portrays a mortal woman Arachne as Athene's rival in the weaving arts. In a contest, when an impertinent Arachne demonstrates a weaving skill that surpasses the skill of the goddess, Athene is enraged and starts hitting her and tearing her tapestry apart. Arachne flees to the woods, where she tries to commit suicide. Athene takes pity on her and grants her a new life as a spider fated to spin and weave forever. This popular interpretation of the myth has undertones at odds with the helpful holy images of Grandmother Spider in indigenous tribes. The original Greek myth may have been changed over the course of time to undermine the spider's (and women's) creative power, for in this version the spider form is given as a sentence, and the act of weaving (creating) thus becomes the compulsory labor of an indentured creature.

Since all acts of creation are the spider's domain, spinning and weaving also have associations to fertility and sexuality. For a woman to create a child, for example, she must bring together all the different elements—chemical, biological, and psychological—and weave them into a single unit. The umbilical cord that nourishes the growing child while the mother "weaves" it into the world is like the spider's "thread of life" that emanates from its body.

This strong connection to the feminine principle and to the power of creating life is a primary reason that the spider was demonized in the male-dominated Judeo-Christian religious tradition, according to the *Bestiary of Christ* by Louis Charbonneau-Lassay. Regarded as an image of Satan, the spider was thought to ensnare men's souls through the seductive wiles of prostitutes. And the spider's ambushing techniques were considered treacherous and Judas-like.

In contrast, Buddhists, who saw the spider as the weaver of the web of illusion and a creator, taught that just as a spider catches flies in its web, so must a seeker of enlightenment capture and destroy the attachment to the illusory world of the senses. Also in contrast to the demonic image are the holy spider figures in countless aboriginal cultures.

The Medicine of Patience   Since weaving requires great industry and patience, Navajo people rubbed spider webs on a baby girl's hands and arms so that when she grew up she could weave without tiring.

In an Osage myth, a spider offers its medicine of patience to a warrior who ventures into the wilderness to find an animal totem. Thinking he knows best which animal to choose, he only tracks large animals, ignoring signs of other ones. One day, with his eyes focused downward on deer tracks, he stumbles into a spider web. A large spider, now at eye level, offers to be a totem for his clan, bringing it the great virtue of patience. "All things come to me," the spider said proudly. "If your people learn this, they will be strong indeed." The warrior, recognizing the wisdom in the spider's words, returns to his village to make the spider the totem of his clan.

A spider taught patience and persistence to Robert Bruce, the fourteenth-century Scottish hero-king. While Bruce was hiding from the English, he watched a spider trying to weave its web across a portion of the ceiling. The spider tried six times but failed each time. Then, as the creature began its seventh try, Bruce watched intensely, knowing intuitively that he was about to see whether or not another attempt to defeat the English army would be in vain. When the spider succeeded on that seventh try, an inspired Robert saw its success as a fortuitous sign. He renewed his campaign and, against all odds, finally freed Scotland from England.

The Intelligent Spider

Native peoples accepted the intelligent awareness of spiders and saw in it a wise knowing of matters beyond human senses, and so they sought the spider's favor and guidance. In the Cheyenne and Arapaho societies, for example, the word for spider actually conveys the idea of intelligence. Even today these tribes hold spiders in high esteem and pray for its intelligent perspective. The spider's wise nature is also the reason that in Pueblo myths the creatrix Spider Woman is sometimes called "Thinking Woman," and the world is considered her brainchild

Today, when people sense that the spider is aware and intelligent, it frightens them, for they pair it with a malevolent intention. It is the most common explanation given to explain a dislike of spiders. In the 1998 science fiction movie *Starship Troopers*, enormous, alien spiderlike creatures with swordlike legs join forces with other giant extraterrestrial insects to annihilate the human race. When the creatures are discovered to be under the direction of a single bug (a jellyfishlike blob of a creature with a tarantulalike face), the fact that it is intelligent is an idea almost too horrifying for the humans to entertain. And when they finally capture it and subject it to sadistic and invasive procedures in a laboratory, the movie audience applauds.

A personal experience, albeit unbidden, can move one beyond the shadowed fears of the culture. Mail carrier and writer Paula Cardran looks at spiders differently now than a few years ago when she sat down on a wooden bridge over a brook near her house. She noticed a long-legged spider sitting quietly on her knee and brushed it off without thinking. Then she had a twinge of guilt and looked around to make sure she hadn't hurt it. She saw it walking over a leaf and up her foot to her leg and back to her left knee where it had been before. It seemed to face Cardran for a moment before turning around toward the stream and crossing its two front legs over each other, as a dog might do. Cardran kept staring at the small creature, wondering if it had intentionally returned to her knee to view the river. "Then I realized the spider had consciousness," she said, "of itself, of me, and of the spatial relationship for getting from the ground, up for a real view." But did it enjoy the view, wondered Cardran, and could the webs that spiders make be the expression of an artistic soul? Cardran didn't have the answer to all her questions, but her perception of the spider had been permanently transformed.

"The act of seeing can transform the person who sees and cause us to see differently for the rest of our lives," says healer Rachel Naomi Remen. It is a phenomenon noted by mystic poets such as Rilke, who called it "divine inseeing." When you "insee," you see through to the essence of what you are looking at.

Arachnophobia   Not everyone is comfortable with the idea of letting spiders climb on them for the view, or for anything else. Nor does watching them bring inspiration to the fearful. In Paul Hillyard's *The Book of the Spider: From Arachnophobia to the Love of Spiders,* he points out that most people are conditioned in childhood to fear spiders. Patience Muffet, the real girl behind Mother Goose's "Little Miss Muffet," apparently suffered from a lifelong fear of spiders because her father, who loved and studied spiders, insisted she swallow live ones as a cure for a variety of minor ailments.

A fear of spiders that is out of proportion to the danger of the situation is called arachnophobia, which usually has a particular spider as a focus—like the Australian huntsman spider, a hand-sized, black, hairy spider. A few years ago a panicky Australian teenager tried to kill a huntsman spider by setting a can of insecticide spray on fire and hurling it at the creature. He burned down his family's home. No one knows if the spider escaped.

Each year this spider is implicated in many disastrous encounters involving people and cars. When people find themselves enclosed in the car with this large ambling creature, they panic and swerve all over the road. Some even drive off the road, hit telephone poles, overturn their cars, and jump out while the car is still moving. Although a few people have been bitten in these circumstances, they didn't suffer from the bite, which feels like a pinprick. Their injuries result from their panic-driven responses.

Some fear is helpful and warns us not to go beyond our understanding, but an inordinate amount of fear that creates panic seldom serves us and may even place us in danger. The distortion of healthy fear comes from misconceptions about the creature and the fear of a painful experience.

From Fear to Fascination   A recent survey in the United States showed that biology classes frequently awaken animal phobias. Sometimes those same classes can be the caldron where the intense fear of an arachnophobe is transformed into an equally intense fascination because both are rooted in an innate affinity for the creature in question. Consider George Uetz, who was terrified of spiders from the age of five when he put his hand in a bush and a large spider ran up his arm. In college, Uetz enrolled in a biology course, unaware that its focus was spiders. Rather than bolting, he stayed. Learning about spiders turned his fear into fascination, and that fascination led him to become the president of the American Arachnological Society and a leading spider researcher.

The Spider Trickster

Twists and turns on one's path, especially wholly unexpected events, were traditionally accepted as the work of the gods—in many cultures, of spider gods twisting the threads of fate. Indigenous people would not have missed the irony of an arachnophobe turning into an arachnologist and are likely to have attributed Uetz's transformation to the influence of this Trickster figure. Only the Trickster—both a mythological figure and an archetypal element of our psyche—could have engineered Uetz's enrollment in that biology class. It was not a decision his conscious personality, understandably concerned with comfort and safety, would ever have made.

The Trickster, as Spider or in its other manifestations (such as Coyote and Raven), personifies the energetic power of the total psyche to overthrow the personality's best ideas about how to proceed, tricking it into taking unexpected action. Since Uetz would not have opted to learn about spiders, the Trickster arranged inner and outer events so that he would unwittingly choose this particular class and "miss" hearing the class description until he was already enrolled and sitting in his seat.

Although feared as an upsetting, unpredictable influence, the Trickster was also considered a cultural hero and sacred creator of the world who brings to people the inspirations and energies of creativity. Consider that Uetz was tricked into discovering work that he is passionate about. His apparent misfortune was actually his good luck—one of the signs that the Trickster is afoot.

Both bad luck and good reside in the Trickster's domain. As a spoiler of plans, the Trickster often brings loss and what we perceive as bad luck, entering a situation to punish pride, arrogance, and insolence. The Trickster also chastises those who seek closure prematurely and, in doing so, cut off the creative possibilities of a situation.

When we feel the Trickster's presence in our life, it helps to know that this energy is aligned with an authentic push in our psyche toward expansiveness. Although its lack of concern for our fears, the culture's taboos, or social appropriateness is unnerving and can feel punitive, the Trickster's demands for a change of direction or for stillness is a call for a necessary change of some kind. Far from being unreasonable, its energies try to align us with deeper patterns of fulfillment—presenting opportunities for growth disguised as frustration, pain, and misfortune.

Trickster Figures   The Oglala Dakota tribes call their Spider Trickster Ikto (or Iktomi) and Unktomi. They say Ikto was the first mature being in the world. More cunning than humans, Ikto, as cultural hero, named all people and animals and was the first to use human speech.

Anansi, the West Indies Spider Man, is also a Trickster figure, as is Ananse, a chief character in the folktales of the African Ashanti people. Like Iktome, Ananse brings divine forces into human life by passing through the hidden, and largely unconscious, boundaries people erect and defend for protection. In myths, Ananse often takes human shape, walking with a limp and speaking with a lisp. A little bald-headed man with a falsetto voice, Ananse lives by his wits, besting other people and animals by cunning and humor.

Although Western culture doesn't consciously acknowledge this constellation of energies or archetype known as the Trickster (except by calling it bad luck), it still operates within us and our society. We tend to think we left behind this energetic pattern and its chaotic influence with the advent of our control-oriented technologies, but we didn't. We only left behind the context through which we might understand its emergence.

If we made room for the Trickster and the energy of our unconscious, we would spend less effort fighting to maintain the status quo and more energy looking for new avenues of growth. We would also laugh at ourselves more often. Personifying this energy, we could resurrect Anansi or Iktomi—or imbue Insect Man, an obscure comic hero from the sixties who could transform himself into any insect, with the power of the Trickster. And working with this energy, we could invite its gifts of grace and creativity, and gain from an outpouring of its benefits.

Good Luck and Protection

The good luck associated with the spider is frequently related to money matters, and the belief in a money-bringing or gift-giving spider is widespread.

The spider is also known to bring good luck and protection to travelers. The myths of the Kiowa tell of a cultural heroine, Spider Woman, who is a protective spirit of travelers. Other stories tell of how spider webs protect travelers fleeing from harm. When Muhammad fled from his enemies at Mecca, for example, he hid in a cave. Suddenly, in front of the cave a tree grew and a spider wove a web between the tree and the cave. When his enemies saw the unbroken web, they didn't search the cave because they thought that no one could have entered it recently. They passed by, and the Prophet emerged unharmed. A similar legend is also told about Jesus when he was hiding from Herod's cruelty.

King Frederick the Great had his life saved by a spider when it dropped down from the ceiling and into his cup of chocolate. Dismayed, Frederick asked for another cup. The cook, who had poisoned the first cup of chocolate, interpreted the king's request for another cup as knowledge about the assassination plot and killed himself on the spot. Only then did Frederick realize that he had been saved by the spider's action. To show his gratitude, and in tribute, he had a majestic spider painted on the ceiling of this room that visitors to the palace can still view today.

A contemporary example of how a spider may intervene in a situation and offer protection comes from native healer Bobby Lake-Thom.[1] He recounts the time when he was washing dishes and a spider dropped down from its web and dangled in front of his face. After getting Lake-Thom's attention, the spider proceeded down into the sink and into the drain. He tried talking to her (for he thought she was a female), and asked what she was trying to tell him. Then suddenly the spider crawled out of the drain and up on the sink and stayed there as though watching him. Curious, he reached down into the drain where she had been and found a shard of broken glass. He realized that if it wasn't for the spider, he probably would have turned on the disposal and sent shards of glass flying out of the drain, perhaps even injuring himself. The spider had protected him, and he thanked her.

Invasion of Spiders

We don't usually welcome spiders into our lives, especially if they come en masse. A few years earlier Japan went to war against the redback spider, a native of Australia. When a dragnet near Osaka captured over a thousand redbacks, health officials went searching for others in response to the public's panic. Emergency shipments of antitoxin were airlifted in from Australia, and urgent updates on the "infestation" were broadcast each night, although no one was bitten.

The people of Australia, meanwhile, were amused at Japan's panic. Australians consider the shy redback spider as more nuisance than threat. Redbacks have a reputation for being timid and easily frightened. If disturbed, they often roll up in a ball and play dead. Every backyard has a few, and it's impossible to live in Australia very long without seeing these spiders.

For the record, the redback's bite does kill a few people around the world each year, but no one in Australia has died since an antitoxin was developed in the 1950s. A bite makes most people sick for a few days, and then they recover.

The assorted "weapons" that spiders and other such creatures possess have evolved to capture food, or for defense, or both. Perhaps we assume that creatures capable of inflicting pain or death spend their lives looking for humans to attack. One of the many distortions in the movie *Arachnophobia* was the portrayal of large, hairy spiders seeking humans to kill. I suspect this movie's success at the box office was a result of feeding this widespread fear.

Spider Venom   All spiders are venomous in the sense that all but one species possess a pair of poison glands. Since spiders use their jaws to employ their venom, they bite, jabbing their fangs into their prey while squeezing venom from these glands (unlike scorpions, bees, and wasps, who have stingers in their tails). Chemically, spider venom is a mixture of many different toxins and digestive enzymes and is being studied for use as a medicine. Spider venom–derived medicines in homeopathy all affect the nervous system, heart, and brain, with each species having its own particular accent. In fact, a spider is credited with helping Constantine Hering, the father of American homeopathy, discover this method of treating disease.

Only twenty to thirty spiders on the planet are potentially dangerous to us—although about five hundred can inflict a significant bite. Most people assume that the large and hairy tarantulas are one of those five hundred because they look dangerous, but that is not true. The ten-inch varieties have a bite that feels like a pinprick.

In North America two species out of three thousand—the black widow and the brown recluse—are poisonous to humans. Knowledge about them should greatly diminish our fear, telling us how to identify them and when to take judicious action.

The Black Widow and the Brown Recluse

The black widow spider is one species that requires caution on our part, although this spider rarely lives up to its reputation. If it is present in our area (and it has a huge geographical range), the first step is learning how to recognize it. The female black widow, the dangerous one of a pair, is a shiny black creature with an hourglass pattern of red or yellow on her underside. Should we encounter one, it will ease our mind to know she is painfully shy. Although her venom is deadly, the chances of receiving even a drop are slim. One reason is that the body of a female black widow spider is only about the size of a green pea. And second, the black widow spends her life in hiding, preferring lumber piles and the nooks and crannies of old building foundations—although be aware, she also likes outhouses and clothing and shoes left outdoors.

If you disturb a black widow, her first reaction will be to curl into a little ball in the middle of her web. If threatened further, she might even leave her web and run away. Statistics on black widow spider bites are usually inflated. One study, conducted before antivenin was developed, revealed that only about fifty cases of human deaths from this spider could actually be verified among hundreds of claims. With antivenin, deaths are virtually unknown, and only 1 percent of untreated bites proves to be fatal.

Like other spiders, the black widow spider has a superior sense of touch and receives messages through the vibrations of her web—for example, when food is available. Rushing toward an insect that lands on her web, she throws silk at it with her hind legs.

Sometimes the vibrations are caused by a cautious male trying to determine whether she is hungry and therefore dangerous. The smaller-sized male is banded and streaked with yellow, orange, or red. Males who are not eaten by the female during or after mating are usually the ones who have a strategy for determining how hungry a potential mate is.

Spider Cannibalism   Male spiders of many species must deal with dangerous females. The black widow male merely tweaks the web of a female. If she doesn't charge out, he takes it as an indication that she isn't starved, and the chances of his mating successfully with her and leaving after the act are good. Sometimes it works, other times it doesn't.

Reports on the black widow focus on the deadliness of her venom and her reputation for eating her mate. I suspect our fears and ambiguous feelings about sexuality contribute to our fascination and horror with her behavior, which is viewed as a cruel, sexual aberration.

Junichiro Tanizaki's famous story "The Tattoo" (1910) is a prime example. In the tale a young girl gets a tattoo of a large spider on her back, which in a mysterious act of satanic-like transfiguration brings out her sadistic leanings. When the tattoo is finished, she becomes cool and calculating (supposedly like the black widow spider) and tells the artist that he will be her first victim.

A short story called "The Spider" (1921) by Hanns Heinz Ewers also plays on the male fear of the erotic danger of women and features a seductive black-haired woman who spins each day in front of her window, luring the male occupants of the room opposite hers to their death. More recently, a made-for-television movie called *The Black Widow Murders* aired. It was based on the true story of a seductive woman who attracted men to her and then killed them.

Men versus Women   These tales reflect the popular theory that there is an inherent conflict between males and females—even in the world of creeping creatures. And in species where the female is bigger than the male and eats him during or after copulation, the hapless males are simply overpowered by the beautiful and insidious females. It's not a new idea. The Aztecs, an aggressive, male-dominated culture, also viewed spiders as malevolent. They interpreted the female's habit of eating the male during copulation as hostility toward men.

It is outside the focus of this book to speculate on the nature of this apparent conflict between men and women or its possible origin in patriarchal cultures, in which men typically exert power over women. That the spider is intricately connected to the feminine is true because of its weaving, an act of creation—the creation of the world, of human beings, and of relationships. And as a symbol of relatedness, weaving is associated with the essence of the feminine nature. Symbolically we could view cannibalism by the female not as hostility to the male, but as an act that returns him to the ground of creation—the source of being and life itself. She becomes then an instrument of the archetypal Spinner of Fate, the one who gives and takes life in the great turnings of the wheel of life.

On the physical side, remembering that Nature's creatures are not possessed of the motivations that drive and/or confuse us will keep us from judging them in a context that doesn't apply. In their realm, unlike ours, death is accepted and cannibalism is commonplace, a survival strategy tied not to cruelty but to energy resources and, as we will see, propagation strategies.

Eagerness in the Redback Male   The behavior of the male redback spider, the species that caused such a panic in Japan, gives us another take on cannibalism. Although the panic in Japan was caused by the fear of being bitten, the redback female's cannibalistic habits did not win her any points. During copulation, she eats the male redback about 65 percent of the time. What's particularly interesting is that spider researchers tell us that the male seemed "peculiarly, almost exuberantly, reconciled to his fate."[2] In fact, he actually flips into his mate's jaws while copulating.

If the Aztecs had investigated the redback spider, they might have had to change their myths to account for the male's eagerness. Those trying to explain the phenomenon today are looking at what advantages there may be in being eaten. One idea is that it allows the male to copulate longer (more than twice the time as males who don't get eaten) and thereby fertilize more eggs. It's an important objective for the male if he wants to pass his genetic material along, especially since the female redback sometimes takes two mates, one after the other. Supporting this theory is the fact that females who eat their first mate are about seventeen times less likely to accept a second mate than females who don't.

Whatever the motivation, judging them by human standards is inappropriate, and projecting malevolence onto the female spider or foolhardiness onto the male doesn't serve the human-spider relationship. What does serve it is letting certain mysteries work in the nonhostile, nonfearful imagination and displacing our anxiety about spiders with information that gives us strategies for coexisting with them.

The Brown Recluse   Another spider in the same family as the black widow, and one that also requires caution, is the brown recluse. Sometimes called the fiddleback or the violin spider, the brown recluse is yellowish brown with a dark brown pattern resembling a tiny violin on its head. Recently the brown recluse, once found only in the Southwest, has spread across North America in suitcases and trunks of clothes. In cold areas, it has had to make its home inside our buildings to survive. Although the brown recluse has killed only six people in a hundred years, it gained notoriety in the 1950s because of a number of bites that resulted in severe tissue damage.

Photographs of unhealed wounds always accompany a talk on the brown recluse. And while it is true that its bite may cause a wound that is stubborn to heal, many people have been bitten with no harm at all— a fact worth noting. With modern communication, we also hear about brown recluse bites more frequently, although we are still left to our own devices to manage our anxiety about them and avoid encountering them. If we remember that this spider is also doing its best to avoid us, we can trust that a good measure of attention when we are cleaning dark, hard-to-reach places will be sufficient to keep most of us out of harm's way.

The Original Networkers

The spider and its web, a universal symbol of connection and relatedness, has returned to modern culture with the advent of the World Wide Web. This cyber-based "spider web" connects computers, their users, and information all over the world.

As the original networker, creator of the first alphabet, and patron of language and writing, the spider and its medicine—creativity, intelligence, industry, and patience—are available to contemporary individuals. When environmental psychologist James Swan was asked to edit a book about networking, he was eager to start the project but developed writer's block. Following his own advice to seek advice from the natural world, he went to a nearby wooded park. After making an offering of cornmeal and singing a prayer, Swan wandered through the wild landscape. Within a few minutes he felt drawn to a particular spot and looked for what might be pulling him. Then suddenly he saw a spider at work weaving its web. He watched the spider for a few moments, and it occurred to him that he was witnessing the original network builder at work. He watched how the spider carefully laid out the structure of the web and then wove it together, one knot at a time and with the greatest patience and attention to its design. Then he went home and drew a picture of the spider and put it over his typewriter. Almost immediately, he reports, the ideas flowed and his book took form.

For the culture at large, spider as networker and the web as a symbol of creativity and relatedness have interesting ties to Peter Russell's global brain and his vision of humanity's potential for evolving into a nervous system or brain for Gaia, the self-organizing entity we call Earth. Russell compares the near-instant interlinking of people all over the world through the communications technology of the World Wide Web with the way the human brain grows. He believes that if the data-processing capacity continues to grow at its present rate of increase, "the global telecommunications network could equal the brain in complexity" in the near future. When this happens, if there is enough cohesiveness and positive interaction, a new order could emerge that would revolutionize humanity in the same magnitude as when the spider gods first wove the webs of Heaven and Earth together to create the universe.

Helping and Relating to Spiders

While spiders are reentering the culture as potently as ever in their new metaphoric garb, actual spiders are losing ground due to habitat loss and pesticides. Protecting the spider is a way of giving back to a creature that still weaves webs in our psyches. Protecting it is also a way to support a balanced ecosystem, since all spiders are vital predators in their specific habitat. One spider in trouble is the great raft spider, Britain's rarest species. Luckily for this hand-sized creature, a company has intervened to help it survive. In 1997, a British water company, perhaps run by a spider enthusiast, set aside twenty million gallons of reserves to raise drought-reduced pond levels in the spider's 325-acre reserve. For six months the water company pumped seventy-two thousand gallons a day into the reserve ponds.

Although some customers were angry that the company was elevating the spider's need for water over their own (an exaggeration, since the company had merely asked them to conserve water to prevent rationing), the company took the criticism in stride and remained firm on its position in regard to helping the spiders. A company spokesperson, replying to complaints with the compassion and wisdom of an elder, said, "How can one possibly equate the life-or-death situation facing the spiders with hose pipe bans? We know we are doing the right thing when one considers the risk to the survival of this rare spider if nothing is done."

Relating to spiders—beyond protecting them and gleaning wisdom from watching them and reflecting on their ways—is an avenue open for exploration, but kindness and compassion are always appropriate. In his 1950 book for laypeople called simply *The Spider*, naturalist John Compton gave the highest marks for loving spiders to a policeman. In 1936 this officer was on duty, keeping traffic moving safely on a busy thoroughfare. Despite his preoccupation with traffic, he noticed a very large spider trying to cross the road. Knowing it would be killed, the policeman held up traffic. The spider crossed with a slow and dignified gait—to the great delight of all those watching.

When people I meet learn about my interest in creeping creatures, many report proudly that they always help spiders out of the house. Some use a scissorlike device with a plastic dome designed to transport spiders from the house without harming them. Another aid, for spiders trapped in the bathtub, is a spider ladder that can be suspended from one of the water taps to let the spider climb to safety on its own.

Helping spiders out of our buildings is a good step toward coexistence—unless of course, as Australian-borne Christie Cox discovered, the spiders belong in the house. When Cox was staying at the home of a friend and professional interspecies communicator, she was left alone one morning and sat down at the kitchen table to eat breakfast. She dropped some food on the floor and bent down to retrieve it. That is when she saw two spiders sitting close to her foot. Their "spiderness and their alarming hairiness" sent her reeling back in fear. She rummaged through the cupboards quickly and found two plastic cups that she dropped over the spiders, immobilizing them before her fear immobilized her. She didn't know whether they were dangerous or not. One part of her wanted to just leave them trapped beneath plastic until her friend returned, but another part of her didn't want to look so incapable. She decided to take them out of the house. She carefully slid a piece of paper under each cup and then, one at a time, took them out of the house and released them into the bushes. She reentered the house, pleased with herself.

When her friend returned several hours later, Cox told her proudly that she had helped two spiders out of the house. Her friend was not pleased, however, explaining that the spiders, fist-sized tarantulas, had been born in the house and were an important part of its ecology, eating flies and keeping the insect population in balance. Later in the day her friend, still deeply upset, told Cox that she had been praying for their well-being, since a storm was approaching and they might be in danger without adequate shelter.

Three days later Cox saw her outside the house in the front, sitting quietly under a tree in the midst of her yard of foot-high grass. She told Cox later that she was calling silently to her spiders to come home. What Cox saw was those two large spiders crawling up out of that huge wilderness of a yard and onto her friend's leg. Later she learned that the spiders communicated to her friend that their adventure in the outside world was interesting, but they had wanted to return to the house. They also conveyed that they were aware of Cox's fear and appreciated the fact that she had been very gentle about taking them out of the kitchen. They forgave her for removing them from their home and suggested that her fear of them was actually a fear of her own creativity.

Cox listened, her natural skepticism flaring up but just as quickly subsiding. She had, after all, witnessed those spiders responding to her friend's silent call.

To acknowledge the intelligent awareness of spiders positions us to learn from them and perhaps to sense, as David Abram sensed, the intricate web of life with its interlocking points of connection that support physical existence. To acknowledge as well that the same awareness poised within the body of a spider may appreciate a thoughtful and considerate response to its presence is equivalent to dropping from our own dragline thread into a sea of possibility—with an act of faith equal to a spider's.

12. *The* LANGUAGE *of the* STING

On this day God is the name by which I designate all
things which cross my willful path violently and recklessly,
all things which upset subjective views, plans and intentions
and change the course of my life for better or worse.

−C. G. Jung

Linda Neale, former director of Earth and Spirit Council, an inter-
faith environmental action group, discovered her uncommon affinity
for scorpions on a hiking trip to the Grand Canyon in 1987. She was
with her young daughter and niece when a scorpion stung her at the
base of her thumb. She tried to brush it off with her other hand and was
stung again. Shaking her hand violently, she managed to dislodge the
creature. The pain was intense, and she realized how vulnerable she
was, with only two little girls to help. The only thing she knew about
scorpions was that they can kill you, and that the small ones are more
dangerous than the large ones. She sat down and called the girls to her,
trying to appear calm while explaining what had happened. She asked
them to get help. They went off and returned with a Boy Scout troop,
but no one in the group knew what to do.

It was then, she recalls, that two paths opened up. She thought of
them as the path of life and the path of death. The death path was waiting around for help, for someone to tell her what to do. The path of life

was walking back to the village and getting whatever help was available. She started walking, and the pain became even more intense. She sang a chant from a tape someone had given her. The words were "Be still and know I am God" (a biblical quote, from Psalms). The scout leader accompanying her wondered if she was becoming delirious. They arrived at a nearby Indian village, and an Indian woman questioned her about the size of the scorpion and whether or not she had any allergies. She said no, and the woman assured her then that she would probably survive.

Senses heightened, Neale continued to be affected by the scorpion experience after returning home from the hiking trip. She started reading about scorpions and thought about her own path, wondering if she was "choosing life" on a regular basis, feeling that something wasn't quite right in her life. Then she had a dream of a giant scorpion outside her bedroom window.

The next day her husband found a metal belt buckle by the side of the rural road where he had been running, very near the spot where her dream scorpion had been. In the center of the buckle was a real scorpion encased in resin—almost identical to the one that had stung her—surrounded by Indian-head nickels. The sight shocked her. She was speechless and suddenly afraid. She knew the buckle was for her.

The sting of the scorpion marked the beginning of a transformation in her life, a death and rebirth. The "deconstruction" took five years and was as painful as it was important. She gave up her life as she knew it and moved in a different direction. The scorpion experiences sustained her, although she often wondered why she needed such a jolt to help her change her life. "I think it is because commitment and loyalty [to choices already made] and stubbornness have always been so important to me. It had to be something big to get my attention," says Neale.[1]

The language of the sting commands our attention, invoking pain and fear and, after the danger has passed, fascination and a heightened sense of awareness.

Creatures that inflict pain and those with the potential to cause death have always intrigued us. It's a universal phenomenon present in every culture and in every age. The sting of creatures that are impervious to our conscious desires initiates us at pivotal times in our lives. Their symbolic role in ancient cultures is intricately intertwined with the archetypes of renewal: birth, death, transformation, and rebirth.

And encoded in our bodies, this archetypal or universal process of initiation, when activated in our psyches, pushes us to grow.

A friend reports that she always sees a centipede on the floor of her bedroom at times when she needs to move on something in her life. She has come to depend on it as a reminder to act now or risk being stung by it into action.

Besides developing a new hive prototype (see the chapter "Telling the Bees"), New York beekeeper Ron Breland writes and lectures on the gift of the sting. Being stung, he says, is an opportunity for wakefulness, but we are free to respond with anger or interest. If we choose interest we can forge a new relationship with the natural world and its creatures.

In an article on the subject, Breland recounts a story from Richard Taylor's *The Joys of Beekeeping* about a hive of "cross" bees.[2] When the cover was removed from this hive, hundreds of bees attacked Taylor and then flew into a nearby field to sting a worker there. The next day the hive returned to its former gentle disposition, leaving him puzzled about the hive's shifts in temperament. Within a week, the field hand, almost recovered, came to Taylor full of questions about how one might become a beekeeper. The stings had brought him "bee fever."

Being stung can also be viewed as the disruptive energies of the Trickster entering our lives, thwarting our best intentions and throwing us into the anxiety that accompanies unwanted events. The Navaho people acknowledged these forces and personified them in their Insect god, a Trickster named Beotcidi, who controlled stinging insects. Irreverent, erotic, and outrageous, Beotcidi brought into people's lives a chaotic or disruptive element. As a universal figure (or in the language of psychology, an archetypal pattern) common to all individuals, Beotcidi hovers on the border of the conscious and unconscious; as a messenger of the potential wholeness of the psyche, he personifies the energies of the shadow and the unconscious, needed by the familiar self to move toward a more expansive version of itself.

The Power of the Small

Wise individuals exercise caution when outside, in the domain of wild and sometimes dangerous creatures. They are more alert, less likely to charge blindly through the area. Such individuals know that an encounter with a species that can hurt us, unlike a carnival ride or a spot on reality television, demands more than our money, wit, or physical presence. It calls forth in us certain qualities—traits of the native hunter or the meditator. We sense real power in the potentially dangerous creature, and unless we panic, we are likely to quiet our own noisy thoughts and restlessness and try to match their depth of silence. Sometimes our well-being depends upon how well we match it.

Silence in the presence of such power anchors us to our own center, where the power can be met and used to transform us. Our sensitivity heightened, a brush with these kinds of creatures typically leaves us raw, as though our terror strips away the layers of comfort that protect us from life. Their ability to hurt us also binds us to the present moment as few things can. And after the moment, when we are returned to safety, we notice that we feel more alive.

Small creatures have power unaccountable for their size. Yellow jackets can make grown men run; so can bees. Tracker and teacher John Stokes thinks small creatures make us aware that we live in an automated world of false power. Because they have real power, they fascinate us and effectively counter our own disproportionate sense of importance. Stokes teaches that "power can't be grasped until you go out in the bush and gain the knowledge of the heart—get humbled by heat, cold, the sting of a bee, the power of the spider."[3]

Angered or confused by the unpredictable and painful encounter, we enter, if only for the moment, the gaps, a transition place where we are not in control. If we don't lash out, if we forgo the heroic stance and allow ourselves to be humbled and temporarily subdued, all manner of insight and fortune await. Confronting real power frees us from the bonds of greed, desire, and numbness, and the concerns of the ego for comfort and control. It also awakens our intuitive and imaginative abilities and gives us rein to approach the big questions about who we are, where we come from, and where we are going. These are the questions that the scorpion awakened in Neale and set her on a new path.

The Saint and the Scorpion

Lashing out at what hurts us or our children is often our first reaction, a culturally supported response that has its origin in the view of the world as a battlefield. For many people, it is the only response they know. Yet there are other responses, like the one found in a Hindu teaching story in which a saint bathing in a river rescues a scorpion, cradling it in his hand as he moves with it toward the riverbank. When the bedraggled scorpion realizes its new dilemma, it stings the saint, but the holy man keeps walking toward the bank. The scorpion stings him again, and the pain is so great that the saint staggers and almost collapses in the river. His agitated disciple, watching from the shore, tells him to put the scorpion down and leave it to its fate, saying that kindness is of no value to such a creature for it is unable to learn from it.

The saint ignores him and continues toward the bank, carrying the scorpion. The scorpion stings him a third time, and the pain explodes into his head and chest. Smiling a blissful smile, he collapses into the river. The disciple rushes into the water and lifts up the saint, who is still smiling and still carrying the scorpion. When they reach dry land, the saint sets the creature down, and it quickly crawls away.

The disciple asks the saint how he can still smile after the scorpion nearly killed him. The saint acknowledges that, indeed, the scorpion's sting almost killed him, but he explains that it was only following its dharma, or nature. "It is the dharma of a scorpion to sting, and it is the dharma of a saint to save its life. . . . Everything is in its proper place. That is why I am so happy."[4]

The saint who responds to the scorpion while staying centered in his own nature is able to match the power of the stinging creature—to match each sting with a deepening of his commitment to save the scorpion's life. Doing so successfully places both man and invertebrate in accord and right alignment with their natures, hence the saint's happiness. He explains to his disciple that a creature like the scorpion will naturally sting, especially when it is alarmed and frightened. Instead of dealing with such incidents of pain in a reactive manner and flinging the scorpion away, the saint demonstrates that we can move more deeply into our own center and from that place meet the power of the sting with the power of compassion.

The "Ain't It Awful?" View

To a mind-set that has embraced the idea of the world as a battle-field, the saint's behavior is more than puzzling, and we are likely to dismiss it as an anomaly peculiar to sainthood. We are more comfortable with killing or running from what hurts us. A director of a county-wide gardening extension service, for example, wrote an article on how to kill scorpions. A visitor brought a dead one to her, and it triggered memories of a time when she stepped on a live scorpion in her house and got stung. Incensed by the stabbing pain in the arch of her foot, she grabbed a book and started smashing the creature. When it was dead, she called Poison Control. They told her that unless she had a severe allergic reaction to the sting, it would only cause local swelling and soreness. "Soak it in ice," they advised.

Later she discovered that nearby house construction was the reason a few scorpions had moved to her home. Their habitat had been disturbed. She also read that they sting only when provoked, as when they are stepped on. Understanding their reasons wasn't enough to quell her fear of having them in her house and the possibility of being stung again. The rest of the article focuses on getting rid of them. She recommends crushing, stomping, smashing, or squashing them and indoor and outdoor pesticide sprays.

This type of article is popular in the culture. It holds up a mirror, showing us what we already believe, so that there is a kind of shared misery in the telling of such a tale—a version of the psychological game "Ain't it awful?" In these kinds of situations, more information about the creature doesn't help. Facts don't alter an emotional bias if the person is unaware that he or she has a bias. Nor do facts help if the person isn't seeking a way to coexist harmoniously. With harmony as the intention, however, more knowledge about the creature feeds the imagination and balances the fear. And even greater help is available when we can step back and view an encounter symbolically.

Necessary Humbling What is often humbled in a painful encounter with another creature—especially a small one—are the self-important, inflated parts of ourselves. Those parts mask our general fear of the unknown and our resistance to the pain of being overcome and changed. "Forget about transformation and renewal," protests our personality, which fights for order and predictability. It is this familiar aspect of self, playing at king or queen, that prefers safety to knowledge. And it is this aspect of self that builds an empire on false power and scrambles for position and visibility among other false leaders.

I suspect that our task, and a monumental one at that, is not to withhold ourselves or defend ourselves from that which would help us grow strong and move closer to our true natures. "What we choose to fight is so tiny, what fights with us is so great," Rilke reminds us in "A Man Watching."[5] When we let go of our resistance to pain and change and actually seek out these transitional places where the subjective and objective worlds intersect—in dread and expectation—we will have altered our way of being in the world enough to open avenues of thought and action previously unavailable.

If we trust that the creatures of the natural world that move into our lives bidden by unseen powers are intent on arousing us and helping us grow, we can learn to submit to them. As Marlo Morgan learned to surrender to the swarms of Australian bush flies, perhaps we can also let go and refrain from erecting elaborate defenses—or engaging in a righteous retaliation. Maybe we can enter the small and great initiations that our soul brings us without doing battle with forces and creatures that are ultimately allies of a fundamental natural self at home in the world. There is power in our defeats and in our surrender, and blessings are due to those messengers who disrupt our familiar world. As Rilke so eloquently explains in the last passage of the same poem.

> Whoever was beaten by this Angel . . . went away proud and
> strengthened and great from that harsh hand, that kneaded him
> as if to change his shape. Winning does not tempt that man.
> This is how he grows: by being defeated, decisively, by
> constantly greater beings.[6]

Allies of Growth   In shamanic traditions it was understood that other species are way-showers to the mysteries and messengers for the divine powers operating within us and within the universe. As initiators, insects and arachnids are impeccable. We can neither appease nor bargain with them. Their task in dreaming and waking is to arouse us out of our complacency and push us past the edge of what is familiar and comfortable. And once beyond the edge, where vision is possible and energy is available, we are transformed and renewed—and we may even return with the powers of the creatures that initiated our transformation.

The arousal methods of insects and the tactics of other species can be very persuasive. A Zen story describes the anxiety that accompanies these passages.

> "Go to the edge," the voice said.
> "No!" they said. "We will fall."

"Go to the edge," the voice said.
"No!" they said. "We will be pushed over."
"Go to the edge," the voice said.
So they went . . .
> and they were pushed . . .
> and they flew . . .[7]

One of the roles animals play is to get the human over the cliff. Some push, others chase. Some use pain to nudge us toward the cliff and away from safety. Stinging and biting insects might torment us until we jump.

If we understood the language of the sting—if we understood the intent of those who can sting us and their alignment with our souls and the forces of growth—we could try to lift ourselves up in surrender. We could appreciate that our fear or anger is a process that includes pride, doubt, helplessness, and self-protection. We could admit that we are afraid of the pain of a biting or stinging creature and fearful of the unknown—despite its promise of renewal. Just accepting our fear can be enough to shift it and allow us to come into a new relationship with the unknown, to see it as mystery and as an important step in initiation. Aligning our personal wills with a greater will, we could then wait with fear, dread, and hope for the visit that marks the beginning of a shift of consciousness and new life.

The Gifts of Pain   This process of growth is universal yet looks so foreign and feels so frightening because we have split our rational awareness from our natural, image-making self. So we can't make sense of it through concepts and rational analysis, nor access the symbols that map the process. And as long as we are alienated from our wilderness self, we are largely cut off from experiencing the spiritual and psychic energy that emanates from its potent symbols and images.

Another reason this process of growth is unfamiliar is that we have been raised to avoid pain and discomfort. Pain-relief products and services permeate the culture, and the context for working with pain has been largely lost.

Stephen Levine has discovered in his work with the dying that our reactions to physical pain offer insight into our attitude toward life in general, and the more we push pain away, the less energy we have for living. Pain stirs our grief and brings up long-suppressed anxiety and unfinished business. Simple awareness has a healing power. He suggests that we can use each moment of unpleasantness—each insect sting, if you will—to learn how to meet all unpleasantness, all pain, and investigate how resistance turns pain into suffering.

Thus discomfort can teach us how to live and take us to places otherwise inaccessible in our normal conscious state. Each incident provides an opportunity to stay in the present moment and bring awareness to the places inside us that recoil and harden in resistance. Softening around them, as Levine advises, lets us penetrate the armor that keeps life at bay and lets us live closer to the mystery. No one can live a pain-free life. Knowing there are gifts in painful experiences helps to redeem them and tempers our responses if it is another species that brings the pain.

In her book *Pain: The Challenge and the Gift*, Marti Lynn Matthews considers pain a guide, a biofeedback system that lets us know what is healthy and unhealthy for us. "There is integrity in pain," says Matthews. "It is not punishment but a force that pushes us into expansion. Without a push, we would never take the leap that would allow us to fly free."

Transforming Weaknesses into Strengths

Some cultures advocate the use of meditation and ritual to transform unpleasantness and discomfort and to further self-understanding, just as Gyelsay Togmay Sangpo did when he deepened his wisdom and compassion by attending to the lice on his body (see the chapter "Insects as Guides and Messengers"). In *A Path with Heart*, Jack Kornfield tells the story of a poisonous tree. On first discovering it, most people see only its danger. Their immediate reaction is to cut it down before someone is hurt. This is like our initial response to dangerous creatures. It is also our first response to other difficulties that arise in our lives, such as when we encounter aggression, compulsion, greed, and fear, or when we are faced with stress, loss, conflict, depression, or sorrow in ourselves and others. We feel great aversion and want to avoid it or get rid of it. In the case of the poison tree, we cut it down or uproot it. In the case of an insect, spider, or scorpion, we poison or stomp on it.

Others who have journeyed further along the spiritual path discover this poisonous tree and realize that to be open to life requires compassion for everything. Knowing that the poisonous tree is somehow a part of them, they don't want to cut it down. From kindness, they create boundaries around it. Perhaps they build a fence around the tree and post a warning sign so that others aren't poisoned and the tree may also live. This is a profound shift from judgment and fear to compassion. Applying it to a stinging and venomous insect, we might caution people when they enter a territory inhabited by such creatures and have vaccines on hand if someone is stung.

Another type of person, who is extremely wise, comes upon the poisonous tree and is happy because the tree is just what he or she was looking for. This individual examines the poisonous fruit, analyzes its properties, and uses it as a medicine to heal the sick. By understanding and trusting that there is value in even the most difficult circumstance, the wise person acts in a way that benefits a great many people. Likewise, those drawn, albeit unwittingly, to study venomous creatures have discovered that the venom of certain scorpion species can be transformed into a drug for treating strokes, and may lead to other useful drugs as well. As mystical poet Jalaluddin Rumi said, "Every existence is poison to some and spirit-sweetness to others. Be the friend. Then you can eat from a poison jar and taste only clear discrimination."

Perhaps, on the deepest levels, we already know that within adversity is a gift. It is why we are so fascinated with creatures that can arouse us and initiate our transformations. In dreaming, our psyche informs us in symbolic language about the role of fear, pain, and death as prerequisites for growth and renewal. And some deep aspect of self must activate the internal and external events, bringing us the creatures and experiences we need to initiate our own rite of passage and move toward healing and growth. We can dream those experiences, or we can unwittingly draw from the natural world the physical presences that will fit our particular needs—the soul will use whatever it can to move us along.

Following shamanic wisdom, we could support our initiations by naming the creatures that we fear as our allies. It's a practical way to begin courting their power. What happens if, following Hildegard of Bingen's lead, we call dangerous creatures "glittering, glistening mirrors of divinity"? Are these not the passwords to open the door to our greater identity? Maybe all we are required to do is to meet adversity and pain with our respectful attention, to learn the language of the sting and its gifts. Instead of killing the creatures with the potential to harm us, seeing with the eyes of wisdom, we can dance around them and allow difficulties to become our good fortune.

The Scorpion

To the average person, scorpions look menacing, although they are not particularly aggressive toward humans and use their venom to capture food and defend themselves from natural enemies. They usually sting people after being disturbed suddenly—a startle response that anyone who has been abruptly awakened from a deep sleep can understand.

Predictably, the popular culture serves up a one-dimensional view of the scorpion. A recent film features open pits of black scorpions and a half man, half scorpion called Scorpion King, who is little more than a killing machine. And in a tale from a *Journey into Mystery* comic book, a scorpion exposed to radiation grows large and menacing to the surrounding humans. He sends them a message by means of thought waves:

> Hear me, Humans! I have always had the seed of
> consciousness! But now your radiation has brought it to life.
> Now after years of utter helplessness, at last I have the strength
> and intelligence to pit myself against you!

The desperate humans finally defeat the scorpion using a combination of hypnosis and trickery before he can gather his brother scorpions together and move against them.

As we have seen in every chapter, the images and practices so prevalent in our culture revolve around power over others—power over a savage natural world bent on destroying us at the first opportunity. It is an uncomfortable way to live, looking over our shoulder. And we don't have to read comics to absorb the ballistic context that prods us into battling these creatures, as we saw in the article by the garden extension director.

Sometimes our fascination for creatures like scorpions is capitalized on by companies who may not understand it but see in it a potential for a product that will sell. A company in the southwestern United States kills tens of thousands of scorpions annually to produce scorpion paperweights, bola ties, and refrigerator magnets. Living scorpions (and

black widows) are encased in a lump of plastic resin and sold as sou-
venirs of the "Wild West." The company obtains its scorpions by paying
people to enter the desert at night with an ultraviolet light. Under ultraviolet radiation, a scorpion glows (perhaps to attract insects), so
these hunters can find and capture them easily. They are then stuffed
into plastic after it is partly hardened to await their death.

Our desire to own dangerous creatures, safely enclosed in plastic or
otherwise rendered harmless, is a sad commentary on our relationship
to wildness and real power. It is also a practice that lets us reconcile our
fascination with our fear. And it may be the force behind the emergence of reality television shows like *Fear Factor*, where we manufacture danger and then film those who have agreed to encounter it
(whether for money or notoriety), living vicariously through them.

Master of Extremes

Surprisingly, those who live in regions where they must coexist
with scorpions rarely prepare themselves with a little bit of knowledge
for the eventual encounter. For example, few people know that the vast
majority of scorpions won't harm you. Only about twenty out of fifteen
hundred known species have poison strong enough to kill an adult man
or woman, and the venom of most of North America's forty or so scorpion species is not deadly to humans. Most scorpion stings feel like the
sting from a bee or wasp—painful, but not life-threatening.

If you live in Algeria, however, you would do well to learn about the
fat-tailed scorpion, responsible for 80 percent of all reported stings—a
third of which prove fatal. Fat-tailed scorpions lived their lives under
rocks or in shallow burrows on hillsides until people built houses on
hillsides; then scorpions used houses for shelter, hiding during the day
and feasting on the insects in the house at night. They especially like
wet places (because humidity and water attract insects for them to eat)
and often crawl into shower heads, baths, and toilets, and congregate
around outdoor water troughs and wells.

Scorpions also frequent shoes for warmth and in Trinidad have
been responsible for human deaths in this way. A necessary precaution
is to always shake out one's shoes before stepping into them. Gandhi,
who believed in the essential unity of all living things, let snakes, scorpions, and spiders move unhindered in his ashram. He saw them as an-

imals fulfilling their lives and believed that humans could safely coexist with them. People in the ashram were advised to look into their shoes before putting them on and walk carefully at night to avoid trampling on any creature.

Most scorpions live solitary lives, meeting only to mate with their own species or kill others. A couple of species, like the stripe-tailed scorpion, are the exception. They fill the spaces in rotted logs, stacked on top of each other like sardines. Another exception is West Africa's black emperor scorpions (used in the movie with the Scorpion King), who look ominous but are gentle animals and, by most reports, reluctant to do any harm. Male and female emperor scorpions live together peacefully and raise their young for two years or longer.

There is much about scorpions to engage the imagination. They live an amazing fifteen to twenty-five years, for example, and before mating, male and female perform an intricate and attractive dance. The longest scorpion gestation periods rival those of sperm whales (sixteen months) and African elephants (twenty-two months), and they give birth to live young. Their average litter is twenty-five babies. The newborns crawl onto their mother's back for protection and transport, and they feed on her back by osmosis.

Masters of extremes, these remarkable creatures don't seem to need much oxygen and can be underwater for several hours and still revive. They can also go without water for three months and without eating for a year. They can survive in the hottest desert and live even after being frozen in ice. And when the French were testing nuclear weapons in the Sahara, scorpions withstood more radiation than any other creature.

Intellectual Appreciation without Love

These attributes and abilities have captured the attention of scientists and science writers alike. What is missing in most reports on scorpions, however, is a feeling connection to these creatures. (A notable exception is Eugene Marais, the author of a mystical and poetical treatise on termites, who had a long friendship with a scorpion and even acted as her midwife!) And it is missing because most of those who study and write about scorpions don't believe it is possible.

As awareness about environmental issues heightens, there is a current trend to champion species people generally don't like, such as scorpions. But the majority champion them in such a way that the emotional bias is left intact. Despite the complex role of the scorpion in ancient cultures, one science writer introduces their historical role this way:

> Throughout history and across almost every cultural boundary, scorpions have had a rotten reputation. And if the truth be known, they deserve it. They're nasty and they're not afraid of anybody. They can kill you or throw you into a seizure. Even those species whose venom is relatively innocuous can deliver stings of incomparable pain, "Like flaming bullets twisting inside you," as a victim once put it.[7]

The emotional context set, she lists the scorpion's admirable abilities, concluding that Nature is strange and wonderful in its myriad of life forms and that we should try to respect scorpions for their abilities. Imagine how much more powerful her call to respect them would be if it were made within a context that invited kinship and peaceful coexistence.

The Destructive Aspect of Scorpions   A recent book on animal symbology draws upon a range of traditions, including ancient forms of animal work and myth-making. The section on scorpions begins by stating that in most mythologies, scorpions are purely destructive. It is a definitive statement that requires an explanation to remind the contemporary reader of the positive role of destruction in life.

As we have already discussed in a variety of contexts, in ancient times destruction was understood as the flip side of growth. To destroy means to destructure, to break apart, and this breaking apart of the old is a prerequisite to new life and new structure. The hull must crack open before the seedling can sprout, the wheat must be ground, and the caterpillar must relinquish its worm body and surrender to the harsh hand of transformation that would reshape its form and give it wings. Symbolically, then, the scorpion is a destructuring agent, a constellation of energies in service of our potential self (and outside the control of the conscious self) and a critical force in the process of renewal.

If we look at the human psyche as the open evolving system it is, we can use system theory to further illuminate this destructuring aspect. System theory teaches that new structures or systems begin to organize themselves once there are enough new elements present to initiate the process. In the psyche, the building of this new aspect is undertaken behind the door of our awareness, for the epicenter of change or growth lies beyond our conscious control. What's more, we don't even sense what has been fashioned within us until the old structure is broken away—that's the destructive part symbolized by the scorpion and the part of the process that hurts. From the personality's perspective, the destructive events are only experienced as disorienting and painful, something to try to eliminate. Luckily, however, we can't eliminate them (although we can distract ourselves or numb ourselves with drugs). Eventually enough pieces are broken so that we can glimpse the new structure underneath—the hidden gift of the soul.

Ancient cultures recognized the scorpion's role in the renewal process. In a stamp seal from 3300 B.C.E., for example, the rosette of the Great Goddess Inanna, goddess of the underworld, is protected by the pincers of two scorpions, a testament to the animal's sacredness and role in the psychospiritual descent. The journey to the underworld, as we saw with the housefly, was accepted as a necessity of life. It was a time of disintegration in which the former identity was lost and the unshielded person had to descend into his or her own forgotten interior realms to emerge, finally, reordered and renewed. The scorpion was associated with that internal call to grow because it held both the weapon of disintegration and the antidote necessary for healing, reintegration, and return.

Demonizing of the Scorpion   The ancient association of the scorpion with the Great Goddess in her destroying aspect led to its becoming a sign of evil in the Judeo-Christian tradition when the female deity it served was demonized. This pronouncement of evil stripped the scorpion of the context through which we once understood its power to destroy and clear the way for new creations. Only remnants of the old context remain. Buffie Johnson's *Lady of the Beasts*, for example, includes pictures of scorpions drawn on Mimbre pottery surrounded with symbols of the goddess, and a Sumerian bowl from the Hassuna Sawarra period, decorated with eight scorpions surrounding a naked divinity figure with windblown hair. The scorpions swirl about her in a double swastika pattern that symbolizes rebirth and infinity.

Ancient Egyptians revered a goddess of writing called Selket (or Serqet), who wore a scorpion on her head. Selket was sometimes portrayed as a scorpion with a woman's head. Despite her fearsome power over death, she appears beneficent when associated with Isis, the Egyptian mother goddess—probably because, as myths tell it, scorpions loved Isis. Selket, when wearing Isis's horns, symbolized resurrection into new life beyond earthly existence. As the link between the living and the dead, she was the one who helped the dead accommodate themselves to their new state of being.

Guardians of Higher Zones

In many spiritual traditions, scorpions were thought to guard the threshold to higher planes of consciousness. Initiates had to prove their readiness to assimilate a new level of being, and they did this by confronting the guardians of the gate. Gilgamesh, the great hero of the Babylonian epic poem of the same name, confronts scorpion guards in his search for the answer to everlasting life.

Myths, fairy tales, and dreams all use symbolic language to show how the archetypal process works in the human psyche. The universal symbols they employ emerge from the collective unconscious, which contains all the archetypes or basic patterns of human experience and self-awareness.

Jungian analyst Marie-Louise von Franz calls myths master teachings that express the purest and simplest processes in human psychic development as it moves toward wholeness. The setting of a myth, then, describes an inner condition. The characters represent integrative or disruptive energies operating within the psyche of a single individual. The animals of myth, like mosquitoes or scorpions, in contrast to fanciful creatures of legend and fable, are usually taken from Nature or depart only slightly from their form in Nature. As links between gods and people, each represents a qualitatively differentiated manifestation of powers, and we can best understand them in a symbolic context.

The ability of the scorpions to wield their destructive power when faced with an individual's unwillingness to grow and change is part of their role as guardians of the gateways of enlightenment. As one of the ancient symbols of the process of spiritual enlightenment, the scorpion that stings itself to death symbolizes the vital energies within us that can illuminate or destroy. These energies, when transformed, become the treasure, the psyche's wholeness. The fire of transformation that this creature controls through its sting can bring insight and growth to an individual as it moves up the spine through the chakras, or energetic centers of development. And as we have noted, these same energies can also collapse in on the person if ignored and allowed to gather at the base of the spine. Since the scorpion venom is said to contain its own antidote, its gift of self-sacrifice and rebirth has, understandably, been both feared and honored.

The symbolism of myths and dreams provides us with a context to redeem painful encounters with other species, firmly positioning them as agents of transformation. It is not a question of believing in this process of human growth or not believing in it. It doesn't wait for our acceptance and understanding. In fact, many times we don't recognize the initiations for what they are until years have passed and we have gained the perspective of time. But myths show us what is and what can be—depending on our attitude and actions.

Dark Night of the Soul   The author who summed up the scorpion's mythological role as merely destructive is lacking a context that includes the role of destruction in growth. He supports his statement by citing the Book of 1 Kings in the Old Testament, which links desert-dwelling scorpions to drought, wilderness, desolation, and a dreadful scourge. But wilderness and desolation in the Christian tradition is also part of the dark night of the soul, the testing of the individual's resolve and commitment to seek enlightenment. If we place symbols in too narrow a context, we are left with a vague negative association that depends on unconscious bias to fill in the gaps.

The author also states as evidence of the scorpion's destructive (and in his view negative) symbology that the Amazonian peoples believed that the scorpion was sent by a jealous creator to punish men for impregnating women whom he himself desired. This belief may be characteristic of a specific local area or tribe, but most native tribes of Central and South America revered a scorpion goddess of the Amazon River called Ituana or Mother Scorpion. Ituana rules the afterworld, receiving the souls of the dead in her house at the end of the Milky Way. She also oversees the reincarnation of souls to new life and nurses the Earth's children from her abundant breasts.

More Discrepancies   In still another contemporary introduction to scorpions, the author states unequivocally that the ancient Chinese believed that scorpions symbolized pure wickedness. Yet in the ancient

Chinese belief system, it is scorpions and other poisonous and venomous creatures that are enlisted to dispel evil perpetuated by spirits, or *gui* (which according to the Chinese calender are most troublesome during the summer, when the yin part of the year begins). In the Ming dynasty even imperial eunuchs wore badges of the five poisonous insects and creatures that combat sinister spirits: the snake, centipede, scorpion, lizard, and toad or spider. Chinese children today still wear aprons with these images on the fifth day of the fifth month.

The discrepancies in interpretation and the slant of mythology and folklore are not only a function of the unconscious bias that operates when people sift through information unwittingly looking for what they already believe. The discrepancies are also a function of how we relate to power and the great fear of the disintegration process so vital to growth.

The Archetypal Influence of the Scorpion

The fact that civilizations around the world, from the ancient Greeks to the pre-Columbian Mayan culture, all saw a scorpion in the same grouping of stars that includes the supergiant red star Antares (typically the "heart" of the scorpion) hints at its archetypal status. Scorpion star symbology was the same in Babylonia, India, and Greece as it was for natives of the Americas.

Ancient astrological myths everywhere placed the Scorpion at the autumn equinox, tying it to the death of summer and the movement into the darkness of winter. In modern astrology, the sign of Scorpio is ruled by Pluto, a planet whose influence changes us from the deepest place inside ourselves. According to Vickie Noble, author of *Motherpeace*, in its relationship to Pluto the "Scorpion represents transformation, death and mysticism—the three central experiences of the shamanistic mysteries." It also rules "the sex organs, the deep unconscious, and the ability to channel healing energies."[8]

Today the scorpion is still a potent symbol, an archetypal initiator of the process through which we strive for psychological maturity and spiritual enlightenment. Those who are actively engaged in this process would do well to study the rich mythology of scorpions, taking special note when they make an appearance in dreams or in our houses, or when we encounter them outside.

216

If, following the native tradition of taking as a guide the first creature you see when you start your day, you see a scorpion, its presence might signal a time of descent leading, in turn, to an opportunity to deepen and grow. Being open to these forces will radically shift the way you experience the descent, although a certain amount of fear and anxiety always accompanies the stripping away of what is outworn and to be discarded. Encountering a scorpion might also relate to our ability to survive a situation of extremes, whether emotional extremes or trying outer events.

If a scorpion has shown up in your life, you might also recognize in this creature a way of being in the world that is similar to your own way of hiding your vulnerabilities behind the threat of stinging words and actions. You might even discover that you have an affinity for scorpions, as one teenage boy found when he met his first scorpion in a pet therapy program.

Scorpion Therapy   In a novel variation of the popular pet therapy visitation programs, volunteers brought scorpions and other creeping creatures to a home for troubled teenagers, along with the usual assortment of dogs, cats, and rabbits. What they discovered is that creatures like the tarantula and scorpion reached certain teenagers in a way that a kitten or rabbit could not. During one visit, when the knowledgeable volunteer talked about the scorpion and the manner in which its fearsome appearance hid a benign temperament, one boy in particular dropped his sullen and withdrawn stance and began asking questions eagerly, as though in the scorpion he had seen a glimpse of something vital and compelling. Perhaps he had recognized his own way of being in the world.

Affinity for certain creatures surfaces in so-called chance meetings. In short, you know when you meet an animal for which you have an affinity because of the intensity invoked in you by it. I suspect whether you name it fascination, fear, or love, it is still just one of the faces of a primordial bond with other species that calls us home inside ourselves.

Laurens van der Post, champion of the "first people," the Bushmen of South Africa's Kalahari Desert, writes that "the task of every generation is to make what is first in us, new and contemporary." If we apply that to the scorpion, our challenge today is to look for new metaphors that combine ancient psychological and spiritual truths concerning creatures of power with the latest scientific observations about their unique form and mode of being in the world.

Sarah the Sensitive Scorpion

A remarkable story shared by dog trainer Vickie Hearne will even open the door to the possibility of relationship with a scorpion, as unlikely as that might sound.

In her book *Animal Happiness,* Hearne tells the story of Warren Estes, a herpetologist who lived with snakes, kangaroo rats, all sorts of insects, and "Sarah the scorpion." According to Warren, Sarah had trouble at holiday times when his relatives came for a visit. They would look at Sarah and express disgust or fear. He said it took some time after his family left for Sarah to feel good again. He also cautioned Hearne that if she was afraid of Sarah, she shouldn't try to hold her because Sarah wouldn't like it.

The visit was memorable for Hearne. What first caught her attention was how Estes talked to Sarah as he held her and how she seemed to respond. He told Hearne how he could tell when Sarah was nervous or relaxed. He spoke to Sarah, stroking her poison sac and telling her how he admired her courage.

Months after the visit, Hearne remembered the look of Warren's desert-rat brown hand and the scorpion named Sarah glistening there. At first, the creature's glisten from her black patent leather–like shell appeared menacing even to Hearne, who loved animals. But as Warren talked about Sarah, it became "the glisten of something very much like consciousness.[9] Hearne decided, as she watched Warren gently hold Sarah "just as she liked to be held," that the knowledge he had gained from his friendship with Sarah was outside the animal rights controversies and did not promote any political point of view.

She didn't really know how to think about Warren and Sarah. She admits the possibility that he understood something at some level, for he never got bitten or stung by any creature. If Sarah had been a dog instead of a scorpion, perhaps Hearne would have more readily accepted what she had seen. Our assumptions about certain species get in our way and make us forget that we all share a language beyond words, a more direct kind of knowing. Encoded in our bodies, this "language of the heart" travels the trajectory of our thoughts and perceptions, arriving before our words.

Warren related to Sarah as an intelligent, spiritual being capable of responding to love—and she was. He could see that she was comforted and calmed when he held her in a gentle loving way, and he had faith in her and didn't worry about being stung. Sensing his love, Sarah also demonstrated her faith in him, relaxing in his hand. In *The Souls of Animals,* Reverend Gary Kowalski says that when we relate to others in this loving way, "we become confidants—literally, those who come together with faith. And it is through faith—not the faith of creeds or dogmas, but the simple 'animal faith' of resting in communion with each other . . . that we touch the divine."

What Hearne saw when Warren held Sarah—just as she liked to be held—was a man and a scorpion resting in communion with each other, touching the divine. If we make room for that truth inside ourselves and ground it in our daily life, it can transform us and everyone we come in contact with; such is the power and inherent healing potential of our connection to other species.

13. The NATION of WINGED PEOPLES

What the caterpillar calls the end of life the Master calls a butterfly.

—*Richard Bach*

In 1998, when the teachers at Chabad Academy in South Carolina needed a visual aid to teach children about the Holocaust, they initiated the "Butterfly Project." They hoped that paper butterflies would help children visualize the true meaning of the number of people lost. Within the year 1.2 million paper butterflies were made and displayed en masse to remember the Jewish children killed in the Holocaust.

In the spring of 2001, the same group launched the "Project of Remembrance and Deeds of Kindness." Again over a million paper butterflies memorialized and honored the soul of each child killed in the Holocaust as well as from all other acts of genocide. On the back of each butterfly, the child who made it wrote a good deed that he or she would perform on behalf of a child who had died and would never have a chance to perform one.

After the terrorist attacks on New York and Washington, D.C., on September 11, 2001, the butterfly healing project began again, this time initiated by butterfly aficionado Maraleen Manos-Jones, to honor the victims and as a reminder that even small acts like making paper butterflies have the power to create great changes in the world. It is "the butterfly principle," discovered by a meteorologist and popularized in the movie *Jurassic Park*. Since the wings of a butterfly generate wind by affecting tiny air currents, a butterfly stirring the air in Hong Kong could thereby influence a storm system over Boston, just as fractional changes in temperature on the ocean's surface turn tropical storms into hurricanes. In short, small changes in dynamic systems produce changes of great magnitude.

A quantum view helps explain the butterfly principle by referencing the unbroken wholeness behind all apparent separateness. It is British physicist David Bohm's "implicate order," out of which all seemingly discrete events arise. It is also the unseen spiritual world that indigenous peoples have always attended to. It means that small events emerging out of this wholeness give rise to nonlocal events, because all is connected. Unseen connections create effects in places and ways we can only imagine.

The power of the butterfly extends beyond the butterfly principle. Its influence over our imagination is a force long recognized in cultures worldwide. This delicate creature is a universal symbol of hope and escape from sorrow and death. Elisabeth Kübler-Ross, a pioneer in the field of death and dying, often speaks of the numerous drawings of butterflies she saw in the barracks at Nazi concentration camps in Europe. They had been scratched into the wooden walls by children and adults incarcerated there. Today pictures of butterflies can be found in almost every hospice, and this symbol of transformation and life beyond death is used extensively by grief counselors, spiritual centers, and support groups for the bereaved.

An Affinity for Beauty

Beauty, not symbolism, is what usually attracts people to butterflies. An American Indian myth teaches that butterflies were created because the Great Spirit wanted people to love Nature and seek out its beauty. Sometimes the pull of their beauty is so great that people pursue an interest in butterflies side by side with other work. Paul Ehrlich, for example, Bing Professor of Population Studies at Stanford University, is an environmental warrior who addresses population issues, nuclear Armageddon, and extinction. And he has an affinity for butter-flies. For over forty years he and his wife travel each summer to the meadows of western Colorado to observe butterflies.

It is not unusual for a butterfly authority to be self-taught, like the late Paul Grey, who was America's leading expert on a particular butterfly genus and a carpenter by trade. Jeffrey Glassberg, president of the National Association of Butterflies, which sponsors the annual butterfly count, is a molecular biologist. Richard Heitzman, an internationally recognized authority on butterflies and moths, earns his living as a U.S. Postal Service mail carrier.

Nature photographer Kjell B. Sandved of Washington, D.C., embarked on a twenty-year journey to thirty countries in order to find and photograph every letter and the numbers 0 through 9 on butterfly wings. Because of his passion and perseverance, almost every elementary school has a beautiful poster of his discoveries.

Affinities can pull at you during any stage of your life. Ronald Boender was a retired electrical engineer who had always enjoyed watching butterflies. He followed that interest and started cultivating plants to attract them in his Florida backyard. It was a life-shaping decision, an act that linked him with the power and resources of a latent affinity. In 1988, he founded Butterfly World in Coconut Creek, Florida, today, one of the largest butterfly research and education centers in the United States.

Legal secretary Ro Vaccaro was stirred to action when visiting Pacific Grove, California, one of the few wintering grounds for monarch butterflies in the United States. One dazzling glimpse of thousands of monarchs was enough. She sent her resignation back to Washington, D.C., and started Friends of the Monarchs. Recently, her 180-member group helped convince the people of Pacific Grove to pass a tax hike to save a butterfly resting site from development.

The Call of the Butterfly

If butterflies have called you into their sphere, you will find food for your passion in Maraleen Manos-Jones's *The Spirit of Butterflies: Myth, Magic and Art*. This extensively researched and enchantingly beautiful book—a celebration of the power of these creatures as spiritual beings—will pull you further into their magic just as they did the author, who now works full time on their behalf.

A chance encounter with a butterfly was Manos-Jones's first call. It landed on her heart and stayed there for an afternoon. The second call occurred a few years later when she was out looking for herbs. She tripped and fell to one knee. Before her, a few inches from her face, was a fat caterpillar. She took it home, recognizing it as a monarch waiting to happen. She fed it milkweed until one day, after it fastened itself to a branch and hung upside down, its skin split and revealed a pale green chrysalis dotted with gold around its rim. Then she waited. The day it emerged, as an orange and black butterfly from the now-transparent chrysalis, a hurricane was raging outside. Manos-Jones didn't release her (she was convinced it was a female) but fed her honey and water from her hand. The bond between woman and butterfly was solidified over the next couple of days as the butterfly explored her human beneficiary, walking on Jones while stretching and flexing her wings. Jones noticed that she often lingered on her shoulders and her forehead, between her brows. When the storm subsided, Jones took her outside and released her. The butterfly took wing, returning a few times to land on Jones as though reluctant to leave. But finally she soared up into the air, catching the wind, and was gone. What remained was a passion for these creatures that would set Jones on her life's course.[1]

Affinity and synchronistic experiences go hand in hand. The forces of affinity seem magnetized or charged in some way and perhaps set up potentialities for fulfillment. I like poet and naturalist David Hope's suggestion that "certain people see things other people don't because those things desire to be seen by them."[2] Seeing involves in some mysterious way the "will" of the creatures that are seen. In the language of the new science, our acts of intention and observation are part of a process that brings forth what we are observing. We literally evoke the potential that already exists in a web of connections that is literally confounding those steeped in traditional science. It means the Manos-Jones-caterpillar-butterfly potential was there waiting for realization, just as all affinities exist as a potential, waiting for our interest and attention.

Perhaps the endangered Palos Verdes blue butterfly wanted Arthur Bonner, a former Los Angeles street gang member and drug dealer, to see its fragility and its struggle for survival in an asphalt-covered world. How else can we explain how deeply the plight of this insect touched this street-smart young man? Interviewed in *People* magazine, Bonner says he learned of its uncertain fate while he was participating in a conservation program aimed at giving at-risk youths a new start, and he identified with the butterfly in a profound way. He followed his feelings and started restoring the habitats it needed to survive. Now an employee of the same conservation program, Bonner says these butterflies facilitated his own metamorphosis into the person he was meant to be, saving some vital aspect of himself from extinction. That is why he is now returning the favor and helping these butterflies recover their presence in the rugged hills of California's Palos Verdes peninsula as well as leading inner-city kids on field trips.

For the Love of Butterflies

Butterflies are easy to love. They don't bite or sting, and their beauty has elevated them above other insects, allowing them to escape most of our negative projections—but not all.

Several years ago a tabloid featured a story about a six-foot butterfly on the rampage (finally shot by a farmer in the Midwest). More recently, a Pulitzer Prize–winning columnist, who cheerfully reflects the biases of our culture in his writing, reacted to what his wife thought was a bat flying around their kitchen ceiling. Only it wasn't a bat; it was a large black butterfly. He took a broom to it anyway, killing it. Perhaps he felt justified because it had frightened his wife and was an intruder of sorts in his home. I think his projections created an enemy out of a benign creature and prevented him from seeing that it was trapped and needed his help, not his aggression.

Luckily, most people find butterflies charismatic, even when we find them on occasion in our homes, confused by walls and windows. Conservationists hope that the butterfly, as the "poster child" of the invertebrates, can generate enough public support so that we will rally to save its endangered habitats, which are also home to countless species that we don't find charming.

As epiphanies of the Goddess, butterflies have been revered throughout the history of our species. The ancient Mexicans worshiped them as their god of love and beauty, regarding butterfly eggs as the seeds from which happiness grows.

A strong association between butterflies and love is also present in the East. The Japanese Emperor Genso reportedly let butterflies choose his loves for him by freeing caged butterflies in his garden and taking note of which maidens attracted them. And Christian myths tell of butterflies originating in the Garden of Eden and then following Eve, whom they loved, when she was banished from this paradise.

Butterflies in Trouble Not everyone working with butterflies has recognized the call of these insects as an honored trust. A number of enterprises, capitalizing on the insect's association with love and happiness, sell butterflies for release at weddings, store openings, and other happy occasions. This may be passion skewed by economics.

Many who understand what butterflies need to thrive are alarmed by this trend to exploit the insects in this way. Robert Pyle, founder of the Xerces Society,[3] the largest insect conservation organization in the world, says that releases of butterflies for our special occasions don't take the butterfly's mating and migration cycles into account. And some individuals are invariably crushed in the rush to release them into the air simultaneously. Another fear is that selling butterflies will tempt some people to take them from overwintering sites, an act that could eventually threaten entire species.

When a person inspired by butterflies isn't unduly influenced by economic concerns, he or she is likely to be concerned with their welfare and take the trouble to find out what they need to survive. Like many other of their less attractive relatives, butterflies are in trouble.

Finely tuned to their environment, they are one of the first to react when the climate changes. In fact, since butterflies, as both caterpillars and adults, are finicky about their surroundings, their presence in a damaged area means that a good measure of balance is still operating.

We generally think flowers are enough to attract and keep butterflies in an area, but they are not. Fog will deter many sensitive species from feeding on the flowers in an area. And butterflies often perceive simple divisions of their territory, such as those created by roads and fences, as impassable.

To complicate things further, many caterpillars feed on just one species of plant—often a plant considered a weed. This need for specific plants has pushed several species in the United States into extinction after development destroyed their habitat. About 80 percent of all butterfly species are hanging on in degraded habitats. About 10 to 20 percent need the real habitat and without it will disappear in the near future. Those butterflies are not going to make it unless we help. Fifteen North

American species are now listed officially as endangered or threatened, and at least seventy-five are candidates for the endangered list.

It is not surprising, given their finely tuned biology, that the absence of butterflies in an area typically signals that pesticides have been used. While many insects suffer from exposure to commonly used pesticides, butterflies fail noticeably and right away—almost always dying out. Predictably, then, the ongoing chemical war against the butterfly's poor relative the gypsy moth, has also hurt butterflies. Even Bt, the natural insecticide discussed in our look at genetic modification, destroys butterfly caterpillars as well as the target insects.

Moths and the Shadow

We are not as likely to include moths in our circle of concern, especially the small drab ones that gather around outside lights. In fact, we don't normally think of moths as beautiful at all. If we were responsible for classifying them, we might readily divide them by beauty and whether or not they fly in the daytime or at night. Most of us assume moths are dull-colored night flyers with featherlike antennae and furry bodies, while butterflies are brightly colored day flyers with club-shaped antenna. But they don't separate out so neatly, because some moths do fly in the daytime; and while many moths have dull coloring and feathery antennae, others do not.

Another distinction is that moths spin cocoons in which to make the change from caterpillar to adult. Butterflies complete their metamorphosis inside a chrysalis, a hard covering that is actually the caterpillar's final molt.

In general, the night-flying habits of most moths have sentenced them to carrying the shadow projections for all but nocturnal butterflies. In Bolivia, for example, the Aymara people took the presence of a certain rare moth as an omen of death. And the ancient Mexicans feared one of the large night-flying moths as a messenger of death.

In early Christian mystical writings, moths symbolized the temptations of the flesh. And the death's-head sphinx moth, a large moth that sometimes makes a strident sound when it flies and has a skull-shaped marking above its thorax, represented Satan and was an emblem of death.

Despite the shadow projections, however, the moth and butterfly are linked in the symbolism of most ancient cultures by their mysterious transformation inside cocoon and chrysalis. Both insects were believed to know the secrets of moving from life to death to new life.

From Caterpillar to Butterfly

Few have witnessed the change in moth or butterfly caterpillar without making a comparison to death, resurrection, and renewal. In ancient religions the butterfly or moth spirit was considered a divine womb. The pairing of the double ax (reminiscent of these insects with outspread wings) with moths and butterflies was a prominent religious image that reflected an understanding that both death and renewal were born from the spirit of these winged creatures.

Indigenous tribes, understanding that the intrinsic patterns of life were reflected in the smallest of creatures, associated the caterpillar's act of transformation and rebirth with the renewal of Nature each spring. The hoop dance of the Plains Indians, for example, is part of the annual celebration of winter's transformation into spring and includes a dancer emulating a caterpillar that turns into a beautiful butterfly.

For the Butterfly clan of the Hopi Indians, the butterfly is a totem, and its spirit is personified in their kachina figures. Every year, young men and women of this tribe perform the Bulitikibi or Butterfly Dance, a ceremonial dance of renewal believed to bring good crops.

Getting Out   As models of growth and transformation, insects in general are without equal. All must molt, a periodical process of shedding their external skeleton. Molting happens in one of two ways. In gradual or simple metamorphosis, which cockroaches, grasshoppers, and preying mantises undergo, the young insects called nymphs have the same general shape and features as the adult (imago). At each instar, or developmental stage, they molt or break out of their exoskeletons and emerge bigger than before. Human bodies grow in a similar way, except that the changes in our skeletons make the transitions more gradual.

The second, more complex solution to growth is called complete metamorphosis and is the one adopted by caterpillars, maggots, and most grubs. It is also the way in which the human psyche grows, which we'll discuss in the next section. Complete metamorphosis has an incubation or pupal stage during which virtually all body tissues break down and are reorganized into a new form—so that immature insects or larvae look radically different from their parents. Recall that maggots don't look like flies and grubs don't resemble beetles. Neither do caterpillars resemble butterflies and moths. The advantage of this form of development, which the vast majority of insects undergo, is that it allows the species to take advantage of very different habitats.

Metaphors of Growth

As we've seen throughout this book, patterns of life are seeded in Nature and prior to our age, were often woven into a cultural or religious context. The stages of simple metamorphosis that a grasshopper undergoes, for instance, were recognized symbolically as being the power we have to free ourselves from earthly concerns. This ability was the reason that the grasshopper was respected as a symbol for the soul in early Christian iconography.

The stages of complete metamorphosis evidenced in beetles, flies, moths, and butterflies mirror in some universal way the stages of any growth that involves changing from one identity to the next. All instances of such radical change include, of necessity, the darkness of an interim period where the process that permits the reorganizing can take place. People of widely diverse cultures and religious orientations, observing this process and its startling result, saw in it a model applicable to human life.

Transforming Ourselves and Society   This image of transformation is as relevant today as it was in ancient times—for groups as well as people. On Earth Day (April 22) 1990, author and educator Norie Huddle wrote and published a book called *Butterfly*.[4] In it she tells the story of the metamorphosis of humanity from a nonsustainable society to a "butterfly civilization" that fulfills humanity's potential, individually and collectively bringing peace, health, prosperity and justice to all the Earth's inhabitants. In her now-popular analogy, she compared where we are today to where the caterpillar is after having consumed enormous amounts food. Like the insect, we are encased in our chrysalis and approaching metamorphosis. For the caterpillar this is a critical time when certain cells, called imaginal cells (that is, cells relating to the insect stage called the imago), begin to develop and the process of building the various parts of what will be a butterfly begins in earnest—although from the outside it looks as though nothing is happening. Huddle says that the culture's imaginal cells are the individuals, groups, and activities that are building new patterns—clumping and clustering together and sharing information. She sees all attempts to hold to the status quo as merely the caterpillar's immune system rigidly and reactively clinging to its old worm ways and not recognizing the imaginal cells as its own—until such time when enough are in place for the winged form to emerge.

In her 1998 book *Conscious Evolution*, futurist Barbara Marx Hubbard picks up Huddle's metaphor to explain the metamorphosis of humanity from its polluting, overpopulating phase through a whole-system transition that eventually promises to fulfill our potential as a fully conscious society. And Willis Harman applied the insect analogy to explain how whole-system change works in our culture and how business will be transformed from its economic and financial foundation to one that values all life-forms and the planet. Like Huddle, he likened where we are in the process of this changeover to the caterpillar within its chrysalis and approaching, through blind instinct (and perhaps grace), its transformation. The communities and organizations already formed and working toward radical change—and under the considerable influence of the feminist, ecological, and spiritual movements—are the imaginal cells in the business community. When the current structure comes down, those "imaginal cells" will be there in full operation and business will have been transformed.

In keeping with the resurgence of butterfly images and metaphors, at the United Nations in New York, when heads of state from around the world assembled on June 26, 1997 to reassess the progress made since the first Earth Summit, Alan Moore, founder of the Butterfly Gardeners Association in Oakland, California, organized a release of butterflies (with careful attention to their pre-release care and climate needs) to symbolize humanity's new awareness of the fragile beauty of the Earth.[5] Moore, who has since then devoted all of his time to raising awareness about the potency of this symbol for the millennium, believes that humanity is emerging out of its chrysalis and beginning a new chapter of evolution in which peaceful coexistence and responsible stewardship will be the norm. For Moore the butterfly is the most appropriate symbol for the renaissance of the Earth and the dawn of world peace, and could inspire people to work harder for that renaissance. A man with many synchronistic butterfly experiences of his own, Moore has also pooled his resources behind the butterfly healing project, hoping that people nationwide will rally around the idea and create and display six million butterflies.

Models of Spiritual Growth

Butterflies and moths model a universal process of transformation and growth. The idea of a hidden life that comes forth when conditions are right is attractive. It gives us hope that a beautiful and winged life is also within us, buried perhaps under layers of societal and familial beliefs. To assist our transformation, all varieties of the spiritual path tell us that our thoughts and actions will help bring about our metamorphosis into the species we were meant to be. Our thoughts and actions are our imaginal cells. Taking our lead from the insects and trusting that at times we too must be in darkness, maybe we can enter life's deep wellspring without erecting elaborate defenses.

In *A Mythic Life*, Jean Houston sees the metamorphosis of society as a renaissance with implications for our personal growth as individuals. She believes that when the door to our "caterpillar self" has been unlocked and the wall to the human soul breached, we will be filled and directed by a flood of new "butterfly questions" about who we really are and what life is about.

In spiritual traditions the human being who works for his or her own transformation into a more perfected state by leaving the agitation, noise, and anxiety of ordinary life has frequently been compared to the caterpillar entering the pupa stage to become a butterfly. The pupa provides an ideal image of serene contemplation and a promise of new life from the perspective of certain Eastern religions. Even today in the Himalayan mountains, some Asian ascetics live for years in almost inaccessible caves, existing on a minimum of food in order to expose their souls more directly to the light of divinity. Afterward they become great gurus, comparing themselves to the huge butterflies that inhabit the valleys of the Indus and the Ganges.

Christian Symbology   In Christian symbolism the caterpillar is a symbol of Christ. According to Louis Charbonneau-Lassay's *Bestiary of*

Christ, in the fifth century the pope declared that "Christ was a worm, not because he was humbled, or humble himself, but because he was resurrected." In fact, all worms that underwent a metamorphosis were emblems of Christ. The transformation of the caterpillar (more than that of any other insect larva) represented the broken body of Jesus transformed into the resurrected body that emerged from the darkness of the tomb. A bright yellow butterfly common in the provinces of western France has become the symbol of the resurrected Christ and is called the Easter Jesus because it is the first butterfly to emerge in March or April.

The caterpillar also represents the Christian man or woman who must pass through two preparatory stages before becoming a butterfly. The first stage, symbolized by the caterpillar, is physical life, and the second stage, symbolized by the chrysalis or cocoon, is death. After death the human soul reaches its goal of resurrection and eternal life, symbolized by the butterfly.

The Darkness of Transformation   For seekers of personal as well as planetary renewal, the goal of wings is often overshadowed by the dying that takes place in the darkness of the cocoon or chrysalis. Those who have witnessed or experienced the struggle that accompanies dying to what is old and outdated within ourselves and our culture might take heart from the fact that the transformation process in other species demonstrates that struggle is an integral part of the renewal pattern. I heard a reportedly true story told of a man who found a cocoon and took it home to await the moth's emergence. One day he saw that the insect had made a tiny hole in the cocoon, and he watched for several hours as the insect struggled to force its body through it. Then it seemed to stop making any progress. In fact, it appeared as though it could go no further. The man, being a kind person, decided to help the moth, so he snipped off the remaining bit of the cocoon with scissors. The moth emerged easily, but it had a swollen body and its wings were shriveled and small. The man watched in happy anticipation for its body to contract and its shriveled wings to expand and unfold. But nothing happened. The moth lived out its life without ever being able to fly. By "saving" it from its long struggle, the man had stopped the process by which blood is pumped into the body and wings in preparation for its winged life.

The Butterfly Soul

Just as the concept of a soul has been recorded in every culture known to history, including our own, so has the idea of a butterfly soul.

In many cultures the butterfly and moth were believed to be the souls of departed ones. The Japanese treat any butterfly that enters their house kindly since they believe souls customarily take butterfly shape in order to announce that they are leaving the body for good. And in the South Pacific Solomon Islands, a dying person tells family members in which shape he or she intends to transmigrate—usually as a bird, butterfly, or moth. From that moment on, the family treats that particular species as sacred.

Today the association between the butterfly and the soul continues. Bill and Judy Guggenheim, authors of *Hello from Heaven*, cite the butterfly and moth as the most frequently mentioned sign of an after-death communication. The following two stories taken from their chapter on butterfly and rainbow signs illustrate the ways these insects contact people.

Love Is Eternal   A retired police officer who had lost his teenage daughter, Diana, in an automobile accident ten months earlier was at home with his wife and some visiting relatives. As they sat outside on lounge chairs, the man noticed a butterfly. Immediately the thought of Diana presented itself. He thought, "If it's you, Diana, come down and tell me." Without hesitating, the butterfly landed on his finger and walked up and down it. Then it went onto his hand and continued to walk back and forth on it. Astonished, he remembers that he was so close to the insect he could see its antennae moving. His wife looked at him as though she knew what he was thinking.

He got up and went into the kitchen, and the butterfly stayed on his hand. He told the butterfly he had to take a shower and that it had to go outside now. He opened the door and pushed it gently off his hand, watching as it took to the sky. It was an unbelievable experience. He had never had a butterfly land on him before. He went in to take a shower and cried. Later, when he attended a conference of the Compassionate Friends, a self-help organization for grieving families, he learned that its symbol was a butterfly.

Luna Moth   Moths also have a long history of bringing messages to people. In Southeast Asia there is a moth that lives on a diet of human tears, a substance that contains various proteins and an apt image of comfort. Maybe the souls of those who have passed away return on wings and in silence to console and drink away the tears of the ones who remain behind.

Other moths bring comfort and assurance by their timely appearances. In the second account from *Hello from Heaven*, a teacher and her husband shared how they lost their teenage son. Two weeks after he died from a heart attack, the mother was in the kitchen when her husband called to her. She went outside to join him, and there, in broad daylight was a large chartreuse moth about five inches wide across its wings. The husband picked it up and placed it on the branch of a nearby bush. They watched it for a long time, and finally it fluttered away. Later she looked it up in a book and discovered it was a luna moth, and *luna* means "moon" in Latin. Her son's hobby was astronomy. He had wanted to be an astrophysicist. She also discovered that the luna moth belongs to the family Saturniidae, and above her late son's desk was a picture of Saturn. These parents believe that their son sent this sign to let them know he was in a new life.

Synchronistic Events

The personal associations that make such occurrences so healing are always present in meaningful coincidences. The events that connect our subjective thoughts and feelings with the outer physical world often bring reassurance or guidance. They return us to a connection with life temporarily overshadowed by doubts, grief, or estrangement of some kind. And there is a magic to the timing of these visits that no amount of factual information or dispersion statistics on a species can dispel. We find ourselves suddenly in the embrace of the natural world, lifted into a terrain crisscrossed with tracks of meaning and seeded with divine forces.

In Helen Fisher's book *From Erin with Love*, a moving account of her daughter's struggle with cancer and her communications to her family after her death, Fisher describes the frequent visits of butterflies. The visits began four days after Erin died. A yellow and black butterfly appeared in the area where they scattered her ashes. Two days later at a ceremony celebrating her life that was held in a natural amphitheater on the campus of the college Erin had attended, a yellow and black butterfly flew down the hill and into the amphitheater. There it fluttered back and forth over the seats of Erin's family and friends, capturing their attention.

During the three weeks following Erin's death, her sister, who lived in a large city, was "literally dive-bombed by a yellow and black butterfly on two different occasions. In each instance it flew straight at her and she could feel the flutter of its wings in her hair." The butterfly continued to appear to Erin's family and friends at significant moments— over two dozen visits in all—bringing them the message that Erin was alive and well, a communication subsequently reinforced and delivered in a variety of ways in the months that followed.

The Moth's Visit   Some visits are not so highly charged as the ones that convey news of a deceased loved one. Yet all speak of a dimension of life, a pattern of deep intentionality, that we are prone to forget. Years ago the presence of a large moth lifted me into this awareness.

The insect descended on cinnamon-colored wings in the early morning hours of a summer day and took shelter in the protected alcove of my front door. Careful not to disturb its meditative posture, I studied the markings, the colorful "eyes" etched delicately on the faintly powdered surface of the outspread wings, the graceful curve of the fringed antennae, and the sturdy hair-thin legs. I knew it was a polyphemus moth because of a childhood interest in butterflies and moths, but I wondered about its presence, as I had never seen one in the area before. It was some hours later, with the moth still on my porch, that I realized an illustration of this kind of moth graced the cover of a book I was currently reading about a medicine woman.

Synchronicity and Grace

Native cultures traditionally viewed synchronistic occurrences as a sign of health. Even today counselors agree that when a person fails to notice synchronistic occurrences in his or her life, it is a sign that something is wrong. When you have a synchronistic experience, you feel seen and affirmed by something larger than yourself and it restores personal power and brings ease.

Synchronistic events accompany crucial phases in our growth and are often called grace. I like spiritual pilgrim Scott Peck's description of grace as more than gifts.

> In grace, something is overcome; grace occurs in spite of something; grace occurs in spite of separation and estrangement. Grace is the reunion of life with life, the reconciliation of the self with itself.[6]

Often what is overcome, if only temporarily, is our general estrangement from life—our grief, our loneliness, or our uncertainty about a particular action. In keeping with the butterfly's role as emissary and as a model for growth and transformation, it should not be surprising that often a butterfly or moth makes an appearance at a critical time in our lives when we are at a junction of some kind. Perhaps we are contemplating a particular course of action or have just embarked on a new inner or outer path.

Flying Boy into Man   Psychologist and men's workshop leader John Lee reports in his book *The Flying Boy* that he had his first out-of-body experience with a butterfly, and that since that time butterflies have appeared to him at just the right moment to remind him of the things he learned that day. The initial experience happened when he was alone on a boat dock reading and a butterfly appeared and landed on his big toe. He followed his intuition and attempted to exchange bodies with it. The butterfly inched its way up his body, finally resting on Lee's hand, where it stayed. He stroked it gently and soon the exchange occurred. After experiencing the interior world of a butterfly for about forty-five minutes, he gently slipped back into his body, having learned lessons that, although untranslatable, would inform his life.

In the months that followed he had periodic experiences with butterflies. His most memorable encounter came when he was working on the early drafts of a manuscript about his journey to find his authentic masculinity. It was winter. A butterfly flittered through his living room and landed on his desk, and its presence felt like a blessing on his work and a reminder of his own metamorphosis from an ungrounded "flying boy" into a man.

Other Signs

Traditionally when prodigious numbers of butterflies, moths, or caterpillars appeared, they inspired fear and were considered signs of doom. In tenth-century Japan, for example, when the warrior Tairano Masakado was secretly preparing for a famous revolt, there appeared in the city of Kyoto a swarm of butterflies so vast that the people were frightened. They believed that the unusual number of insects was a portent of evil and that the butterflies were the spirits of the thousands who would die in the coming battle.

Message from the Monarchs Insects in large numbers don't always spell doom, as Sherry Ruth Anderson, coauthor of *The Feminine Face of God* and more recently *The Cultural Creatives*, discovered. When her father was seventy-five, Anderson first learned of his fascination with monarch butterflies and the mystery of their migration. He would ask her, clearly puzzled, "How can they make the long journey?" Even when she researched the phenomenon and presented her findings on the mechanics of migration, he would still shake his head and wonder out loud how they could accomplish the journey when they are so small and frail. He had somehow sensed a correspondence between himself and the delicate monarchs and their ability to make such a journey, for he was weakened after just coming through his second heart bypass in a decade. Eventually, Anderson understood that when he asked about the monarchs, he was really wondering about his own journey.

Later that year, when her father lay dying in a coma, the family gathered. Anderson's niece Catherine was there and asked to talk to her grandfather privately. After a long time in his room, she emerged, eyes red from crying. Later Anderson and her niece headed for a walk on the beach. Catherine shared that she was angry with her grandfather and had wanted to let him know how upset she was that he never even tried to get to know her. And now it was too late.

As they strolled along, they began to notice that they were being enveloped by a mass of orange and black butterflies—monarchs. Hundreds of them were keeping pace with them as they walked. In all her years of growing up in that area, Anderson had never seen more than two or three butterflies at a time. She kept thinking about her father and his fascination with monarchs, but she didn't say anything to her niece. Then Catherine stopped and nodded toward the butterflies.

> "This is Pop-pop," she said calmly, using the name she'd called my father when she was a child . . . "He's come to say good-bye to us. It's okay now. It's okay how he was, not understanding us and making mistakes. I forgive him." She paused, reflecting. "I'm glad he was my grandfather."[7]

When she finished speaking, the multitude of butterflies that had been accompanying them changed direction, flew directly into the wind, and swiftly disappeared. Anderson says she wanted to tell Catherine how these long-distance survivors had been coming for a whole year to visit her grandfather, the survivor in the hospital bed preparing for his own long journey, but she was speechless. Two days later her father died, completing his journey "just fine."

Dragonfly Questions

The Oglala Sioux grouped flying creatures together, calling them the "Winged Peoples,"[8] and associated them all with the powers of the wind. Included in this group were birds, butterflies, moths, and dragonflies.

If it is true, as the ancients believed, that the more simply constituted creatures respond more readily to the unseen energies that have proved so maddeningly elusive to scientists, it is likely that insects at one time or another—especially the Winged Peoples—will be involved in a meaningful coincidence that happens to us—especially if we are open to them and pay attention.

In an essay included in Arielle Ford's *More Hot Chocolate for the Mystical Soul,* author and speaker Tom Youngholm describes a transformative experience with a dragonfly that flitted in front of his face and then landed on the knuckle of his left thumb. After soaring off again, the insect returned to land on the same spot. In that moment there was a silent exchange that Youngholm still can't find the words to adequately describe. He considers it the deepest connection he had ever felt with anyone or anything—a moment of grace at a time when he was mourning the death of his mother.

When the dragonfly left, Youngholm was flooded with questions about his life and his choices. His experience follows Jean Houston's idea that when the door to our "caterpillar self" is unlocked and the wall enclosing the human soul is breached, we will be filled and directed by a flood of new "butterfly questions" about who we really are and what life is about. Only in this example, the wall is breached by another of the Winged Peoples, the dragonfly, and so it was, perhaps, "dragonfly questions" that filled Youngholm.

The Winged Peoples

Flying creatures are linked in our imaginations by their ability to take to the air, a feat much admired in native cultures. They were also grouped together because of the widespread belief that they were messengers from other realms. Not only did they bring messages from the dead, but they also were believed to bring messages from other kingdoms intimately connected to Earth. Interspecies communicator Penelope Smith agrees that some forms of life, including butterflies, dragonflies, and hummingbirds, play the role of interkingdom or interdimensional messengers. These envoys adjust their vibrations to interact with the life rhythms of several dimensions and often convey messages from other animals or plants.

In *Animals: Our Return to Wholeness*, Smith shares the story of Marcia Ramsland, who received a message from a young white pine tree—via a butterfly. Ramsland had observed a yellow-green cast on the tree and considered chopping it down when a butterfly appeared in front of her and telepathetically advised her not to. Realizing that the butterfly was acting in the tree's behalf, she took its advice. In time, the tree's color changed to a more normal appearance, showing that it was not deteriorating, as the woman had thought, but had only been going through a growth phase.

Interestingly, another butterfly-tree partnership captured the imagination of the nation. A then-twenty-three-year-old woman who calls herself Julia Butterfly camped out in the branches of a 200-foot-high redwood for over two years to stop Pacific Lumber Company from cutting it down. "My spirit led me here, and I mean to stay with it," she would explain to reporters. When asked about her name, she said she had an intense spiritual experience with a butterfly as a child. The insect had landed and remained on her hand during a long and trying walk, fascinating and fortifying her.

In folklore, there is a long association between butterflies and moths and the realm of Nature spirits or fairies. Ted Andrews, author of *Animal Speak* and *Animal Wise*, rich books on the mystical powers of other species, says that prior to giving a workshop on fairies and elves, he was meditating at a nearby Nature center in preparation. When he opened his eyes, he was surrounded by a dozen or more black and yellow butterflies. Several were even in his lap. The occurrence was significant to him. He knew that in traditional angelology, yellow and black are colors often associated with the archangel Auriel in her role of overseeing the activities of the Nature spirits. He took the butterflies as a positive indication of the supportive energy that would accompany him at his workshop.

The clairvoyant Austrian scientist Rudolf Steiner also connected insects to Nature spirits. He maintained that insects were a vital link between the physical world and the wavelengths of these energies—especially the fire spirits.[9]

That insects operate using wavelengths undetectable to our human senses has already been established by traditional science. In fact, Philip Callahan, the scientist who discovered how plants communicate to insects that they are sick and how insects communicate with each other, thinks that a vast communication grid is operating, composed partly of billions of insect antennae that receive wavelengths and link Earth to the cosmos in a symphony of vibration. I like this image of continual communication between the universe and insects (and all life forms right down to cells). And it echoes the perennial wisdom passed down in traditional cultures that everything in creation is sentient and capable of communication. It also makes the notion of insects acting as messengers of invisible realms very plausible, given their numbers and communication apparatus.

Helping the Messengers

The weaving of scientific and esoteric knowledge provides a backdrop of complexity and mystery in keeping with the enormous mystery of our existence, here and beyond. The winged messengers' communications underscore the interdependence of our inner life and outer experiences, all held within the web of some vast, if largely unknown universal network. All support the idea of a consciousness-directed universe in which our intent is of utmost importance and our every thought, word, and action is witnessed.

The way into the numinous underlining of our existence begins with a step out of the familiar house of the self, past the end of the known road, and into the borderland places (which the insects love) with only our intention and attention. To plan for experiences that confirm our deepest longings for meaning and connection requires that we stay alert. Inattention is a major impediment to these kinds of experiences. Another obstacle is the fact that many species of the winged tribe are endangered. If we allow these species to disappear from the Earth, their habitat replaced by concrete and the clamor and neon lights of shopping malls and amusement parks, will they only be able to contact us in dreams? And if they are no longer a part of the physical world, who will inspire us with their beauty, give us hope by letting us witness their transformations, and bring us comfort and the assurance that our loved ones, who have passed on, are close by and just fine?

Will those of us who are the recipients of the Winged Peoples' messages respond to their plight? Will those groups who have chosen the butterfly as their symbol of hope give hope to the creatures on Earth who are propelled by the beneficent unseen energies of creation? Will they add their voice to the voices already protesting the demise of the plant-loving caterpillars and the eradication of the water-bound dragonfly larvae, innocent victims of our current agricultural practices and war against the gypsy moth and mosquito? Can we assure them that there will be a place for them to live and thrive and perpetuate their kind? And will all of us who love their beauty speak on their behalf and stand up to people who, for whatever reason, are unable to value them over economic concerns?

What rejoicing there will be among all forms of consciousness when we can acknowledge the role of the Nation of Winged Peoples as messengers of those realms within and beyond our living Earth and follow them when they beckon us. And what celebrations we can initiate when our own imaginal cells mature and we can finally see in these creatures a reflection of our own winged life, ready to unfold and take flight.

14. Strange Angels

I have sent you nothing but angels.
—Conversations with God
by Donald Neale Walsh

Ancient peoples looked to dreams and visions—and the creatures that appeared in them—for guidance, warning, wisdom, and creativity. Since other species were seen as messengers from the Creator, it was a priority for these people to understand the message.

The shaman or healer who knew how to "read" an animal did not learn it from a dream sourcebook or bestiary but by observing the creature and reflecting on its ways. Encoded in its appearance and unique living strategies was its message.

Although we have access to many facts about insects, we are not adept at translating those facts into meaning—especially in dreams. We are likely to interpret a dream in line with the biases of the culture, until we realize that there is a bias. Even Carl Jung changed his beliefs about insects as merely "reflex automata," when he learned late in his life that bees are capable of language and are therefore, in all probability, conscious and capable of thought.

In a popular dream glossary, the assumption of insect as adversary and as an object of fear or distaste is clearly evident: Termites are reduced to meaning "slow destruction." Cockroaches are equated with "dirt, . . . neglect, carelessness, [and] lack of pride or self-worth." Scorpions imply "vengeance," beetles "the destruction forces at work in our lives, especially in our seed-thought and affirmations," and flies "a real pest."

The cultural bias comes through clearly in these descriptions. So does a lack of knowledge about insects that would honor their visit as "Other," expand our symbolic vocabularies, and lend our dreams more creative possibilities. Imagine a glossary that interpreted termites as altruistic and vital to the growth of the "trees" of our minds, that is, vital to the healthy formation and structure of our thought, abilities, and characteristics. What they eat in a dream then might be our outgrown ideas, the deadwood of our minds.

Even indigenous people who have been educated in Western thought fall prey to the bias of our culture toward certain species. A recent book on American Indian Nature symbols by a native healer who holds a master's degree in sociology and psychology contains a mixture of native lore and Western prejudice. For those species our culture has branded pests, he reiterates the cultural bias as though it were a general native view calling flies a pestilence bringing disease and messages of envy and inclement weather. He also says that the kinds of flies that feed on dead things and garbage are bad signs representing evil and dark forces.

In his statements we find little of the native view of flies as navigational wonders and guardians of fish, or of flies' ancient connection to valor. Also absent is an acknowledgment of the destructuring or recycling powers of flies, so vital to life's cycles of renewal. Instead, the Western myths that limit the fly to being only a carrier of disease and filth and the Judeo-Christian condemnation of the fly as evil are restated.

The same Westernized native also condemns cockroaches. He considers them dirty, a "bad insect," and an unfavorable sign that warns of forthcoming sickness and undesirable visitors. He also notes that sorcerers work with these kinds of insects, sometimes sending swarms of them against other people.

Again we see the Western view of cockroaches as dirty, disease-spreading creatures. His statement that they can be sent on evil missions is reminiscent of the heroine Marcia in the story "The Roaches," who sent cockroaches to kill her neighbors.

Contrast his statements with the insights in *Buffalo Woman Comes Singing* by Brooke Medicine Eagle, who writes of the time when the women of the Dawn Star shaman lineage began to signal her by sending shiny black insects with copper wings. She had a numinous dream in which she met an insect of great power and called her "Insect Grandmother." In the dream Brooke followed her into a cave that appeared to be an immense crystal geode. In her words:

> Insect Grandmother stood on her back legs and indicated other beetles scurrying around the room. Making each word clear, distinct, and emphatic, Grandmother said, "This is a communications room. My people use these crystals to communicate with each other over very long distances.[1]

When Brooke Medicine Eagle awoke, she understood that the insect elder was letting her know that crystals—long believed to have energy-augmenting abilities (and in dreams a symbol of the Self and the union of matter and spirit)—can be used for communication in more direct ways than our technologies have currently employed.

Interpenetrating Worlds

An openness to insects can take an individual outside common opinion and the pull of the collective shadow. Those who study insects are apt to dream about them. British zoologist Miriam Rothschild says she knows of no knowledgeable entomologist who has not dreamed of a rare, desirable, or fantastic species of butterfly.

Although entomologists are not a group likely to record and work with their dreams, Thomas Eisner, the father of chemical ecology, has admitted that he dreams about the insects he studies. In an interview he says that when he studied the ornate moth, he became so attuned to it that he dreamed he *was* one. And in another dream he was an insect talking to other insects about a dream in which he was a human being!

Since the boundaries between waking and dreaming experiences are never fixed, but fluid and permeable, our feelings about insects naturally impact our dreams and our ability to understand them. It is not uncommon for a dream creature to make an appearance as a physical creature in the daylight hours, or for one we encounter in the day to visit us in a dream.

L. Hugh Newman, an eminent British butterfly specialist, wrote that when his butterfly-collector father had made plans to go to an unfamiliar little village in Sussex to search for a rare moth, his father dreamed the night before that he was in the village walking down a street toward three giant oak trees. When he reached them, he stopped and looked at the trunk of the center tree and there was the moth he was seeking. When he woke up, he told his wife about the dream, and they laughed, dismissing it as just wishful thinking. But when he arrived at the village later that day, he recognized it from his dream. In fact, he was on the street with the three oaks. He walked toward them, feeling the unreality of his situation. When he looked on the trunk of the center tree, there was the moth, just as he had dreamed it.

These kinds of improbable occurrences hint at a unifying pattern that weaves inner and outer events together. If we are attentive to both waking and dreaming encounters, we have the chance to see the way they work together, building on each other and nudging and informing us as we grow and move into greater expression.

In *Spirits of the Earth*, Bobby Lake-Thom shares the story of how, on a cold winter night, his daughter was meditating and focusing on a ritual for menstruation, when a butterfly appeared in her room. Lake-Thom heard her talking and laughing loudly. When he checked on her, she was sitting on the edge of the bed, but still in a quasi dream state. She pointed to a butterfly (invisible to Lake-Thom), calling it "Grandmother." She told her father that the butterfly was now human size and kept changing from a young girl to an old woman. It wanted her to come over and give her a hug. He told his daughter that Grandmother was a good spirit and to give her a hug. In the morning, as his daughter was relaying her beautiful dream to her parents—convinced that it was just a dream—a butterfly flew out from her bedroom. Lake-Thom and his wife explained to their astonished daughter that it was an ancestor spirit wanting to communicate with her during this spiritual time of menses.

In *Healing Dreams* Marc Ian Barasch reports that a lama told that he could learn, not only how to transform his dreams, but to change his waking reality, because there wasn't any difference between the two. It brought to mind an incident in which he had changed his reality: He was sunning in a friend's yard when a bee landed on his bare chest.

Having spent years trying to overcome his revulsion to insects, he assumed an attitude of benign curiosity. "I soon became entranced by the rainbow sheen of its wings, . . . the incessant dipping motion of its antennae and tapping of its legs. It became a dream bee, an apparitional creature that I had never really seen before."[2]

He forgot his fear of being stung and shared a surreal interlude with the bee, watching it use its back legs to scrape off its load of pollen and deposit it on his chest in a tidy yellow pile. Then it calmly flew away with a sudden whirl of its wings.

Marc realized that if he had seen the bee as a dangerous insect, he would have swiped at it, either killing it or driving it away. His aggression would have changed the dynamics of the encounter and might have even caused the bee to perceive him as a threat and sting him. "I had changed my 'waking dream' of the bee, and . . . the perception had altered my experiment's outcome."[3]

Marc adds that this kind of "dream yoga" is practiced not as a mental trick but as a way to wake up from our so-solid delusions. This in turn unblocks the flow of compassion for our fellow beings.

Messages from the Shadow

By letting go of any prejudice we may harbor against insects, we allow them their role as the bearer of blessings and affirmation. But insects also bear the task, not always pleasant for the dreamer, of revealing unconscious material.

In a recent book on the healing power of dreams, the author writes that insect dreams are almost always unpleasant. Since she didn't offer any further explanation, I don't think she understood that what is unpleasant is having our attention drawn to neglected or out-of-balance areas in ourselves. Pushing past our defenses, insects alert us to issues that we have ignored or denied.

A woman who dislikes both her job and her apartment, but has not taken any steps to change her situation, dreams that she is in a room with human-size cocoons hanging from the ceiling. Many are withered, as though the occupant has long since died, but others are not. Suddenly an enormous caterpillar emerges from one of the cocoons. It is very angry and wants to sting her. She backs away as it approaches.

The threatening behavior of the caterpillar appears to be a call to action and an expression of the pent-up energies within the dreamer that demand transformation and a more expressive life. The dreamer is stuck, and so too is the caterpillar stuck with its worm body. Perhaps it is angry at having been deprived of its transformation into a winged creature by what we can assume is the dreamer's lack of action.

A different dreamer had a similar dream, in which she is in a small, dimly lit, poorly ventilated room. She opens a cupboard. An insect flies out, stinging her, and she cries out in pain. The setting of this dream illustrates where the dreamer reports she is in her life—closed in and barely able to see or breathe. A flying insect is trapped with her, perhaps a winged self, who, released from its confinement in the cupboard, promptly stings her. Perhaps the insect is trying to arouse her so that she can make some necessary changes. Or maybe by stinging her and making her cry out, the insect helps her express her frustration and despair.

When a dream insect has something to tell to us, it usually pursues us, lands on us, or bites or stings us. In these dream situations no thoughts of goodwill can turn the insect away from its mission. When they need to get our attention and steer us in a new direction or reveal emotions that have been suppressed, they are simply unstoppable.

In a northwestern contemplative community, a woman who has a very positive attitude toward insects dreamed that she was walking by a path leading into the forest. On the path, coming out or going in, a man is struggling to escape from a swarm of bees. Then the bees start to move toward her, and she begins to send good thoughts to them, but they attack and sting anyway. She puts her head down in a protective gesture. The back of her neck gets stung, and angry welts appear.

If we allow the insects their role as messages and remember the language of the sting, the dream interpretation moves down a different track than if we assume they are simply the problem. The dreamer walks by the path leading into the forest, sending the bees good thoughts so they won't sting her. They attack and sting anyway. What does their insistence mean, and who was the man who also struggled to escape them?

As we learned in the chapter on bees, a swarm is homeless, having left a hive or nest to seek a new one. Why then are they responding as though they were being threatened? Do the bees want her to leave the road and follow the path through the forest? What energies swarm inside the dreamer, homeless energies not bridled to the road but to a new path? What is angry and aroused in the dreamer that she cannot eliminate by thinking good thoughts or putting her head down and shielding herself? Is she refusing to deal with something directly? Do the stings cause the angry welts or just allow them to appear?

Confronting the Shadow

Awake or while dreaming, the shadow usually appears as the enemy—something threatening or repulsive. It is easy to see, then, how our psyches might borrow an insect form to reveal an aspect of self the dreamer needs to work on. All the forms of tyranny and exploitation that alienate one part of the population from another and permit us to control, manipulate, and treat as alien the nonhuman world emerge from the shadow and are revealed in our dreams. In those dreams, we harm ourselves by despising and rejecting parts we have been taught are "not us."

Dreamworker and author Jeremy Taylor says that working on our dreams is a critical part of learning to "love the enemy" both within and without. "Dreams reveal that the despised and feared other is actually a challenge to our own narrowness," and when we work with our dreams, he assures us, compassion and growth will replace the fear of others and our feelings of alienation.

As an added incentive to work with shadow material, it helps to know that the shadow contains our undeveloped talents and gifts as well as our "negative" side. In fact, paradoxically, within the shadow is the very thing we need most for our healthy development. Myths the world over teach that renewal always comes out of what we consciously despise and reject. In order to receive the shadow's gift, we must overcome the fear or revulsion evoked by its dark (unconscious) aspect.

It helps also to know that confronting the shadow is not a one-time affair. It is a task that must be undertaken at every level of growth and development. During each cycle, the shadow takes on new forms, and each time, it requires that we find our courage and engage in honest self-reflection to facilitate a reconstellation of the energies within the psyche and reach a new balance point.

Understanding the Message

When a dream insect directs our attention to something we would prefer not to see, we defend ourselves against it and its message in a specific manner. James Hillman says, in his illuminating essay "Going Bugs," that the way we defend ourselves or get rid of the insect indicates the source of suffering. For example, a woman who dreams she cuts a bee in two—dividing it into better and worse or perhaps rational and instinctual—performs the dissection to feel safe. She creates safety by dissecting problems with sharp practical distinctions.

Another dream from Hillman's essay begins with the dreamer looking up to see insects crawling on the ceiling. He crushes them with a broom, sweeping them out of his upward-looking attitude and restoring his view of a blank ceiling. Hillman calls this response taking the heroic stance. Exercising his personal will, the dreamer obliterates from his view (that is, he denies) what is new, unknown, and therefore threatening.

Insects and Images of Illness   The same dream authority who described most insect dreams as unpleasant says that diseases sometimes take the form of insects in our dreams. I would add for clarification that insects point out the disease or malfunction by their presence. Since most insects are destructuring agents whose job it is to recycle what is dead or dying, they are attracted infallibly and automatically by the very existence of the malfunction. Their presence is a warning, a signal that something is out of balance and has called them to disassemble it if it can't be brought back into balance.

Following Jung's lead, James Hillman suggests that diseases and afflictions are a divine process through which the gods reach us. In this view, dream insects that reveal physical diseases are divine instruments helping to provide the illness or affliction that leads us to a sense of soul. Sickness is not the awareness-heightening peak experience that we typically strive for, but it does rivet our attention and sensitize us to the movement of the psyche and its needs.

So we can follow the insects in our dreams and let them lead us to what is not functioning, and we can bless them for sensitizing us to whatever part of the body needs to "speak." Without the affliction, we would likely remain unconscious of how that part is functioning, and without the imagery, we won't hear its message.

Healing Dreams

In some ways, all dreams are healing dreams, even when they upset us or when we don't understand their message. Healing happens on many different levels, with and without conscious awareness.

Healing dreams help us in our life's work, affirming and clarifying a path already taken. Insect artist Gwynn Popovac, introduced in the first chapter, had a dream that not only reaffirmed her desire to create insect portraits but also presented her with the essence of her style—quick, short strokes in pen, pencil, and paint—as a satisfying and appropriate way to join with and reflect the vibration of insects. She dreamed:

> I was walking on a sidewalk with a group of friends. When the concrete ended, everyone stopped walking but myself. I continued off into an uncultivated area, a sort of marsh, and looped around. When I returned to the sidewalk and rejoined my companions, my head was filled with a high-frequency whirring of insects. I felt as though I were hearing something only I could hear, something I would have to try to translate to them in the best way I knew how—through my insect portraits.

Transpersonal Healing Dreams   Dreams with archetypal themes have an unmistakable intensity and a message that encompasses yet transcends the personal. Some reflect conditions in the culture. In the following dream, ants direct the dreamer's attention to what is wounded and needs healing in herself and in the culture. The ants also signify that energy is available for healing the wound. At the time the dream occurred, the dreamer was actively searching for a path of service and had no obvious connections to insects. She dreamed:

> I am driving in my mother's white car. Ahead, coming toward me, is a black boy riding a bike and steering it in a haphazard fashion. I don't know which way to swerve to avoid hitting him, so I stop the car. He continues toward me and stops just short of hitting the front bumper. I get out and walk to the front of the car. The boy on the bike has disappeared, and in his place is a

man's head torn off at the neck. The man appears to be from India. Thin and impoverished-looking, he reminds me of one of Mother Teresa's "poorest of the poor." He has ants crawling all over him. They are in every orifice—his eyes, ears, mouth, and the ragged neck area, which looks like raw meat. He moans softly, moving his head in obvious pain and distress. I am repulsed. I don't want to touch him, but I know I must. I say, "Can I help?" He doesn't answer, but turns toward me, and I repeat, more firmly now, "Can I help?" He says weakly, "You want to help me?" and I say with resounding clarity, "Yes!"

Since a full interpretation of this dream lies outside our intention to highlight the role of ants, we must risk flattening it and confine ourselves to a few ideas. A shadow figure comes directly at the dreamer, turning into a living head severed from the body and in obvious distress. The head or rational thinking faculty has been disembodied, ripped away from the torso and its instinctual wisdom and heart. The image suggests that the masculine has been forcibly separated from the feminine, a simplistic but telling image for modern society. Ants are swarming all over the open wound of the neck as well in the eyes, ears, nose, and mouth. They are aroused as though their nest has been violently disturbed.

Remembering that the ant colony has long been thought of as a single living organism, compared in its functioning to the human body, we can see how on one level this severed head with its agitated ants could depict a rupture in the human community. As a sister-based society and symbol of the feminine, ants could also represent the altruistic propensity within an individual to voluntarily sacrifice himself or herself for the benefit of the whole.

When an ant nest is disturbed or any part of it destroyed, every ant in the vicinity of the broken structure comes to help repair it. In the dream the ants are swarming all over the openings in the severed head where new things might be heard, sensed, seen, or digested to invoke healing. Perhaps they bring the energy of the colony, the consciousness of community and wholeness, to heal the split, motivating the dreamer to affirm her own altruistic inclinations, that is, her willingness and capacity to serve society as a healing agent.

The Queen Bee's Willing Death   In another dream with transpersonal themes, a schoolteacher with no outer connections to bees enacts a sacred ritual where she deliberately kills a queen bee, who comes happily to her death.

> I am walking in a big open space purposefully collecting the queen bee from each field. I feel a strong sense of my own femininity as I perform this task.
>
> I approach each field with a delicate white cloth in my hand. The queen bee comes to me happily, as though it is her duty to sacrifice herself for "the purpose," although what that purpose might be is still unclear to me. We communicate with each other, our hearts joyful, understanding that the time has come. I feel only pure love toward this insect and become one with her as I suffocate her under the cloth. She is my sister.
>
> As I walk to the next field, I feel a deep sense of honor and respect for my sisters, the bees, and I celebrate with them in this collection process. We become one.

In this multilayered dream is another community of insects comprised of socially cooperating individuals who work toward the benefit of the whole. The fact that most of the bees in the hive are female and are ruled by a queen makes the beehive a sacred feminine symbol.

An image of a willing death is also in the dream—what tribal societies call a "give-away." The death is a "good death," for the one killed is willingly sacrificing her life for some great purpose that supersedes her personal survival instinct, uniting human and bee in the sacred act.

Interestingly, in Nature a queen bee is occasionally killed by the entire colony in a formalized death ritual known as "balling the queen." All members of the colony participate, forming a solid ball around their mother and suffocating or crushing her. Observers have always assumed that the action was a collective act of homicide triggered by some offense by the queen—which says more about the observer than the bees. This dream suggests that a deeper truth is operating. There is a cyclical nature to the queen's life, an appropriate end and closing of a circle of life. The act of taking her life is not done against or without her permission. In fact, she enables it in some inexplicable manner, and it is through her willing sacrifice that some greater purpose is fulfilled.

The Black Butterfly Vision   Blackfoot Indians believed that butterflies, as emissaries of the Great Spirit, brought dreams and news to the dreamer. A black butterfly brought the bliss of heightened awareness to psychologist Richard Moss in a vision described in his book *The Black Butterfly: An Invitation to Radical Aliveness.*

Visions are waking dreams. The person is awake but his or her consciousness is altered and normal time and space parameters do not apply. Moss was in a meditative state after several days of unease and anxiety, coupled with a period where ordinary boundaries were blurred. He observed a black butterfly and a white butterfly dancing together in the air. They landed on a nearby branch, and to his amazement and delight, they mated, wings opening and closing as one. Then they resumed their dance. Suddenly the black one flew to him, landing between his eyebrows, and in that moment his life changed forever. "All of creation became a single consciousness, a state of indescribable glory and unspeakable peace."

Moss's heightened sense of awareness filled him with a flood of knowledge. His experience of unity, delivered by the black butterfly, forms the core of all mystical and religious traditions, underneath the myriad of techniques and cultural trappings. Dreams and visions give us access to our expanded identity that resides behind the thoughts and experiences. They put us in touch with the vast Self, which knows that all things are a part of itself and that our souls touch the souls of every creature.

Although visionary experiences like the one Moss describes are unusual, an increasing number of people report experiences of oneness in which ordinary boundaries of perception that separate us from others blur, giving way to a direct bodily knowing of the unity behind form.

Destroyer Turned Benefactor

In tribal societies, healing dreams and visions were the domain of the shaman, but anyone who had a vision or dream visitation by a creature had a responsibility to act on it in some way. In some tribes, members organized themselves into clans or societies with special rituals and responsibilities based on the appearance of another species in a dream, vision, or physical encounter. Among the Comanche Plains Indians, for instance, was a Wasp Tribe that may have been organized around such a dream. A vision or dream alone, however, was not enough to guarantee someone membership in the society. The person would have to display behavior indicating that he or she had received the creature's blessing or favor.

In the Blackfoot tribe a warrior formed the Mosquito Society after a powerful lucid dream. It started while he was hunting in a place thick with mosquitoes. Swarms descended on him and bit him so relentlessly that he wondered if they were going to kill him. He took off his clothes and lay on the ground in an act of surrender. The mosquitoes quickly covered him, biting him until he lost all feeling and then consciousness.

Suddenly, he heard strange voices singing, "Our friend is nearly dead!" Although his physical eyes were shut, he saw red and yellow mosquitoes sitting in a circle singing and then dancing with claws attached to their wrists and heads adorned with long plumes. Then the voice addressed him: "Brother, because you were so generous and let us drink freely from your body, we give you the Society of Mosquitoes and make you the leader."

The warrior opened his eyes and sat up. The mosquitoes had gone, and he was alone in the woods. He returned home and shared the dream with the tribe's elders and shaman, who agreed that he should create the Society of Mosquitoes.

Note that in the dream, the man had to surrender and approach his death before the gift was given. Wise individuals—that is, ones who are psychologically ready—will surrender to the forces that come for them and afterward receive the gifts of their animal-destroyer.

Since we can't change or control this process, imagine how much easier it would be if we embraced it. What if we didn't regard sobering experiences that humble us or leave us in pain and reminded of death as nightmares? What if we welcomed them as opportunities to move into a more satisfying life? When we insist on renewal without fear or pain, and on resurrection without death, we run from what appears to be a nightmare and subvert the intention of our deepest identity.

Granted, we might always long to be imbued with knowledge of soulful matters without being bitten or stung, but if we resist the impulse to fight with the forces who come for us, we'll discover that in the midst of the fear and darkness is the gift we need the most in order to infuse our lives with new purpose and will.

The Power Animals in Dreams

As we discussed in the chapter on the language of the sting, the way we meet and work with adversity determines the outcome. In all shamanic traditions, the one who attacks and destroys the initiate is the one who becomes the ally and teacher after the trials of initiation have been endured. These confrontations with power resemble descriptions by yogis of the awakening of the kundalini (the energy of inner consciousness) and by accounts of the path to enlightenment. So surrendering to the creature—losing the fight—changes misfortune into triumphant victory, adversary into ally and protector, in what Joan Halifax in *The Fruitful Darkness* calls a kind of "psychological homeopathy."

Sometimes confrontations with power involve a particular animal with whom we have a special connection. In *Shakti Woman,* Vickie Noble writes of the "power animals" that appeared in her dreams. Her first power animal as an adult was a human-sized Mexican orange-kneed tarantula. As a child she had been terrified of spiders and would scream if she saw one until someone came and killed it or took it away. She had frequent nightmares of spiders and at age nine had a secret compulsion to trap yellow and black garden spiders in a jar. Then, she confessed, she would make a small fire and drop them into the flames. She refers to it as a "terrible fascination" and was relieved that this obsessive activity only lasted about three weeks before disappearing. As an adult she later understood that her behavior was not so much a psychological aberration as it was an intuitive and compelling recognition of the spider's alchemical power of transformation for her.

She remained hysterically afraid of spiders until after her first marriage ended and she was learning how to be self-sufficient. She opened the garage door and met a black widow spider at eye level. Worried that it might bite her children, she decided to kill it and performed the act calmly, without hysterics. She was surprised that she didn't feel any anger or fear, and she was able to deal with the spider without calling for help. She showed its lifeless body to her children and warned them to not touch that kind of spider.

That was the turning point. From then on, her hysteria about spiders disappeared as though it had never existed. Five years later, when her shamanic path opened and spiders began to visit her, she was ready. In the first dream an enormous Mexican tarantula appeared and taunted Noble. "Dark and hairy with knees of orange crystal, gemlike and fantastical . . . she danced and jumped in the dream." Noble was properly awed, dwarfed, and scared. She awoke hysterical and in a cold sweat.

In the years to come Noble entered periodic dreaming confrontations with this same spider in a gradual process of healing and rebirth. She always dreaded the spider's return, yet paradoxically looked forward to each opportunity as an initiation in which she had another opportunity to meet the spider in a more courageous and creative way. Even the tarantula's shedding its skin taught her to leave her old tight self behind and allow a new, more expansive self to emerge—one filled with new health and abilities. Other tarantulas also visited her in dreams over the years. Some were black with red interlocking rings on their backs, and there was one that was her pet and drank milk from a cup she placed on the floor. Finally, she danced with them.

Consider that in this modern age of diminishing and caged wildlife, dreams may be the only vehicle left where insects and other animals can reach us and help us contact the vital forces of our own threatened nature. And when the dream swarm of bees stings us, or the tarantula grabs us by the neck and tears away our flesh, breaking the bones that contain our understanding, we have unwittingly entered the spaces governed by the personal and transpersonal jaws of transformation and growth. Do we surrender, or do we harden in fear and reach for poison? Can we live in the spacious heart of life and learn to dance with these creatures, or do we cling to the hard edges of the uncertain and frightened mind?

Today, whenever Noble discovers that she is sharing the house with black widow spiders, she either lives in harmony with them or escorts them politely outside to a more appropriate place for them to live. She feels blessed by the presence of spiders and understands them to be messengers of the Great Goddess. They no longer come as opponents in her dreams; they are allies now.

Insect as Angel

One of the most interesting views of insects in dreams is James Hillman's angelic interpretation. He says that underneath our culturally driven aversion, insects may simply remind us of the supernatural and the miraculous, a notion touched on briefly in the cockroach chapter when we discussed insects as "Other," not alien. Like insects, angels direct our attention to the relationship *between* fields of experience, widening our awareness of an autonomous order. And a fear of insects, which is often without a rational basis, has more in common with awe than ordinary fear. Religious visions are as disquieting as they are fascinating and at the onset always invoke fear and dread.

One of the dictionary definitions for *angel* is "a messenger, especially of God." After looking at the ways in which the insects, aligned with our most fundamental identity, continually assist us, conveying all manner of information to our benefit, the interpretation of insect as angel is not so unreasonable as it might appear at first glance.

Insects, like angels, have remarkable powers. They can live everywhere, partaking of all the elements of the natural world. As models of transformation and growth, they can multiply, transform, and camouflage themselves endlessly. And as bearers of information outside the boundaries of what we know, they bring new worlds to our attention—which is what angels are supposed to do. By resolutely drawing us in dreams out of our comfortable human perspective, insects also bring us the potential of new consciousness. Sometimes it is the consciousness of a hive or colony and a degree of cooperation and commitment that few human groups ever obtain. Other times it's the consciousness of transition that lives on the edge of chaos, where new energy and vision are available.

Perhaps insects are D. H. Lawrence's angels knocking at our door: "What is the knocking? What is the knocking at the door in the night? It is somebody who wants to do us harm. No, no, it is the three strange angels. Admit them, admit them."[4]

The Golden Cockroach

To close this brief look at insects in dreams, I want to share one last dream from a woman whom tribal people would call a "universal dreamer." Marcia Lauck's visionary dreams, some of which are published in *At the Pool of Wonder: Dreams and Visions of an Awakening Humanity*, which she coauthored with artist Deborah Koff-Chapin, are not personal dreams, although they have touchstones to her personal life. Rather these dreams emerge from a sacred, transpersonal realm where all the archetypal patterns of humanity reside—a realm outside the familiar boundaries that most of us travel at night. They speak of the evolution of humanity's consciousness, its initiations, and the new ideas and cultural developments present at each stage. The following is an unpublished dream she had during the time this book was being written.

Dreaming opens in the moisture-laden night air of the South Pacific. In the humid dark, all is silent but for the rhythmic chirping of the nocturnal insects. I am part of a ceremonial circle of women elders. We are the Dreamers who spin the great medicine wheels into the field of time and space, and we come from every continent on Earth. Our work this night is to bring down a new field of energy, a new pattern to initiate an evolutionary shift in planetary consciousness. As we move into the innermost reaches, the atmosphere thrums. There is a gathering acceleration of consciousness. Images of wombs, passageways, and deep ruby throats of flowers flash by in lightning succession and then we are spun beyond reckoning, travelers on a mission into frequencies unnamed by human beings.

The dream folds into itself, and when our circle re-emerges, I am in the center, held in the arms of the others as I labor to bring forth the fruits of this night's work. Contractions ripple through my body and the great waves push the new life into our midst. We look, wondering what the imago of this new cycle will be. At our feet, in the center of this sacred circle, is a shimmering golden roach. Small sounds of satisfaction emerge from the others. This is a good omen for the future. The insect, seemingly lit from within, grows in luminosity and size until it becomes the dream. As I come back to waking, I feel it at the shoreline of human consciousness, embedded in the archetypal ground.[5]

The pairing of gold, that enduring essence that symbolizes the soul, with the ancient insect who preceded us and has since accompanied humanity on its evolutionary journey signifies that some great work is under way—a deep reconciliation and healing called forth from the primordial wisdom that is held in the heart of creation. Lauck explains that "just as there is a unique task for each individual to unfold through the process of individuation, there is also a transpecies, planetary task that must engage all of us desiring to remain part of this world's story."[6]

Myths the world over teach that the seed of personal and collective renewal is always to be found in something humble, in what has been despised and rejected. What quality, what energies does the golden cockroach bring to a world that no longer knows its true name? And how can we do our part? Admit them, admit them.

15. Following Mantis

The Word came with Mantis, and the Word was with Mantis.
—*Sir Laurens van der Post*

When people speak of the praying mantis, they speak of presence. Taking liberty with Denise Levertov's poem "Come into Animal Presence," a fitting tribute to the praying mantis might read:

Come into Mantis presence, . . .
Those who were sacred have remained so,
holiness does not dissolve, it is a presence
of bronze . . .[1]

Part of this insect's appeal is its huge eyes and attentive demeanor. A flexible neck lets it move its head freely and direct its gaze to its surroundings. Many people report that its stare seems quite human, as though it were coolly observing them.

The confident demeanor of the praying mantis isn't just show. It's known for holding its own. Artist Gwynn Popovac has a snapshot of a praying mantis that had just caught a hummingbird. And biologist

Ronald Rood remembers seeing his first mantis in the middle of a busy street in Connecticut, standing its ground defiantly.

The praying mantis's reputation for courage is legendary. A story included in *One Hundred Ancient Chinese Fables* tells of the time when Duke Zhuang of the state of Qi was out on a hunting expedition and saw a large insect in the road. It lifted its front legs, ready to fight with the wheel of his carriage. The duke asked his driver what kind of insect it was, and the driver replied that it was a praying mantis—the one insect that only knows how to advance and never retreats and is so confident about its abilities that it routinely overestimates it own strength and underestimates its foe.

Impressed, the duke remarked that if the praying mantis were a man, it would be considered the bravest man in the world. He told his driver to turn the carriage to avoid the mantis. When men of courage heard about the duke's response to the insect, it is said that they thought so well of the duke that they pledged loyalty to him unto death.

The Art of Hunting

Most of us have seen a praying mantis. Two thousand species are scattered throughout the world, ranging in size from less than half an inch to more than five inches. In the United States, all species are known as the gardener's friend because of their appetite for other insects. The praying mantis is also prey for other animals—especially bats. But even for bats, the praying mantis is no easy meal. A single ear located in the middle of its underside often helps the praying mantis escape these skilled night predators.

An exceptional hunter, the praying mantis uses an effective sit-and-wait approach to hunting. Its superior vision and reflexes let it seize its prey with lightning-fast precision (the time required to strike and capture has been recorded on high-speed film at fifty to seventy milliseconds). Perhaps this is why people often mistakenly call it the "preying" mantis. Its hunting prowess has even inspired a style of gung fu (kung fu) that employs the mantis's mastery of stillness as it waits for unsuspecting insects.

The famous Zen Buddhist teacher D. T. Suzuki found the stillness of the praying mantis a striking example of one of the great Zen articles of faith—that of action through nonaction. This attribute also inspired a form of meditation called gi gong (chi kung), in which one directs one's life force through the body to strengthen and heal it.

The Prophetess In *Animal Speak*, an animal symbolism book by Ted Andrews, the praying mantis is associated with the "power of stillness." People with this creature as their totem are directed to be still and open up to prophecy. This connection between the praying mantis and prophecy dates back to the ancient Greeks. They called the praying mantis a prophetess or seer, one who sees the future. They believed that when the praying mantis saw a traveler, it could discern the traveler's destination and what dangers awaited him or her on the road. Better yet, it could show them with a clear gesture in which direction to proceed to avoid the trouble.

Early Christian symbology adopted the popular belief in the praying mantis's power of divination and its willingness to use this power on behalf of travelers. They called the mantis an image of the "Good Guide." As the guide of souls, the insect was also a symbol of Christ, helping those who have strayed from the path of righteousness.

The praying mantis continues to direct people who are open to its presence. In *Reinventing Medicine,* Larry Dossey shares the story of how, while writing his popular *Recovering the Soul*, he was sitting at his desk thinking about the spiritual implications of nonlocal mind and how distant, intercessory prayer is infinite, universal, and cosmic. His wife brought in a large bouquet of cosmos from the garden. As he admired them, he saw one of the stems move. It was a praying mantis. Dossey felt a shiver up his spine. One of his themes—prayer in the cosmos—had literally sprung to life, and knowing the future was another nonlocal theme he had been exploring. It was as if the praying mantis were a cosmic prophet who had come to say, "You're on the right track. Don't hold back."

The Mantis as Cruel The praying mantis, like other insects, suffered when authorities of the Judeo-Christian tradition began to view its habits under the microscopic lens of a language and an analysis removed from nature's cycles and the regenerative female power of life. Whereas the Egyptians, Greeks, and early Christians honored the praying mantis, the Christian tradition from which our contemporary version stems did not. In Charbonneau-Lassay's *Bestiary of Christ*, for instance, the habits of this insect were pronounced cruel.

What was deemed cruel was not just the fact that the praying mantis feeds only on living things, but also the fact that the female frequently devours the male (starting with his head) during sexual intercourse. Those who judge the mantis as cruel often point to the Asmat tribe of New Guinea, for whom the praying mantis was a totem. The Asmats practiced head-hunting, a practice related to their fertility and initiation rites. They believed that the vital energy was concentrated in the brain. When they killed their enemies, it was important then to confiscate their heads, extract their brains, and eat them to render their enemies harmless and assume their strength. They also saved the skulls of deceased friends and used them as headrests. Calling them "father," they believed that these headrests protected them when they slept at night.

Cannibalism   Although we have already touched upon cannibalism, more needs to be said to shift its power over our imagination to a new track. The fact that the female praying mantis often begins to eat the male while they are still engaged in intercourse is an act that has horrified many unsuspecting entomologists new to the study of these insects. And it still causes nervous laughter today. For all our lack of knowledge about insects, this is one fact that, once heard, is never forgotten because it reinforces our misgivings about insects.

As mentioned in regard to the black widow spider, entomologists suspect that cannibalism may be a propagation strategy for males in some species. It also boosts energy reserves and is common among insects. In a ladybug clutch of fifteen-plus eggs, for instance, most eggs hatch over a period of two or three hours. Any eggs not hatched within this time period are eaten by siblings that emerged earlier. Some 5 to 10 percent of all ladybugs die this way—or we could think of it as living on through their siblings. The ladybug larva that eats its egg-bound sibling greatly increases its chance of living long enough to catch its first aphid—a challenging endeavor at this stage when aphids are larger than they are.

Praying mantis specialists are still debating why cannibalism occurs during copulation. Some biologists have proposed that the male mantis needs to lose his head to copulate successfully—that is, its brain, concerned with surviving, inhibits the mating instinct in some unknown but important way. Others disagree. A few evolutionary biologists have proposed that the male mantis, like the male redback spider, goes willingly to his death to provide his partner with enough nutrients to help her produce more offspring. His reward? Babies that carry his genes.

The Feminine Ground Switching to a symbolic lens, it is easy to see why the praying mantis was a symbol for ancient female power: the female insects are larger and stronger than the males and wield, like all females, the power of creating life. And their size and creative capacity may be (as noted about spiders and the patriarchal Aztec society) one of the reasons our male-dominated society is so troubled by the behavior. Yet, if we only draw those correspondences that reflect our confusion and pet theories about sexuality, we diminish the praying mantis and reduce its behavior to an abnormal and bizarre act.

Taking an imaginative approach, perhaps the "exuberance" of the redback spider as he flips himself back into his mate's jaws holds the key to explaining the behavior in all other species whereby the male is devoured while mating. J. W. Goethe says in "The Holy Longing": "I praise what is truly alive, what longs to be burned to death." Maybe these males are "truly alive" and on the deepest levels of being accept the necessity of dying in order to be transformed and reborn. By taking the act out of the narrow framework that reduces it to something foolhardy, the willing surrender of the males can be viewed as a great teaching about how everything is renewed. To be eaten means to be assimilated, to undergo transformation by death. As Goethe concludes in the same poem:

> And so long as you haven't experienced
> this: to die and so to grow,
> you are only a troubled guest on the dark earth.[2]

So while completing his final task, it is the fortunate male who returns to the feminine ground from which all things come. It is the ending of one phase and the beginning of another, occurring in one great moment of union. By rejoining the female, both male and female become whole, and from this point of unity they are reborn and live again in their young, and so the cycle begins again.

And perhaps Nature, in her wisdom, has wired in certain circuitry that makes the act not only a good propagation strategy but a peak experience as well. Some studies suggest that the brain releases chemicals under life-threatening conditions that block pain and produce a euphoric feeling. Mystical sources say that violent acts of dying (as when one animal kills and devours another) are not what they appear to be. There is an understanding, what Barry Lopez calls a "conversation of death," and once it occurs, as the strike to disable and kill is made, the consciousness of the one dying leaves the body immediately. What we observe then in the struggle of the body is not conscious agony but reflex.

By moving past our immature fears of sexuality and our dread of being overcome, we stop being "troubled guests on the dark earth" and open ourselves to the imaginative power of the mantis—a power illuminated in the mythology of the Bushmen. Through these people, who lived in intimate communion with Earth and Heaven, we may rediscover that in the praying mantis "those who were sacred have remained so. Holiness [has] not dissolve[d], it is a presence of bronze."[3]

The Creative Pattern

For the Bushmen, the praying mantis is the Spirit of Creation and a manifestation of their God come to Earth. In Bushman myths, Mantis is the great hero-God and Trickster—both self-destroyer and self-renewer—complete unto himself. Although Mantis has supernatural powers, he is also very human and often gets into trouble by the tricks he plays on others. But the trickery of Mantis is not malicious. He is continually trying out different ways of behaving, learning from his mistakes, and trying again. And most of all, like us, he is trying to learn about himself.

One creation story says that Mantis was present at the very beginning of the world, and that the sacred Bee carried him over the dark, windy waters that covered the new Earth. Since honey was an image of wisdom for the Bushmen, it was fitting that its maker carry their God to his new home. After hours of flying, Bee laid Mantis to rest in the heart of a white flower floating on the water's surface. Then, before dying, Bee planted within Mantis the seed of the first human being. Mantis came alive in the morning sun and created the first Bushman at the same spot.

The exploits of Mantis (called Xhui, Cagn, Kaggen, and Kaang) form the body of Bushman mythology. Other African tribes who revered the praying mantis borrowed from the Bushman culture and from each other's cultures. But it is in Bushman mythology that Mantis expresses his full creative power.

The Bushmen believed that Mantis created all things, giving them their names and colors. Mantis also protects people from illness and danger, sends precious rain, and determines whether or not a hunt will be successful.

The stories about Mantis refer to a time when other species were considered people too, not just humans. Mantis accomplished many miraculous feats through these animal-people—although he also had his own kind of magic. For example, Mantis could bring dead people and animals back to life again, and when confronted by danger, he often grew wings and flew away—usually to the water, which symbolizes a place of renewal and new beginnings. Mantis was also a great dreamer. Just before disaster struck, Mantis would have a dream that would tell him what to do to avert it. Other stories tell how he transforms small and unobtrusive things into something radiant—a significant aspect of the creative pattern he embodies. For example, he used an ostrich feather to create the moon and turned ashes into the Milky Way.

Teachings of the First People

Much of what we know about the myths and stories of the Bushmen is a result of the dedication and work of the late Laurens van der Post, who was born in the heart of their ancient land. As a child, van der Post was taught by his family's Bushman servants to pray to Mantis. Little did he know that this exposure would work its way into him so deeply that as an adult, when he realized that the Bushman tribes were dying out (persecuted by other African tribes and by white colonists), he would return to live with them and record their stories and myths.

Van der Post thought it significant that even though the Bushmen resided in a land that contains the greatest diversity of animal and insect life, these people did not choose a bigger, more powerful animal to be their God. They chose an insect. Van der Post believed they selected an insect because their instinct was not deceived by size and appearance. They chose Mantis as the image of their greatest value because no other animal could represent the creative pattern inherent in all life as well as Mantis. In Mantis is a blending of the full range of human and divine characteristics. Mantis is a creator come to Earth to experience all that he can—just as many spiritual paths teach that *we* are creators, here on Earth to experience all we can and learn to manage our power wisely.

The Bushmen are as close to the first people or race on Earth as we will ever see. As root people, they epitomize what it means to be "primitive"—living without the sophisticated cultures that other indigenous people developed. The Bushmen's imaginative powers and intuition, as well as the keenness of their physical senses, emerge from their mystical participation in a sentient universe. Why their images are important to us today has everything to do with how they mirror the archetypal wilderness or primitive self that we have banished to the unconscious in our own technologically sophisticated but image-starved consciousness.

Creative Pattern of Renewal It was van der Post's belief that the long procession of animals, birds, reptiles, and insects in the Bushman's imagination and society corresponds to psychological elements in our contemporary psyches. In other words, every creature or element that plays a role in the Bushman myths has a specific symbolic meaning in our collective unconscious. As van der Post worked to decipher the "ancient, hieroglyphic code" of these creations of the Bushman imagination, he uncovered a transcendent creative pattern, an archetypal "foundation in spirit" whose activation he believed was absolutely critical to our ability to make the right decisions at this time of crisis on the Earth.

The creative pattern of renewal that van der Post identified is essentially a religious pattern. Calling it largely undefinable, he risks defining it as a desire and capacity to create a new and greater expression of life. Rachel Naomi Remen might call it life turning toward its true nature or soul. This universal pattern or blueprint makes us aware of our continually expanding inner range of impulses and potentials. It also links us to humankind's beginning as conscious beings on Earth and the inadequacy of any static state of existence. If we attuned to this inner creative pattern—an expression of our wilderness self—van der Post was convinced that we would have "the power to achieve a greater and more authoritative statement of life and personality."[4]

So, attuning to the Mantis within—the oldest, most natural image of God—we touch this underlying pattern and begin to restore our intuitive self to its rightful place in our consciousness. By doing so, we also embrace what is despised and rejected in ourselves and in our society, and, as Mantis teaches, allow this underpinning of spirit to be transferred into an inner source of great creativity and radiance.

Visits by Mantis   Mantis still appears in contemporary dreams and in synchronistic visitations as though directing us toward this inner blueprint. Sharon Callahan, whom we met in the bee chapter, remembers feeling the presence of God when she first encountered a praying mantis as a six-year-old. She was playing outside when she saw her cat corner something on the patio. Drawn to investigate, she bent down until she was suddenly face to face with a large insect. Although at the time she didn't know what kind of insect it was, its presence captivated her. While waving its "arms" as though it were trying to box with the cat, the insect kept its large eyes fixed on her with an expression so human, so conscious, that young Sharon was astonished.

She offered it her hand, and it climbed onto it without hesitation. Lifting it to the highest willow branch that she could reach, she waited for it to move to safety. It didn't move right away, however, but stayed still, keeping its eyes on her face. It was a revelatory moment—although Callahan would not be able to put it into words until many years later. As an adult she describes the encounter as an epiphany. Throughout the years at pivotal times, she notes, a praying mantis appears—sometimes in person, other times in a dream or even in an object of art—but always with the "shiny conscious eye of that first encounter—God looking at me through the eye of the Mantis."

Mantis is also known to visit those engaged in learning about the Bushman people and their insect God, often through Laurens van der Post's book *A Mantis Carol*. This quiet yet startling true story of a series of synchronistic events begins with a dream of a praying mantis and ends with van der Post's journey from England to the United States, where he meets a woman who had known an exiled Bushman in New York City.

I first read *A Mantis Carol* in 1984. I remember the time not only because the book is a remarkable and moving tale, but also because a praying mantis showed up on my office door when I was halfway through reading it. A vision of miniature perfection, it surprised and delighted me. I hadn't seen one since I was a child, so its visitation at that moment, after I had just learned that it was the Bushmen's God, spun me out of my normal preoccupations and filled me with the wonder that accompanies improbable events.

A Quest for Meaning   *A Mantis Carol* begins with a letter written by New York psychologist Martha Jaeger to van der Post about her recurring dreams of a praying mantis. When these dreams came with greater frequency, she renewed her search to discover what the insect signified.

As a psychologist, Jaeger believed that everything that emerges from the human psyche has a meaning that wants acknowledgment and expression from the dreamer. Yet nothing in her experience seemed connected to this insect image. It was as though it had emerged out of an unknown part of her psyche, a dimension hidden from her clear desire to explore this inner realm in herself and others. Since she had no connection to the physical insect, its dream appearance seemed subversive, undermining her understanding of dreams and her work as a dream analyst.

Then someone sent her one of van der Post's books about the Bushmen of South Africa and their God. She read it eagerly and then contacted the author and flew to England to meet with him.

In several meetings, as van der Post shared with her what he knew about the part played by the praying mantis in the life and imagination of the Bushmen and how he saw its role in inspiring a healthy modern society, her dreams of the mantis confirmed for him what he had already suspected: This particular pattern of the imagination was critical to understanding the nature of human imagination everywhere.

He told Jaeger about his conviction that the Bushman's conscious mind corresponds in some important way to our dreaming self, and that unfamiliar images, like her dream mantis, surface unbidden from our unconscious, trying to inform us of an "unknown and profoundly rejected self." It was the resurrection of this "first" self that he believed was absolutely vital if we are to heal our fractured spirits and make ourselves whole again.

Directed by Mantis   What he said made sense to Jaeger and transformed her dream pattern, which had seemed so meaningless, into a source of revelation. Her natural self was calling to her, demanding restoration. On her return home to New York, she had another dream with a praying mantis that confirmed the change she felt inside.

In the dream it was late summer, and she was walking barefoot in the grass. Looking down, she saw in the middle of her right foot, where her toes joined it, Mantis sitting firmly and happily. She awoke filled with "an indescribable sense of well-being and a re-belonging to life, happier than she had ever felt before."

She knew what the dream meant because van der Post had told her that the powerful and gentle eland, an antelope that is the Bushman hunter's primary prey, was dearest to Mantis's heart, and that Mantis was thought to sit between the eland's toes. It was an appropriate seat of command because when the eland's foot comes down on the desert sand, its toes snap together with a sharp click that sounds like the snap of an electrical current. It is in this position—at the source of this "electricity"—that Mantis sat, as if to say, "The way of this animal is my way." Van der Post thought it was like a first commandment to the Bushman spirit, directing the people to follow all that the eland evoked in their minds and hearts in order to follow their God.

For Jaeger the dream meant that she had restored her natural self to its rightful position of command. She thus decided that nothing could be better than to be directed in your life by one of the purest, most natural images of what people called God—or, as van der Post had once described Mantis to her, "the voice of the infinite in the small." She knew that a part of herself that had been arrested for many years was on its way again, expanding and informing her, and her dreams of praying mantises ceased.

After her return home, she wrote van der Post and asked him to come to the United States and lecture about the Bushmen and this creative pattern. He agreed. At one of his first stops he walked up the front steps to his hosts' home, and on the door "in an attitude of profound contemplation, as if waiting for a temple door to open, sat a large praying mantis." His hostess said that although she had lived there for many years, she had never seen a praying mantis before. Van der Post said, "If I had had doubts, they were gone. I was traveling under Mantis's auspices."

Under the Auspices of Mantis

Synchronistic events involving a praying mantis that occur when the recipient is involved in some way with learning about the Bushmen may be more common than we realize. It is as though the insect comes to accentuate the importance of the teaching or to inform us that we are under its guardianship. For example, while the mythologist Joseph

Campbell was at his New York City high-rise apartment reading about the role of Mantis as the hero/God in Bushman mythology, he felt a sudden impulse to open a nearby window. When he did, he looked out to the right, and there was a praying mantis walking up the building and onto the rim of his window. Campbell said it was large, even for a mantis, and as Campbell studied the insect's face, he could see its resemblance to the face of a Bushman.

Several years ago *The Sun* magazine invited its readers to share their favorite insect stories. A woman from Northern California wrote that while working on a difficult master's thesis outside at a table beneath an orange tree, she felt she was being watched. She looked up and saw a praying mantis on one of the tree's low-hanging branches. The next day another one came to the table. One by one they came, until six different species surrounded her. She and her husband searched the backyard, wondering whether it had been overrun by the insects, but they only appeared around the table where she was working. Over the next five weeks as she worked on her thesis, the praying mantises kept her company, two or three on the table, five or six in the tree or adjacent greenery.

She had recently given her husband *A Mantis Carol* as a birthday gift. While she was outside surrounded by them, he was inside reading about the Bushmen and their God. The day after she finished her thesis, they all disappeared.

A friend of mine from Wisconsin, who was raised as a Catholic but found herself interested in other spiritual paths, went to Pendle Hill, a Quaker training center just outside Philadelphia, for a retreat. This was the same Pendle Hill that van der Post spoke at during his visit to the United States, since Martha Jaeger was chairman of the Conference on Religion and Psychology of the Quaker Society of Friends and had arranged the event.

My friend had recently heard about *A Mantis Carol*, but she hadn't read it when she arrived at Pendle Hill. Guests of this center share the chores of meal preparation and cleanup, so she was wiping down the table when she noticed on one of the chairs what she thought was a green bean. Closer inspection revealed the green bean to be a large praying mantis. She called to another woman in the dining area, "There's a praying mantis here!" The other woman came over with a woven cloth in her hand and with the greatest reverence urged the insect onto it. Then she took it ceremoniously to the door and outside.

When my friend returned home, she read *A Mantis Carol,* and it confirmed all she had experienced during her retreat, which was a turning point in her life.

Psychotherapist Deike Begg shares in her book *Synchronicity* that shortly before she and her husband had set off on holiday, their good friend Laurens van der Post had died. One afternoon her husband was reading *Yet Being Someone Other,* van der Post's account of how Jung had announced his death to him by means of a seagull while en route to South Africa. Suddenly he became aware of a praying mantis crawling across the window and peering in at him. Neither he nor Deike had seen a mantis in Majorca before. He continued reading and in the next paragraph found the only reference to a mantis in the book. He remembered then in van der Post's last letter to him, his friend had written, "We shall meet before long," and he felt that van der Post was just keeping his word and saying goodbye—once again traveling under mantis's auspices.

Following Mantis

The pattern of renewal so evident in primitive tribes and in the dreams of every individual in every culture shows over and over again that the renewal of life—that our source of renewal—comes out of what is small and humble. Depth psychologists agree, telling us to look for it in what we despise, reject, and ridicule. Both ancient wisdom and contemporary paradigms of self and world testify to the power and hidden radiance inherent in the vast kingdom of the insects and imply that re-visioning our relationship to the insects will bring about a renewal of spirit beyond our wildest imaginings. Like the gift hidden in the midst of the Shadow, it seems that what we need most, individually and culturally, is this aspect of self and of the living Earth that our contemporary minds have rejected.

Living their lives on automatic (ironically, in the same mechanical way we accuse the insects of living), many people report having lost the animating aspect—their soul, if you will—that gives life continuity and infuses it with meaning. Gone, too, is the feeling of belonging to the Earth and of being known by the plants, the animals, and the stars. Yet, according to the beetle in Daniel Quinn's dream shared in the preface, the other nations of consciousness are close by. They hear our cries for help and answer in myriad ways. We are the ones who must remember how to listen.

Daniel Quinn's beetle told him that he was needed in the forest off the main path and that the other species had a secret to reveal to him. Quinn thinks the secret is that the insects and other animals are part of us, and we are part of them. We are not strangers on Earth, but rather have grown out of life like the mosquito and the butterfly. In fact, it is because we belong to the community of life that we are so desperately needed. Without our participation, the community cannot be whole any more than we can. By removing ourselves, we have fractured the spirit of the Earth community as well as our own spirits.

The process of retrieving our wilderness self and restoring it to its rightful place in our psyches is more than a first step toward healing the loss of soul that we have come to accept as a normal condition. This personal and cultural reclamation project has power beyond what we understand. Recognizing and undertaking the task means we have positioned our will in full accord with the pattern of renewal inherent in all life. When that pattern is invoked by our intention, it will call in all manner of help to assist in our transformation and movement into greater wholeness. And when we inhabit our true natures, our outer lives will also become more true to what is most genuine and unique in each of us.

An important part of the restoration work involves regaining the capacity to see the divinity in all modes of being—whether in a distressing guise or a pleasing one—and crying out in recognition.

A Rumi poem translated by Robert Bly says:

> You should try to hear the name the Holy One has for things . . .
> We name everything by the number of legs it has;
> The other one names it according to what they are inside.[5]

To find out who they are inside and hear the name the "other one" has given them takes time and perhaps regular conversations with bugs. Francis Ford Coppola, the flamboyant American filmmaker who is known for the *Godfather* trilogy, takes time now in his late fifties to talk to insects. One evening, as he and Fred Ferretti of *Gourmet* magazine ate dinner on the veranda of Coppola's Napa Valley farmhouse, a mosquito landed on a spot of spaghetti sauce on the tablecloth. Coppola noticed it but continued to eat, quietly letting the insect take its fill. Later, over dessert, Coppola told Ferretti, "We don't kill the bugs here.

We kill nothing here. . . . I talk to the bugs, the grasshoppers, the spiders." When Ferretti asked, "About what?" Coppola replied, "I am always trying to understand the scope of our existence, knowing that we are allowed to see only a piece of it. That's what I want to write about and to film. And I will."

Coppola is intuitively following Mantis. He has turned toward the insects to learn how to see the macrocosm in the microcosm and free his imagination to find the correspondences that exist between human beings and the natural world.

He is not alone. Many are turning now, answering an inner call, and all must eventually undertake the inner and outer journey to the bug-infested worlds that surround us. We must participate in their powers and try to sense the larger patterns of communication that sustain all life streams. We must also welcome, if not seek, personal contact with the small ones, understanding that new meaning must be lived and grounded in our physical life before it can be truly known.

The time has come for humans and the insects to turn toward each other, as Thomas Berry has written in the foreword. It is time to cross the vast distance between false power and the power at the heart of creation where the insects await our return. The voice of the infinite, carried by butterfly and bee, beetle and fly, cockroach and spider, and countless others, bids us to remember their true names and open ourselves to their teachings.

What insect do you rejoice in where you come from?

Postscript

The morning that I sent copies of the original manuscript to publishers for their consideration, a large praying mantis appeared over my front door. As I lifted my hand toward him, he climbed down the door and onto my hand. I photographed him, aware of the significance of his visit that morning and knowing that the book was traveling under Mantis's auspices. His picture appears on the cover of this book.

Notes

CHAPTER 1   COMING HOME

1. Condensed version of Larry Millman's "The Old Woman Who Was Kind to Insects." From *A Kayak Full of Ghosts.*

CHAPTER 2   CLEARING THE LENS

1. Interview with Brian Swimme, in Renée Lertzman, "Experiencing Deep Time: Brian Swimme on the Story of the Universe," *The Sun*, May 2001, p. 12.
2. Laurens van der Post, "The Creative Pattern in Primitive Africa," *Eranos Lectures* 5 (Dallas: Spring Publications, 1957), pp. 6–7.
3. Jane Goodall, *Reason for Hope: A Spiritual Journey,* (New York: Warner Books, 1999), p. 277.

CHAPTER 3   INSECTS AS GUIDES AND MESSENGERS

1. Geshe Sonam Rinchen, *The Thirty-seven Practices of Bodhisattvas: An Oral Teaching,* trans. and ed. by Ruth Sonam (Ithaca, N.Y.: Snow Lion Publications, 1997), pp. 8–9.
2. Stephen T. Butterfield, "The Face of Maitreya," *The Sun*, February 1989, pp. 20–25.
3. Daniel Brooks in Jennifer Ackerman, "Parasites: Looking for a Free Lunch," *National Geographic*, October 1997, pp. 83.
4. Berlin Snell, "Little Big Top: Maria Fernanda Cardosa Reinvents the Flea Circus," *Utne Reader*, May–June 1996, p. 68.
5. Arne Naess in Pat Fleming, Joanna Macy, Arne Naess, and John Seed, *Thinking Like a Mountain: Toward a Council of All Beings* (Philadelphia: New Society Publishers, 1988), p. 79.

CHAPTER 4   MY LORD WHO HUMS

1. Called campaign diseases, typhoid and dysentery were common among troops in active service and, until recently, caused more deaths than wounds. By the end of the nineteenth century, again as overall sanitation

improved, they were largely eliminated in Europe and North America, but they still claim lives in countries where inadequate sanitation practices and overcrowding permit the parasite to be transmitted easily.

Nearly all recent outbreaks of typhoid in developed countries have been traced to immigrants, refugees, or visitors returning from infected places—not flies. Sometimes the microorganism responsible for the symptoms we call typhoid is carried in the bowels of a healthy person. If such a carrier is employed in the kitchen of a large institution, he or she may spread the disease. Public health officials make tracking and immunizing human carriers an ongoing priority.

2. Lynn Margulis and Dorion Sagan, *Microcosmos: Four Billion Years of Microbial Evolution* (New York: Summit Books, 1986), p.15.

CHAPTER 5   THE COUNSEL OF BIG FLY

1. Robert Hass, ed. *The Essential Haiku: Versions of Basho, Buson, and Issa* (New York: HarperCollins, 1994), p. 188.
2. Marlo Morgan, *Mutant Message Down Under* (Lees Summit, Mo.: MM Co., 1991), p. 70.
3. Maria Rainer Rilke, "A Man Watching," in *News of the Universe: Poems of Twofold Consciousness*, chosen and introduced by Robert Bly (San Francisco: Sierra Club Books, 1980), pp. 121–22.
4. Karen Hild, personal correspondence.

CHAPTER 6   DIVINE GENIUS

1. James Swan, *Nature as Teacher and Healer: How to Reawaken Your Connection with Nature* (New York: Villard Books, 1992), p. 115.
2. Ibid.
3. Christin Lore Weber, *A Cry in the Desert: The Awakening of Byron Katie* (Barstow, Calif.: The Work Foundation, 1996), p. 23.
4. William Jordan, *Divorce among the Gulls: An Uncommon Look at Human Nature* (San Francisco: North Point Press, 1991), p. 125.

CHAPTER 7   GO TO THE ANT

1. Anthony de Mello, *Taking Flight: A Book of Story Meditations* (New York: Doubleday, 1983), quoted in *Spiritual Literacy: Reading the Sacred in Everyday Life*, by Frederic and Mary Ann Brussat (New York: Touchstone, 1996), p. 190.
2. Piers Vitebsky, *The Shaman* (Boston: Little Brown and Company, 1995), p. 68.
3. The clairvoyant scientist Rudolf Steiner saw striking similarities between the ant heap and the human being—with every part (ant or human cell) communicating and cooperating with every other part. He also attributed much of the natural world's ability to renew itself to the production of formic acid—made in Nature especially by stinging insects. Probing Nature and the cosmos with his spiritual vision, Steiner saw in formic acid (and bee venom) the chemicals essential in our process of incarnation and as it exists

in Nature, the physical basis for the Earth's soul to be able to unite with the physical earth.

4. For more information about Dances with Ants, contact Kerry Louise Gillett at kerrygillett@aol.com or 1-877-433-6474.

5. Robert Shapiro and Julie Rapkin, *Awakening to the Animal Kingdom* (San Rafael, Calif.: Cassandra Press, 1988), p. 53.

CHAPTER 8   LORDS OF THE SUN

1. Henry David Thoreau, *Walden*. (New York: Thomas Y. Crowell, 1961), pp. 439–40.

2. As an insider, entomologist Robert Van den Bosch could see the corruption in his profession firsthand. In 1978 he wrote *The Pesticide Conspiracy,* a book whose thesis is that corruption lies everywhere in the pest-control field. In his book, he blasted the Entomological Society of America, which he saw as having been bought by the chemical companies and wined and dined by the "pesticide Mafia" (Graham, *The Dragon Hunters*, p. 289). Other books since then continue to detail how chemical companies (and now biotechnology companies) have manipulated scientific studies, the EPA, and the public to keep harmful products on the market.

3. Critics of GM crops also argue that these plants may have unanticipated allergens or toxins, or have their nutritional value reduced in unexpected ways. They point out that those who shuffle genes around also risk removing or inactivating substances presumed to be undesirable in food, but which may actually have an unknown but essential quality such as a natural cancer-inhibiting ability. Critics say danger is also present when modified virus genes are inserted into crop plants. Dr. Joseph Cummins, professor emeritus of genetics at the University of Western Ontario, is one concerned scientist who warns "it has been shown in the laboratory that modified viruses could cause famine by destroying crops or cause human and animal diseases of tremendous power ("Eminent Scientists Comment on the Dangers of Genetically Engineered Foods," www.geocities.com/ Athens/1527/scientists.html). Finally, added to the real risks of genetically altered plants touched on in this section, the check to ensure quality in one giant agrochemical conglomerate has already failed.

4. An example of a new approach is seen in the work of soybean farmers who call themselves the Practical Farmers of Iowa. This group began a tillage system and planting techniques that have completely replaced a carcinogenic herbicide. And Jim Bender, author of *Future Harvest*, outlines how he turned his acres of corn and soybeans into a chemical-free farming operation by staggering planting times, using crop rotation and diversification, and reintegrating livestock.

Readers interested in exploring other visionary solutions are encouraged to read Kenny Ausubel's *Restoring the Earth,* which fosters a sense of optimism that we will find a way to heal our soils, plants, and animals and grow healthy food. *Secrets of the Soil* by Peter Tompkins and Christopher Bird (New York: Harper & Row, 1989) also offers solutions— both innovative and nontraditional—for reversing serious agricultural problems. Also read Janine Benyus's *Biomimicry: Innovation Inspired by Nature* (New York: William Morrow & Co., 1997). Benyus introduces us to "biomimics"—people learning from (not about) Nature, including those who are trying to grow food plants the way Nature grows plants. In her chapter on agriculture, she recounts the mounting problems with current practices and believes revamping the way we grow food is the most important idea in her book—and the most radical: Following Nature, "agriculture in an area would take its cue from the vegetation that grew there before settlement. Using human foods planted in the patterns of natural plant communities, agriculture would imitate as closely as possible the structure and function of a mature natural ecosystem" (p.13). And this approach is already in practice. Wes Jackson, a California university professor who returned to his home state of Kansas and started a school that focused on sustainable living practices, shows how a prairie-based, chemical-free form of agriculture will benefit farmers and their ecosystems—as well as the consumer.

5. Machaelle Small Wright, *Behaving As If the God in All Life Mattered: A New Age Ecology* (Jeffersonton, Va.: Perelandra, 1983), p. 85.

6. Ibid., p. 86.

CHAPTER 9   TELLING THE BEES

1. The bees have conveyed to Alison Yahna that they are working with humans to help us find the path to harmony with each other and Nature. They stress the importance of understanding the power of human consciousness to manifest. Thus, when we direct a stream of goodwill and love, the desire for health and well-being, as "prayerful" thought forms toward the bees, those prayers help them to manifest health and well-being on the physical plane. The bees have suggested that by coming together in groups to pray through dance and song within a "temple" that mimics the higher vibrational order/pattern of their hive, humans will be assisted in making an evolutionary leap, integrating the individual consciousness into the reality of Unity Consciousness. "All is one!" is their vibration, she adds.

    Yahna is in the planning stage of building a temple as a place for dance and prayer on the island of Hawaii. Please contact her if you are interested in working with the bees in this way. Alison Yahna c/o Judith Giauque-Yahna, 3023 SE Clinton St., Portland, OR 97202; beeoracle@hotmail.com; (503) 233-9644.

2. Peter Russell compares the near-instant interlinking of people worldwide through the communications technology of the World Wide Web with the way the human brain grows. He believes that if the rate of data-processing capacity continues to grow rapidly, this global telecommunications network will eventually equal the brain in complexity. When this happens, if there is enough cohesiveness and positive interaction, a new order could emerge that would revolutionize humanity.

3. Gunther, personal correspondence, March 1998.

4. Ron Breland has been a commercial photographer, plantsman, and beekeeper for thirty years and operates a bee sanctuary and research facility in Columbia County, New York. He is experimenting with both conven-

tional hives and prototypes of his own design including a hive formed as a dodecahedron, out of pentagonal shapes. Within the shape is a rounded basket in which the bees cluster. In sacred geometry the dodecahedron represents renewal, resurrection and the form that is closest to the first level of spirit. Breland believes that the hive can become a vessel for spiritual forces strengthening the bees on all levels. For more information contact him at (845) 353-0513 or 323 Strawtown Road, West Nyack, NY 10994.

5. Sharon Callahan, personal correspondence, February 1998. Contact her at Anaflora Flower Essence Therapy for Animals, P.O. Box 1056, Mt. Shasta, CA 96067; (530) 926-6424; www.anaflora.com and www.animalliberty.com.

CHAPTER 10 BLOOD RELATIONS

1. Quoted in Gilbert Waldbauer, *Insects through the Seasons* (Cambridge: Harvard University Press, 1996), p. 202.

2. Steward Edward White, *The Forest* (1903), in Sue Hubbell, *Broadsides from the Other Orders: A Book of Bugs* (New York: Random House, 1993), p. 80.

3. Dorothy Shuttlesworth, *The Story of Flies* (Garden City, N.Y.: Doubleday, 1970), p. 29.

4. Gordon Harrison, *Mosquitoes, Malaria and Man* (New York: E. P. Dutton, 1978), p. 5.

5. An account from that time period makes no attempt to disguise its racist underpinnings. "With weapons in hand to destroy the lower forms of life that made men ill, Europeans could move into the tropical lands and supplant the lower forms of human life who were then in possession. The battle against disease and the battle for civilization were demonstrably one" (Harrison, p. 4).

6. Believing that the great difference in susceptibility was due to racial differences, the conquerors defined their mission to overtake other lands in heroic terms. The self-deception went something like this: the white race would eliminate tropical diseases, which they perceived as the cohorts of "barbarism." Since diseases like malaria "permitted backward, slothful races of man to . . . [control] what were obviously the richest lands on earth, and so letting their riches go to waste" (Harrison, p. 5), the Caucasian race would change all that.

7. Genetically, the black race is relatively resistant to one form of malaria, a fact demonstrated among African Americans. The sickling trait, an inherited abnormality of hemoglobin (the "working" constituent of red blood cells) also produces an inherited immunity to a malignant form of malaria indigenous to sub-Saharan Africa. Children with a sickle cell gene from both parents are likely to develop severe and often fatal anemia, but those with genes from only one parent have a mixture of normal and abnormal hemoglobin that usually doesn't affect them and gives them resistance to the malignant malarial parasite. They can get malaria, but the parasite doesn't thrive. The child survives the attack to eventually become an adult protected by an acquired immunity. So in a small agricultural community, the sickling trait has allowed the survival of the group.

Like the sickle cell gene, two other abnormal hemoglobins (hemoglobin C

and E) also protect populations in Africa and Asia, and an enzyme defect connected to the red blood cell metabolism protects malaria patients from death.

CHAPTER 11   SPINNERS OF FATE

1. Bobby Lake-Thom, *Spirits of the Earth: A Guide to Native American Nature
   Symbols, Stories, and Ceremonies* (New York: Plume, 1997), p. 13.
2. "Breakthroughs: Of Sex, Somersaults, and Death," *Discover*, November 1995,
   p. 34.
3. Christie Cox, unpublished manuscript.

CHAPTER 12   THE LANGUAGE OF THE STING

1. Linda Neale, unpublished manuscript, 2001.
2. Ron Breland, "The Language of the Sting: Dying to the Old Way," *Earthlight:
   Magazine of Spiritual Ecology*, Spring 2000, pp. 24–25.
3. John Stokes, "Finding Our Place on Earth Again," *Wingspan: Journal of the
   Male Spirit,* Summer 1990, p. 6.
4. Harish Johari, *The Monkeys and the Mango Tree: Teaching Stories of the Saints
   and Sadhus of India* (Rochester, Vt.: Inner Traditions, 1998), p. 58.
5. Rainer Maria Rilke, "A Man Watching," *News of the Universe: Poems of Twofold
   Consciousness*, ed. and trans. by Robert Bly, (San Francisco: Sierra Club,
   1980), pp. 121–22.
6. Ibid.
7. Natalie Angier, *The Beauty of the Beastly: New Views of the Nature of Life*
   (Boston: Houghton Mifflin, 1995), p. 97.
8. Vickie Noble, *Motherpeace: A Way to the Goddess through Myth, Art, and
   Tarot.* (San Francisco: Harper & Row, 1982), p. 100.
9. Vickie Hearne, *Animal Happiness* (New York: HarperCollins, 1994), p. 68.

CHAPTER 13   THE NATION OF WINGED PEOPLES

1. Maraleen Manos-Jones (email: mmjbutterfly@msn.com;
   www.spiritofbutterflies.com) encourages every butterfly enthusiast to support the Michoacan Reforestation Fund. For every dollar donated, a tree can
   be planted by locals in the mountains of Mexico to create buffer zones
   around the butterfly sanctuaries. This solution offers dignity through
   economic self-sufficiency to the mountain people and protection to the
   monarchs' hibernation area. For more information and to help, contact Bob
   Small, Director, Michoacan Reforestation Fund, 628 Pond Isle, Alameda, CA
   94501; (510) 337-1890.
2. David Hope, *A Sense of the Morning: Inspiring Reflections on Nature and Discovery* (New York: Fireside, 1988), p. 47.
3. The Xerces Society, based Portland, Oregon, the only conservation organization solely devoted to the protection of invertebrates. A world leader in biodiversity conservation and public education, this organization will need all
   of our support if we are to stop the extinctions. Becoming a member is a
   way of giving back to the insects. Write the Xerces Society at 4828 Southeast
   Hawthorne Blvd, Portland, OR 97215, or call (503) 232-6639 for membership
   information.

4. In 1982 Norie Huddle got the idea that by looking more closely at the actual process of insect metamorphosis, that is, at what specifically happens inside a chrysalis, we might gain insight into our own process of transformation. She did just that and then wrote *Butterfly* (New York: Huddle Books, 1990), a book that is part of her Best Game on Earth, a "consciously redesigned game of life" aimed at bringing about universal peace, health, prosperity, and justice on Earth—the "Butterfly Era of Human Civilization." For more information, contact Huddle by email at nhuddle@intrepid.net or write her at 664 Cherry Run Rd., Harpers Ferry, WV 25425; website:www.bestgame.org.

5. For more information about Moore's vision of the butterfly as a symbol for a new era on Earth, contact him by email at bflyspirit@aol.com or write him c/o Butterfly Gardeners Association, 1563 Solano Ave. #477, Berkeley, CA 94707.

6. M. Scott Peck, *The Road Less Traveled*, in *Daybook: A Weekly Contemplative Journal* (Grass Valley, Calif.: Iona Center, January 14–February 10, 1991), p. 2

7. Sherry Ruth Anderson, *Noetic Science Review*, Autumn 1995, p. 27.

8. Joseph Epes Brown, *Animals of Soul: Sacred Animals of the Oglala Sioux* (Rockport, Mass.: Element, 1992), p. 40.

9. For more information about the spiritual nature of butterflies and their connections to plants and Nature spirits, see Rudolf Steiner, *Man as Symphony of the Creative Word* (Sussex: Rudolf Steiner Press, 1991), and Karl Konig's lectures on biodynamic agriculture presented in *Earth and Man* (Wyoming, R.I.: Bio-Dynamic Literature, 1982).

CHAPTER 14   STRANGE ANGELS

1. Brooke Medicine Eagle, *Buffalo Woman Comes Singing* (New York: Ballantine Books, 1991), pp. 249–50.

2. Mark Ian Barasch, *Healing Dreams: Exploring the Dreams That Can Transform Your Life* (New York: Riverhead Books, 2000), p. 309.

3. Ibid.

4. D. H. Lawrence, "Song of a Man Who Has Come Through," in *The Rag and Bone Shop of the Heart: A Poetry Anthology,* ed. by Robert Bly, James Hillman, and Michael Meade (New York: HarperPerennial, 1993), p. 20.

5. Marcia Lauck, private correspondence, March 1997.

6. Marcia Lauck, "Dreamtime and Natural Phenomena: The Release of Transformative Energy into Collective Consciousness," *Dream Network: A Journal Exploring Dreams and Myths*, 14 (4), p. 27.

CHAPTER 15   FOLLOWING MANTIS

1. Denise Levertov, "Come into Animal Presence," in *Poems 1960–1967* (New York: New Directions, 1983), p. 23.

2. J. W. von Goethe, "The Holy Longing," in *News of the Universe: Poems of Twofold Consciousness,* trans. and ed. by Robert Bly (San Francisco: Sierra Club Books, 1980), p. 70.

3. Levertov, "Come into Animal Presence," p. 23.

4. Laurens van der Post, "The Creative Pattern in Primitive Africa," *Eranos Lectures* 5 (Dallas: Spring Publications, 1957), p. 21.

5. Jalaluddin Rumi, "The Name," in *News of the Universe: Poems of Twofold Consciousness*, trans. and ed. by Robert Bly (San Francisco: Sierra Club Books, 1980), p. 268.

Selected Bibliography

Abram, David. *The Spell of the Sensuous: Perception and Language in a More-Than-Human World*. New York: Pantheon Books, 1996.

Ackerly, J. R. *My Father and Myself.* (1968, p. 174) in Keith Thomas, *Religion and the Decline of Magic: Studies in Popular Beliefs in Sixteenth- and Seventeenth-Century England*. Hammondsworth: Penguin University Books, 1973.

Adam, Frank. "Quantum Honeybees." *Discover*. November 1981, pp. 81–88.

Aivanhov, Omraam Mikhael. *The Key to the Problem of Existence*. Fréjus, France: Editions Prosveta, 1985.

——. *Sexual Force or the Winged Dragon*. Fréjus, France: Editions Prosveta, 1984.

Altea, Rosemary. *Proud Spirit: Lessons, Insights, and Healing from the Voice of the Spirit World*. New York: William Morrow & Company, 1997.

Anderson, Sherry Ruth. *Noetic Science Review*. Autumn 1995, pp. 25–27.

Andrews, Ted. *Animal Speak: The Spiritual and Magical Powers of Creatures Great and Small*. St. Paul, Minn.: Llewellyn Publications, 1994.

Angier, Natalie. *The Beauty of the Beastly: New Views of the Nature of Life*. Boston: Houghton Mifflin Company, 1995.

Barasch, Marc Ian. *The Healing Path: A Soul Approach to Illness*. New York: G. P. Putnam's Sons, 1993.

Bardens, Dennis. *Psychic Animals: A Fascinating Investigation of Paranormal Behavior*. New York: Henry Holt & Co., 1987.

Begg, Deike. *Synchronicity: The Promise of Coincidence*. London: Thorsons (HarperCollins), 2001.

Berliner, Nancy Zeng. *Chinese Folk Art: The Small Skills of Carving Insects*. Boston: Little, Brown and Co., 1986.

Berry, Thomas. *The Dream of the Earth*. San Francisco: Sierra Club Books, 1988.

Bly, Robert, trans. and ed. *Selected Poems of Rainer Maria Rilke*. New York: Harper & Row, 1981.

Boone, J. Allen. *Kinship with All Life*. San Francisco: Harper & Row, 1954.

Boyd, Doug. *Rolling Thunder*. New York: Dell Publishing Co., 1974.

"Breakthroughs: Of Sex, Somersaults, and Death." *Discover*. November, 1995, p. 34.

Breland, Ron. "The Language of the Sting: Dying to the Old Way." *Earthlight: The Magazine of Spiritual Ecology*, Spring 2000, pp. 24–25

Brooke Medicine Eagle. *Buffalo Woman Comes Singing*. New York: Ballantine Books, 1991.

Brown, Joseph Epes. *Animals of Soul: Sacred Animals of the Oglala Sioux*. Rockport, Mass.: Element Books, 1992.

———. *The Sacred Pipe*. Norman: University of Oklahoma Press, 1953.

Brussat, Frederic, and Mary Ann Brussat. *Spiritual Literacy: Reading the Sacred in Everyday Life*. New York: Scribner, 1996.

Butterfield, Stephen T. "The Face of Maitreya." *The Sun*, February 1989, pp. 20–25.

"Butterfly Man." *People*, February 26, 1998, pp. 131–32.

Callahan, Philip S. *The Soul of the Ghost Moth*. Old Greenwich, Conn.: Devin-Adair Co., 1981.

Caldwell, Mark. "The Dream Vaccine." *Discover*, September 1997, pp. 85–88.

Campbell, Joseph. *The Hero with a Thousand Faces*. Princeton, N.J.: Princeton University Press, 1949, 1968.

Campbell, Joseph. *Way of the Animal Powers: Mythologies of the Great Hunt*. Vol. 1. New York: HarperCollins, 1988.

Carroll, Lewis. *Through the Looking Glass and What Alice Found There*. New York: Clarkson N. Potter, 1972.

Carson, Rachel. *Silent Spring*. New York: Houghton Mifflin, 1962, 1994.

———. *The Sense of Wonder*. New York and Evanston: Harper & Row, 1956.

Charbonneau-Lassay, Louis. *The Bestiary of Christ*. Translated by D. M. Dooling. New York: Parabola Books, 1991.

Cheng, Nien. *Life and Death in Shanghai*. New York: Penguin Books, 1986.

Cherry, Ron H. "Insects in the Mythology of Native Americans." *American Entomologist* 39 (1993), pp. 16–21.

"Chiquinho of the Bees: The Boy Who Talks to Animals" ("Chiquinho da abelha, o menino que fala com os bichos"). February 1980.

Clausen, Lucy W. *Insect Fact and Folklore*. New York: Macmillan Company, 1954.

Combs, Alan, and Mark Holland. *Synchronicity: Science, Myth, and the Trickster*. New York: Paragon House, 1990.

Compton, John. *The Spider*. New York: Nick Lyons Book, 1987.

Cooper, Gale. *Animal People*. Boston: Houghton Mifflin, 1983.

Cooper, J. C. *Symbolic and Mythological Animals*. London: HarperCollins, 1992.

Costello, Peter. *The Magic Zoo: The Natural History of Fabulous Animals*. New York: Saint Martin's Press, 1979.

Cousineau, Phil. *Soul Moments: Marvelous Stories of Synchronicity—Meaningful Coincidences from a Seemingly Random World*. Berkeley, Calif.: Conari Press, 1997.

Covell, Victoria. *Spirit Animals*. Nevada City, Calif.: Dawn Publications, 2000.

Desowitz, Robert S. *The Malaria Capers: More Tales of Parasites and People*. Research and Reality. New York: W. W. Norton & Company, 1991.

Disch, Thomas. "The Roaches." In *Strangeness: A Collection of Curious Tales*. Edited by Thomas M. Disch and Charles Naylor. New York: Charles Scribner's Sons, 1977, pp. 175–84.

Dossey, Larry. *Recovering the Soul: A Scientific and Spiritual Search*. New York: Bantam, 1989.

———. *Reinventing Medicine: Beyond Mind-Body to a New Era of Healing*. San Francisco: HarperSanFrancisco, 1999.

Eagle, Brooke Medicine. *Buffalo Woman Comes Singing*. New York: Ballantine Books, 1991.

Eberhard, Wolfram, ed. *Folktales of China*. Chicago: University of Chicago Press, 1965.

Elkins, James. *The Object Stares Back: On the Nature of Seeing*. New York: Simon & Schuster, 1996.

"Eminent Scientists Comment on the Dangers of Genetically Engineered Foods." http://www.geocities.com/Athens/1527/scientists.html.

Estés, Clarissa Pinkola. *Women Who Run with the Wolves: Myths and Stories of the Wild Woman Archetype*. New York: Ballantine Books, 1995.

Evans, Arthur V., and Charles L. Bellamy. *An Inordinate Fondness for Beetles.* New York: Henry Holt & Company, 1996.

Ferretti, Fred. "Master of Movies and Wine." *Gourmet*, April 1998, pp. 60–63.

The Findhorn Community. *The Findhorn Garden: Pioneering a New Vision of Man and Nature in Cooperation.* New York: Harper & Row, 1968.

Fisher, Helen M. *From Erin with Love*. San Ramon, Calif.: Swallowtail Publishing, 1995.

Fleming, Pat, Joanna Macy, Arne Naess, and John Seed. *Thinking Like a Mountain: Towards a Council of All Beings.* Philadelphia: New Society Publishers, 1988.

Ford, Arielle. *More Hot Chocolate for the Mystical Soul.* New York: Penguin Group, 1999.

Frank, Adam. "Quantum Honeybees." *Discover*, November, 1997, pp. 81–88.

Gadsby, Patricia. "Why Mosquitoes Suck." *Discover*, August 1997, pp. 42–45.

Garfield, Patricia. *The Healing Power of Dreams*. New York: Simon & Schuster, 1991.

Gillett, J. D. *The Mosquito: Its Life, Activities, and Impact on Human Affairs*. New York: Doubleday & Co., 1972.

Gimbutas, Maria. *Language of the Goddess*. San Francisco: Harper & Row, 1989.

Goethe, J. W. von. "The Holy Longing." In *News of the Universe: Poems of Twofold Consciousness*. Translated and edited by Robert Bly. San Francisco: Sierra Club Books, 1980, p. 70.

Goleman, Daniel. *Emotional Intelligence: Why It Can Matter More Than IQ.* New York: Bantam Books, 1995.

Goodall, Jane. *Reason for Hope: A Spiritual Journey*. New York: Warner Books, 1999.

Goodwin, Brian. *How the Leopard Changed Its Spots: The Evolution of Complexity*. New York: Simon & Schuster, 1994.

Gordon, David George. *The Compleat Cockroach: A Comprehensive Guide to the Most Despised (and Least Understood) Creature on Earth*. Berkeley, Calif.: Ten Speed Press, 1996.

Gould, Stephen Jay. "Of Mice and Mosquitoes." *Natural History*, July 1991, pp. 12–20.

Grossman, Warren. *To Be Healed by the Earth*. New York: Seven Stories Press, 1998.

Graham, Frank Jr. *The Dragon Hunters*. New York: Truman Talley Books (E. P. Dutton), 1984.

Griffin, Donald R. *Animal Minds*. Chicago: University of Chicago Press, 1992.

——. *Animal Thinking*. Cambridge: Harvard University Press, 1984.

Guggenheim, Bill, and Judy Guggenheim. *Hello from Heaven*. New York: Bantam 1996.

Halifax, Joan. *The Fruitful Darkness: Reconnecting with the Body of the Earth*. New York: HarperCollins, 1993.

——. *Shaman: The Wounded Healer*. New York: Thames and Hudson, 1988.

Hall, Mitchell. "Some Animal Tales." *Orion Nature Quarterly*, Spring 1990, pp. 62–64.

Hall, Rebecca. *Animals Are Equal: Humans and Animals—The Psychic Connection*. London: Century Hutchinson, 1980.

Harman, Willis. "Biology Revisioned." *Noetric Sciences Review* 41 (Spring 1997), pp. 12–17, 39–42.

Harman, Willis, interviewed by Sarah van Gelder. "Transformation of Business." In *Context* 41 (1994), pp. 52–55.

Harrison, Gordon. *Mosquitoes, Malaria and Man: A History of the Hostilities since 1880*. New York: E. P. Dutton, 1978.

Hass, Robert, ed. *The Essential Haiku: Versions of Basho, Buson, and Issa*. New York: HarperCollins, 1994.

Hearn, Lafcadio. *Kotto: Being Japanese Curios, with Sundry Cobwebs*. New York: Macmillan, 1927, pp. 57–61, 137–69.

——. *Kwaidan: Stories and Studies of Strange Things* (1904). Rutland, Vt.: Charles E. Tuttle Co., 1971.

Hearne, Vickie. *Animal Happiness*. New York: HarperCollins, 1994.

Hillyard, Paul. *The Book of the Spider: From Arachnophobia to the Love of Spiders*. New York: Random House, 1994.

Hillman, James. "Going Bugs." *Spring: A Journal of Archetype and Culture*. Dallas: Spring Publications, 1988, pp. 40–72.

——. *Kinds of Power: A Guide to Its Intelligent Uses*. New York: Currency Doubleday, 1995.

Hillman, James, and Margot McLean. *Dream Animals*. San Francisco: Chronicle Books, 1997.

Hogan, Linda, Theresa Corrigan, and Stephanie Hoppe, eds. *And a Deer's Ear, Eagle's Song, and Bear's Grace: Animals and Women*. Pittsburgh: Cleis Press, 1990.

Hölldobler, Bert, and Edward O. Wilson. *The Ants*. Cambridge: Harvard University Press, 1990.

Hope, David B. *A Sense of the Morning: Inspiring Reflections on Nature and Discovery*. New York: Fireside, 1988.

Houston, Jean. *A Mythic Life: Learning to Live Our Greater Story*. San Francisco: HarperCollins, 1996.

Hoy, Michael J. "Amazing Boy Talks to Animals—and They Obey His Commands." *Manchete Revista Semanal* 1452, February 16, 1980, p. 40–41.

Hubbard, Barbara Marx. *Conscious Evolution: Awakening the Power of Our Social Potential*. Novata, Calif.: New World Library, 1998.

Hubbell, Sue. *Broadsides from the Other Orders: A Book of Bugs*. New York: Random House, 1993.

Huddle, Norie. *Butterfly*. New York: Huddle Books, 1990.

James, Mary. *Shoebag*. New York: Scholastic, 1990.

Jensen, Derrick. *A Language Older Than Words*. New York: Context Books, 2000.

Johnson, Buffie. *Lady of the Beasts*. New York: Harper & Row, 1988.

Jordan, William. *Divorce among the Gulls: An Uncommon Look at Human Nature*. San Francisco: North Point Press, 1991.

Johari, Harish. *The Monkeys and the Mango Tree: Teaching Stories of the Saints and Sadhus of India*. Rochester, Vt.: Inner Traditions, 1998.

Jung, Carl. *Synchronicity: A Causal Connecting Principle*. Princeton, N.J.: Princeton University Press, 1973, p. 94.

Junichiro, Tanizaki. "The Tattoo." In *Modern Japanese Stories*. Edited by Ivan Morris. Rutland, Vt.: Charles E. Tuttle Company, 1962, pp. 90–100.

Keen, Sam. *Faces of the Enemy: Reflections of the Hostile Imagination*. San Francisco: Harper & Row, 1986.

———. *Hymns to an Unknown God*. San Francisco: Harper & Row, 1994.

Keller, Evelyn Fox. *A Feeling for the Organism: The Life and Work of Barbara McClintock*. New York: W. H. Freeman & Co., 1983.

Kelly, Peter. "Understanding through Empathy." *Orion Nature Quarterly*, Winter 1983, pp. 12–16.

Kennedy, Des. *Nature's Outcasts: A New Look at Living Things We Love to Hate*. Pownal, Vt.: Storey Communications, 1993.

Knutson, Roger M. *Furtive Fauna*. New York: Penguin Books, 1992.

Koehler, Philip G., and Richard S. Patterson. "Cockroaches." In *Insect Potpourri: Adventures in Entomology*. Edited by Jean Adams. Gainesville, Fla.: Sandhill Crane Press, 1992, pp. 147–49.

Kornfield, Jack. *After the Ecstasy, the Laundry: How the Heart Grows Wise on the Spiritual Path*. New York: Bantam Books, 2000.

———. *A Path with Heart: A Guide through the Perils and Promises of Spiritual Life*. New York: Bantam Books, 1993.

Kowalski, Gary. *The Souls of Animals*. Walpole, N.H.: Stillpoint, 1991.

Lake-Thom, Bobby. *Spirits of the Earth: A Guide to Native American Nature Symbols, Stories, and Ceremonies*. New York: Plume, 1997.

Laland, Stephanie. *Peaceful Kingdom: Random Acts of Kindness by Animals*. Berkeley: Conari Press, 1997.

Lame Deer, John (Fire), and Richard Eredoes. *Lame Deer Seeker of Visions*. New York: Simon and Schuster, 1972.

Lappé, Marc. *Broken Code: The Exploitation of DNA*. San Francisco: Sierra Club, 1984.

———. *Evolutionary Medicine: Rethinking the Origins of Disease*. San Francisco: Sierra Club, 1994.

Lauck, Marcia. "Dreamtime and Natural Phenomena: The Release of Transformative Energy into Collective Consciousness." *Dream Network: A Journal Exploring Dreams and Myths* 14, no. 4 (1995), pp. 25–27.

Lee, John. *The Flying Boy: Healing the Wounded Man*. Austin, Tex.: New Men's Press, 1987.

Lertzman, Renée. "Experiencing Deep Time: Brian Swimme on the Story of the Universe." *The Sun*, May 2001, pp. 6–15.

Levertov, Denise. *Poems 1960–1967*. New York: New Directions, 1983.

Levine, Stephen. *Healing into Life and Death*. New York: Doubleday, 1987.

Locke, Raymond Friday. *Sweet Salt: Navajo Folktales and Mythology*. Santa Monica, Calif.: Roundtable Publishing Company, 1990.

Longgood, William. *The Queen Must Die: And Other Affairs of Bees and Men*. New York: W.W. Norton & Co., 1985.

Macy, Joanna. *World as Lover, World as Self*. Berkeley: Parallax Press, 1991.

Manos-Jones, Maraleen. *The Spirit of Butterflies: Myth, Magic, and Art*. New York: Harry N. Abrams, 2000.

Margulis, Lynn, and Dorion Sagan. *Microcosmos: Four Billion Years of Microbial Evolution*. New York: Summit Books, 1986.

Matthews, Marti Lynn. *Pain: The Challenge and the Gift*. Walpole, N.H.: Stillpoint Publishing, 1991.

Mercatante, Anthony S. *Zoo of the Gods: Animals in Myth, Legend, and Fable*. San Francisco: Harper & Row, 1974.

Millman, Lawrence. *A Kayak Full of Ghosts: Eskimo Tales*. Santa Barbara, Calif.: Capra Press, 1987.

Moore, Daphne. *The Bee Book*. New York: Universe Books, 1976.

Moore, Robert, ed. *A Blue Fire: Selected Writings by James Hillman*. New York: Harper & Row, 1989.

Moore, Thomas. *Care of the Soul: A Guide for Cultivating Depth and Sacredness in Everyday Life*. New York: HarperCollins, 1992.

Morgan, Marlo. *Mutant Message Down Under*. Lees Summit, Mo.: MM CO., 1991.

Moss, Richard. *The Black Butterfly: An Invitation to Radical Aliveness*. Berkeley: Celestial Arts, 1986.

Myss, Caroline. *Anatomy of the Spirit: The Seven Stages of Power and Healing*. New York: Harmony Books, 1996.

Nahmad, Clair. *Magical Animals: Folklore and Legends from a Yorkshire Wisewoman*. London: Pavilion Books Limited, 1996.

Nielsen, Lewis T. "Mosquitoes Unlimited." *Natural History*, July 1991, pp. 4–5.

Noble, Vickie. *Motherpeace: A Way to the Goddess through Myth, Art, and Tarot*. San Francisco: Harper & Row, 1982.

———. *Shakti Woman: Feeling Our Fire, Healing Our World*. San Francisco: HarperSanFrancisco, 1991.

Nollman, Jim. *Dolphin Dreamtime*. New York: Bantam New Age Books, 1987.

———. *Spiritual Ecology: A Guide to Reconnecting with Nature*. New York: Bantam Books, 1990.

Pearlman, Edith. "Coda: An Inordinate Fondness." *Orion Nature Quarterly*, Autumn 1995, p. 72.

Perera, Sylvia Brinton. *Descent to the Goddess: A Way of Initiation for Women*. Toronto: Inner City Books, 1981.

"Pest Control: Cockroaches Equipped with Tiny Electronic Backpacks Scuttle around Japanese Lab at Scientists' Commands." *San Jose Mercury News*, January 10, 1997, p. 27A.

Peterson, Brenda. "Animal Allies." *Orion Nature Quarterly*, 1994.

Quammen, David. *Natural Acts: A Sidelong View of Science and Nature.* New York: Dell Publishing, 1985.

Quinn, Daniel. *Providence: The Story of a Fifty-Year Vision Quest.* New York: Bantam Books, 1994.

Reichard, Gladys A. *Navaho Religion: A Study of Symbolism.* Princeton, N.J.: Princeton University Press. 1950.

Rilke, Maria Rilke. "A Man Watching." In *News of the Universe: Poems of Twofold Consciousness.* Translated and edited by Robert Bly. San Francisco: Sierra Club Books, 1980, pp. 121–22.

Rinchen, Geshe Sonam. *The Thirty-seven Practices of Bodhisattvas: An Oral Teaching by Geshe Sonam Rinchen.* Edited and translated by Ruth Sonam. Ithaca, N.Y.: Snow Lion Publications, 1997, pp 8–9.

Ritchie, Elisavietta."The Cockroach Hovered Like a Dirigible." In *And a Deer's Ear, Eagle's Song, and Bear's Grace: Animals and Women.* Edited by Theresa Corrigan and Stephanie Hoppe. Pittsburgh: Cleis Press, 1990, pp. 53–56.

Rodegast, Pat, and Judith Stanton. *Emmanuel's Book III: What Is an Angel Doing Here?* New York: Bantam Books, 1994.

Rood, Ronald. *Animals Nobody Loves.* Brattleboro, Vt.: Stephen Greene Press, 1971.

———. *It's Going to Sting Me: A Coward's Guide to the Great Outdoors.* New York: Simon and Schuster, 1976.

Rumi, Jelaluddin. "The Name." In *News of the Universe: Poems of Twofold Consciousness.* Translated and edited by Robert Bly. San Francisco: Sierra Club Books, 1980, p. 268.

Russell, Peter. *The Global Brain Awakens: Our Next Evolutionary Leap.* Palo Alto, Calif.: Global Brain, 1995.

Ryan, Lisa Gail. *Insect Musicians and Cricket Champions: A Cultural History of Singing Insects in China and Japan.* San Francisco: China Books and Periodicals, 1996.

Saunders, Nicholas J. *Animal Spirits.* Boston: Little Brown & Co., 1995.

Schul, Bill. *Life Song: In Harmony with All Creation.* Walpole, N.H.: Stillpoint Publishing, 1994.

Shapiro, Robert, and Julie Rapkin. *Awakening to the Animal Kingdom.* San Rafael, Calif.: Cassandra Press, 1988.

Shealy, C. Norman, and Caroline M. Myss. *The Creation of Health: The Emotional, Psychological, and Spiritual Responses That Promote Health and Healing.* Walpole, N.H.: Stillpoint Publishing, 1993.

Sheldrake, Rupert. *Seven Experiments That Could Change the World: A Do-It-Yourself Guide to Revolutionary Science.* New York: Riverhead Books, 1995.

———. *Dogs That Know When Their Owners Are Coming Home: And Other Unexplained Powers of Animals.* New York: Crown Publishers, 1999.

Shepard, Paul. *Thinking Animals: Animals and the Development of Human Intelligence.* New York: Viking Press, 1976.

Shiva, Vandana. *Biopiracy: The Plunder of Nature and Knowledge.* Boston: South End Press, 1997.

———. "Vandana Shiva and the Vision of the Native Seed." In Kenny Ausubel, *Restoring the Earth: Visionary Solutions from the Bioneers.* Tiburon, Calif.: H. J. Kramer, 1997,

Skafte, Dianne. *When Oracles Speak: Understanding the Signs and Symbols All Around Us.* Wheaton, Ill.: Quest Books, 1997.

Smith, Penelope. *Animal Talk.* Point Reyes, Calif.: Pegasus Publications, 1989.

———. *Animals: Our Return to Wholeness.* Point Reyes, Calif.: Pegasus Publications, 1993.

Snell, Marilyn Berlin. "Little Big Top: Maria Fernanda Cardosa Reinvents the Flea Circus." *Utne Reader.* May–June, 1996, pp. 67–71.

Spangler, David. "Decrystallizing the New Age." *New Age Journal.* January/February 1997, pp. 70–73, 136

Spears, Robert. "Gypsy Myths: News, Information, Alternatives and Opinion about Coexisting with the Gypsy Moth." http://www.erols.com/rjspear/gyp_welcom.htm.

Spielman, Andrew, and Michael D'Antonio. *Mosquito: A Natural History of Our Most Persistent and Deadly Foe.* New York: Hyperion, 2001.

Steiger, Sherry Hansen, and Brad Steiger. *Mysteries of Animal Intelligence.* New York: Tom Doherty Associates, 1995.

Steiner, Rudolf. *Nine Lectures on Bees: Given to Workmen at the Goetheanum (1923).* Translated by Marna Pease and Carol Alexander Mier. New York: Anthroposophic Press, 1947.

Steingraber, Sandra. *Living Downstream: An Ecologist Looks at Cancer and the Environment.* Reading, Mass.: Addison-Wesley, 1997.

Stevens, J. R. *Sacred Legends of the Sandy Lake Cree.* Toronto: McClelland and Stewart, 1971.

Stokes, John. "Finding Our Place on Earth Again." *Wingspan: Journal of the Male Spirit.* Summer 1990, pp. 1, 6–7.

Suzuki, David, and Peter Knudtson. *Wisdom of the Elders: Honoring Sacred Native Visions of Nature.* New York: Bantam Books, 1992.

Swan, James A. *Nature as Teacher and Healer: How to Reawaken Your Connection with Nature.* New York: Villard Books, 1992.

———. In *Voices on the Threshold of Tomorrow: 145 Views of the New Millennium.* Edited by Georg Feuerstein and Trisha Lamb Feuerstein. Wheaton, Ill.: Quest Books, 1993.

Swift, W. Bradford. "Down the Garden Path: How Ten Thousand Years of Agriculture Has Failed Us: An Interview with Daniel Quinn." *The Sun* 7 (December 1997), pp. 7–12.

Taubes, Gary. "Malarial Dreams." *Discover.* March 1998, pp. 109–16.

Taylor, Jeremy. *Dream Work Techniques for Discovering the Creative Power in Dreams.* New York: Paulist Press, 1983.

Teale, Edwin Way. *The Golden Throng.* Binghamton: Vail-Ballou Press, 1940.

———. *Grassroot Jungles.* New York: Dodd, Mead & Co., 1966.

"The Year in Science: Ebola Tamed—for Now." *Discover.* January 1996, pp. 16–18.

Thoreau, Henry David. *Walden.* New York: Thomas Y. Crowell, 1961.

Thurmon, Howard. *The Search for Common Ground.* New York: Harper & Row, 1971.

Tompkins, Peter, and Christopher Bird. *The Secret Life of Nature: Living in Harmony with the Hidden World of Nature Spirits from Fairies to Quarks.* San Francisco: HarperSanFrancisco, 1997.

——. *Secrets of the Soil: New Age Solutions for Restoring Our Planet.* New York: Harper & Row: 1989.

van der Post, Laurens. "The Creative Pattern in Primitive Africa." *Eranos Lectures* 5. Dallas: Spring Publications, 1957.

——. "Creative Patterns of Renewal." *Pendle Hill Pamphlet* (121). Chester, Pa.: John Spencer, 1962.

——. *A Far-Off Place.* New York: William Morrow and Company, 1974.

——. *A Mantis Carol.* Covelo, Calif.: Island Press. 1975.

——. "Wilderness: A Way of Truth." In *Wilderness The Way Ahead.* Edited by Vance Martin and Mary Inglis. Forres, Scotland: Findhorn Press, 1984, pp. 231–37.

Vitebsky, Piers. *The Shaman.* Boston: Little Brown and Co., 1995.

von Franz, Marie-Louise. *Alchemy: An Introduction to the Symbolism and the Psychology.* Toronto: Inner City Books, 1980.

——. *The Psychological Meaning of Redemption Motifs in Fairytales.* Toronto: Inner City Books, 1980.

Walker, Barbara. *The Woman's Dictionary of Symbols and Sacred Objects.* New York: Harper & Row, 1988.

——. *The Woman's Encyclopedia of Myths and Secrets.* San Francisco: Harper & Row, 1983.

Waters, Frank. *Book of the Hopi.* New York: Ballantine Books, 1963.

Werber, Bernard. *Empire of the Ants.* New York: Bantam Books, 1999.

Wheeler, W. M. *Ants: Their Structure, Development and Behavior.* New York: Columbia University Press, 1910.

Willow, Sara. In "Stories of Animal Companions." *SageWoman.* Spring 1995, pp. 26–27.

Wilson, Edward O. "Ants." *Wings: Essays on Invertebrate Conservation.* Fall 1991. pp. 4–13

——. *Biophilia.* Cambridge: Harvard University Press, 1984.

——. *The Diversity of Life.* Cambridge: Harvard University Press, 1992.

——. *On Human Nature.* Cambridge: Harvard University Press, 1978.

——. *Sociobiology: The New Synthesis.* Cambridge: Harvard University Press, 1975.

Wolkomir, Richard. "The Bug We Love to Hate." *National Wildlife.* December–January 1993, pp. 34–37.

Wright, Machaelle Small. *Behaving As If the God in All Life Mattered: A New Age Ecology.* Jeffersonton, Va.: Perelandra, 1983.

——. *Perelandra Garden Workbook.* Jeffersonton, Va.: Perelandra, 1987.

Youngholm, Thomas. "The Pond." In Ford, Arielle, *More Hot Chocolate for the Mystical Soul: 101 True Stories of Angels, Miracles and Healings.* New York: Plume, 1999, pp. 278–84.

Credits

Index